W

INVENTING THE PINKERTONS

or, Spies, Sleuths, Mercenaries, and Thugs

INVENTING THE PINKERTONS

or, Spies, Sleuths, Mercenaries, and Thugs

BEING A STORY OF THE NATION'S MOST FAMOUS
(AND INFAMOUS) DETECTIVE AGENCY

S. Paul O'Hara

JOHNS HOPKINS UNIVERSITY PRESS / BALTIMORE

© 2016 Johns Hopkins University Press
All rights reserved. Published 2016
Printed in the United States of America on acid-free paper
9 8 7 6 5 4 3 2 1

Johns Hopkins University Press
2715 North Charles Street
Baltimore, Maryland 21218-4363
www.press.jhu.edu

Library of Congress Cataloging-in-Publication Data

Names: O'Hara, S. Paul, 1975– author.
Title: Inventing the Pinkertons, or, spies, sleuths, mercenaries, and thugs :
    being a story of the nation's most famous (and infamous) detective
    agency / S. Paul O'Hara.
Description: Baltimore : Johns Hopkins University Press, 2016. | Includes
    bibliographical references and index.
Identifiers: LCCN 2015046698 | ISBN 9781421420561 (hardcover : alk.
    paper) | ISBN 9781421420578 (electronic) | ISBN 1421420562
    (hardcover : alk. paper) | ISBN 1421420570 (electronic)
Subjects: LCSH: Pinkerton's National Detective Agency. | Pinkerton,
    Allan, 1819–1884. | Private investigators—United States—History. |
    Industrial relations—United States—History. | Labor—United
    States—History.
Classification: LCC HV8087.P75 O43 2016 | DDC 363.28/90973—dc23
    LC record available at http://lccn.loc.gov/2015046698

A catalog record for this book is available from the British Library.

*Special discounts are available for bulk purchases of this book. For more informa-
tion, please contact Special Sales at 410-516-6936 or specialsales@press.jhu.edu.*

Johns Hopkins University Press uses environmentally friendly book
materials, including recycled text paper that is composed of at least
30 percent post-consumer waste, whenever possible.

Contents

CHAPTER SEVEN. *In which the frontier closes and Pinkerton practices*
are exposed   122

A cowboy detective and a labor spy / Surrounded with lice, Pinkerton
detectives, and other vermin / Pinking the Pinkertons / Conclusion:
Anarchists and detectives, reconsidered

CHAPTER EIGHT. *In which the modern state takes on the duties of the*
Pinkerton agency   144

Birdy Edwards and the last myth of the Pinkertons / The modern state
and the detectives / Stool pigeons, company gunmen, and the New Deal /
Conclusion: Dashiell Hammett, Pinkerton

CONCLUSION. *Pinkerton's Inc.*   158

Illustrations follow page 84

Acknowledgments

This project has incurred a large number of debts; my apologies to anyone I have forgotten to include. This began as part of a National Endowment for the Humanities institute entitled "American Immigration Revisited." I would like to thank the institute's organizers, Alan Kraut and Maureen Murphy Nutting, as well as my fellow participants. I presented an early version of this project at the "Power and the History of Capitalism" conference at the New School for Social Research. Jean-Christophe Agnew, Oz Frankel, and others at the conference offered many helpful comments. My colleagues in the history department at Xavier have helped at every step of this process. Many read drafts along the way. I would especially like to thank Rachel Chrastil, Amy Whipple, David Mengel, Frank Rzeczkowski, and Julia O'Hara, who not only offered suggestions but also let me bounce half-baked ideas about French cultural theory, Chartism, the Special Irish Branch, Robin Hood, western outlaws and lawmen, Mexican mine strikes, and Tom Horn off them for years. Maggie Bell compiled information on the history of dime novels, Steve Towne shared some of his own research on Civil War spies, and Carey Cummings, a bona fide member of the Baker Street Irregulars, sent me all kinds of information on Sherlock Holmes and Dashiell Hammett. Liz McMahon shared her thoughts on an early version of the introduction. Robert J. Brugger at Johns Hopkins University Press believed in this project and stuck with it through several substantial revisions. I greatly appreciate his patience. The staff at Johns Hopkins University Press has been fantastic, and the anonymous readers of the manuscript offered thoughtful commentary. My thanks to all.

It is difficult to envision completing this project without a lot of additional support. My thanks to my father (who wondered, jokingly I hope, why he worked for so long in the plant only to have his son write about the Pinkertons) and my mother (who introduced me to Irish radicals and revolutionaries long ago). Julie's role in this has been immeasurable; she is the first and most important sounding board for all of my ideas. None of this would be possible without her. Both Jerry and Charlie have endured many stories about bandits, outlaws, strikers, and detectives, but their enthusiasm for stories has enhanced my enthusiasm for stories. I hope that someday they will like this collection as well.

INVENTING THE PINKERTONS

or, Spies, Sleuths, Mercenaries, and Thugs

Pinkerton's National Detective Agency, or heroes and villains of the Gilded Age

I N 1886, the Haymarket jury believed what agents of Pinkerton's National Detective Agency had to say. The prosecution argued that a criminal conspiracy existed among the anarchists of Chicago to foment violence and revolution. Anarchists, the theory went, had designed the rally held in Haymarket Square on May 3 to lure the police into an ambush. The events of the Haymarket riot, where an unidentified assailant threw a handmade bomb into the ranks of the Chicago police, killing seven, and the police responded with gunfire into the crowd, killing at least four, were the responsibility of the anarchists. The jury saw the eight defendants' own collections of explosives and dynamite, which established the means of the bombing. They heard the rhetoric of the defendants' speeches and newspaper editorials, in particular anarchist threats against the Chicago Police and Pinkerton detectives, which suggested a motive for anarchists to attack authority figures. Undercover Pinkerton agent Andrew C. Johnson then provided the vital links between the public rhetoric of the anarchists, their stockpile of bombs, and their secret plans for specific acts of violence. Hired by a private association of Chicago industrialists to root out worker radicalism within the city, Johnson claimed to have infiltrated several workers' militias and been privy to their plans for acts of terror.[1] Convinced by Johnson's testimony, the jury convicted all of the accused anarchists; seven were sentenced to death. On November 11, 1887, four were hanged.[2]

However, when Illinois governor John Altgeld pardoned the three living Haymarket anarchists in 1893, he assumed the opposite about the testimony of Pinkerton agents. The trial was deeply flawed for several reasons, he declared, including its reliance on Pinkerton agents in the employ of industrialists.[3] The presence of Pinkerton detectives seemed to be the cause of the violence, and when workers clashed with Pinkerton guards and spies, they were challenging private capital, not the authority of the state. Perhaps, the new thinking went, labor unrest and violence were less a criminal and radical fringe of discontented foreign populations and more a genuine (and perhaps justified) response to the rise of a plutocratic elite who hired their own spies and thugs, a system that critics came to call "Pinkertonism." Much of this had to do with the public's reaction to the events in Homestead, Pennsylvania, in 1892, when three hundred Pinkerton guards in the employ of Andrew Carnegie clashed violently with steel strikers. In just a few short years, with Homestead as the hinge, public opinion about labor violence and the legitimacy of the Pinkerton agency had dramatically shifted. What had seemed in 1886 to be a moral force of detectives and agents that protected society by infiltrating dangerous international criminal conspiracies had become a despised tool of capital intent on crushing dissent and worker resistance. The meaning of the agency changed because of both their actions, such as at Homestead, and broader changes in the public opinion that surrounded them. The agency, within both political discourse and the cultural imagination, had become the apotheosis of industrial violence and corporate power in Gilded Age America.

Yet the Haymarket trial and the Homestead strike were neither the first nor the last time that the American public debated the political role and cultural reputation of the Pinkerton agency. Nor would it be the only time that the Pinkerton detective served simultaneously (and paradoxically) as both a state-sponsored vanguard of law and order and an arm of plutocratic power. In an age of new market discipline and territorial expansion, Pinkertons served as a quasi-official extension of the state where the state had little other representation. As rapid industrialization triggered bloody labor conflict, the agency became, for all intents and purposes, capital's private army. It was the muscle of industry at a time when industry tried to crush dissent and consolidate its control. The Pinkerton detective, in both action and reputation, came to symbolize, for good and bad, the new industrial order.

Americans in the Gilded Age were familiar with Pinkerton's detective agency and spoke and wrote often about it. The imagery of the Pinkerton detective was fodder for romantic and sensationalist novels, whose readers craved such stories, as well as for models of frontier justice (and injustice) as the frontier was closing. For the Victorian age, the Pinkerton detective could either epitomize the ideal of Victorian masculine propriety or provide a rugged and violent alternative to this model. Famed undercover agents such as Kate Warne could subvert notions of the masculine detective even further. The political purpose of the Pinkerton agent and the agent's cultural resonation were flexible, meaningful, and contradictory long before Haymarket and would remain so long after Homestead. As a cultural and political touchstone of industrial conflict, the purpose and meaning of the Pinkertons did change between 1886 and 1893, yet from the agency's founding in 1852 to its vow to reject labor work in 1937, the agency's purpose and cultural resonance had always been contested and ambiguous.

This book traces the histories and meanings of the "Pinkertons" because Pinkerton's National Detective Agency was a pivotal institution in the formation of American monopoly capitalism.[4] Through the Pinkertons, American capitalists implemented and enforced new structures of order on industrial frontiers. At the same time, the company's folkloric reputation within dime novels, detective fiction, and sensationalist papers allowed for often-contradictory narratives of law, order, criminality, resistance, masculinity, and adventure. The state, at the federal and local level, not only refused to limit the scope and power of the agency but also actively legitimized the Pinkertons by hiring and deputizing the agents. The state both exercised its power and contracted out its authority through its use of the agency; only during specific moments did the state choose to reestablish its legitimacy by pulling back some of the power it had granted to the Pinkertons. The agency was simultaneously a tool for capital, a myth in American folklore, and a manifestation of state power. At the nexus of industrial order, folklore, and state authority stood a public desperate to make sense of the changes that surrounded them. As the Pinkertons reinvented themselves to fit their time, so too did others reinvent them to explain the tensions of the age.

ALLAN PINKERTON founded his agency in the early 1850s as a form of "special," or private, police. For banks and railroads, Pinkerton provided security and investigation beyond what "official" sheriffs were willing to offer. To separate himself from the tradition of "thief takers" who collected rewards, Pinkerton promised the professionalism of detectives paid per diem. At the behest of Chicago industrialists, the company's agents tracked down counterfeiters, exposed embezzlement within railroads and express companies, and protected company property. Pinkerton detectives also held a number of official and quasi-official posts, including sheriff's deputy, police detective, and agent for the US Postal Service and Treasury. During the Civil War, Pinkerton gained national fame for providing private protection for Lincoln and military intelligence for the Army of the Potomac. Between 1865 and 1884 agents were involved, as private detectives and labor spies, in many of the key political and cultural moments of the era. First at the request of express companies and later as a personal vendetta, agents pursued but never caught Jesse James and his gang across Missouri. Pinkertons infiltrated and helped crush a suspected conspiracy of Irish miners (the Molly Maguires) in Pennsylvania. Undercover agents penetrated the ethnic neighborhoods of industrial cities to root out suspected anarchists. In the west, they chased train robbers and defended the interests of large cattle barons against outlaws and rustlers. In the coalfields of Illinois, they safeguarded company property from the potential violence of striking miners and protected strikebreakers as well. In short, Pinkerton agents filled the role of state power where capitalists tended not to trust the actual authorities of the state and served to bring market discipline and industrial order to frontier areas.

The desire for order upon which Pinkerton built his agency and his reputation also led city and state officials to create professional police forces, construct urban armories, and mobilize a national guard. However, industrialists often found such institutions of order unreliable. Capitalists tended not to trust the loyalty of sheriffs or the composition of militias along rail lines and in newly created industrial towns. Instead, they turned to privately hired agents to ensure order and protect their interests. As undercover agents, Pinkerton detectives could infiltrate ethnic and artisan societies and crush worker dissent. In addition, Pinkerton agents held the power to define criminality; even when they were not deputized, they still seemed to carry the weight of official authority. The Molly Maguires in Pennsylvania and anarchist conspiracies in Chicago seemed to exist because undercover agents said they existed. Moreover, the American public understood these conspiracies as threats because Pinkerton agents held the power to define threats to society. To challenge the Pinkertons was not only an act of defiance toward capitalism, progress, and industrial order but also a criminal act. The all-seeing and unblinking eye of the Pinkerton logo symbolized a kind of "architecture of surveillance," a vast network of faceless eyes that watched every move.[5]

However, the Pinkerton eye, emblazoned with the promise "we never sleep" and evoking the political vigilance of the prewar "Wide Awake" militias, was more than a threat of surveillance; it was the company brand.[6] Industrialists in the immediate postwar period worried about the need for discipline and the potential for crime. Allan Pinkerton built his agency into a powerful and lucrative business by exploiting these perceptions of disorder. His company helped invent the concept of a national detective agency, and for years the Pinkertons dominated this business. His reputation and biography were part of the brand and were advertised as such. Through a series of books chronicling the adventures of his detectives, he tied his reputation directly to the emerging literary genre of detective novels. Such stories guided readers through the modern world because they promised that crime was an abnormality that could be contained and that the power to place the world in order (a power held by the detective) always proved stronger than the criminal's power to disrupt social order. At the same time, sensationalist descriptions of Pinkerton agents fed readers' guilty pleasures of delving into criminal worlds and anarchic chaos. Labor periodicals, exposés, and dime novels would offer very different understandings of the Pinkerton agent. Critics would point out that Pinkerton's business was not establishing order but fomenting disorder; continued chaos meant continued employment. Further, counternarratives often portrayed Pinkertons as the hired assassins of new industries intent on crushing traditional communities.

Between Pinkerton's death in 1884 and the Homestead strike in 1892, the purpose of the agency shifted as it began to send armed guards to engage strikers and patrol mills in numerous labor conflicts, becoming a despised enemy of labor and a symbol of corporate power. It was this new reputation that prompted labor leader Terence Powderly to say that "when the Pinkertons fire upon the people, they do so from behind the breastworks of capital." Armed clashes between Pinkertons and striking workers continued to grow in scale and violence until the Homestead conflict between strikers and the "paid assassins of the Master of the Mill," as one paper reported, captured the imagination and horror of the American public. As capital's private army, the Pinkertons were now understood by many to be a protector of plutocratic power, and their presence was seen as a direct cause of disorder. Pinkerton guards were increasingly defined by their own criminality.[7]

Yet even as the purpose of the agency shifted, Pinkerton detectives were always more than the sum of their actions. Public perceptions of order, disorder, foreign populations, bandits, detectives, and secret societies drove both the popularity of and the backlash toward the Pinkerton detectives. Americans in the long Gilded Age were in the process of reinventing their sense of nation during a time of great upheaval and anxiety. Some feared the end of artisanal autonomy and free labor; others felt the need for social reform. Some advocated the moral suasion and planning of Victorian propriety; others preached the new ideologies of benevolent paternalism, associationalism, or social Darwinism. Critics embraced the vibrancy and resiliency of American immigrant communities or the wild mythologies of the American west. These were the issues that Gilded Age Americans debated and the anxieties they confronted, and Americans used the Pinkertons (both literally and figuratively) to make sense of these issues. The success of the agency was built on a self-generated reputation that both reflected and fed the anxieties of the age. Hence, the cultural image of the Pinkertons forced a maturation of cultural narratives that helped Americans understand the new social realities of the age. Because of the contradictions among Pinkerton's official powers, the agency's employment by private interests, and its cultural reputation, an important gap emerged between what we might call the new "logic of capitalism" (which uprooted traditions and enforced new rules of order) and the "folklore of industrial society" (which allowed for resistance, reinvention, hidden transcripts, and the arts of resistance and subordination).[8]

Pinkerton detectives were actors and agents within this culture, but they were also subject to the interpretations of others, hence the agency's desperate desire to control its own narratives and meanings. Pinkerton's public reputation was part of an episteme of power which dominated the Gilded Age; the meaning of the agency was shaped through the interplay between both "legitimate" and "excluded" histories. In the process, "Pinkertons" became a key component in a new industrial folklore that portrayed them alternately as sleuths, spies, assassins, and union busters. In recurring yet adaptable tales, they served as both heroes and villains within American popular culture.[9] This folkloric reputation, along with the ambiguity of their quasi-official role, made the agency both infamous and problematic. Tales of Pinkerton exploits and outrages could be comedy, satire, tragedy, or romance. The Pinkerton detective functioned as synecdoche, metaphor, and metonym for industrial capital; the agency served as a metahistory of the industrial age.[10]

The malleability of the Pinkerton detective within American cultural narratives helped to provide vastly different story lines, all while offering the lure of authenticity. Yet the Pinkertons themselves were often steeped in mystery. Nearly all the "official" information about Pinkerton exploits came from Allan Pinkerton, and he was far from a reliable narrator. Like so many other notable Victorian figures who often crafted their own images through memoirs and half-truths, Pinkerton existed in the twilight area between reality and outright fiction; he and his detectives were figures of usable myth and folklore. Pinkerton's early career was and remains shrouded in mystery, self-aggrandizement, and reinvention—deepened by the fact that Pinkerton's files were destroyed in the Chicago Fire of 1871. The tales Allan Pinkerton told of his early career and time during the Civil War were written from memory. Decades before Rudyard Kipling would describe his friend Theodore Roosevelt as a master "spinner" able to control stories and myths, Allan Pinkerton had already mastered this feat.[11] Yet controversy and contradiction also plagued Pinkerton. Contested claims, persistent rumors, and self-serving misstatements were key components of his public persona. The company founder and spokesman (and lightning rod of criticism) was as much a fictionalized cipher as a real figure.[12]

Given the agency's profound awareness of its own constructed reputation on the public stage, it was also able to hide some deep contradictions. Allan Pinkerton was a former Chartist dedicated to the ideologies of free labor (and abolitionism) whose company increasingly found itself rooting out worker resistance.[13] After his death, Allan continued to be the public face of the company even as his biography shifted to accommodate the company's new role as armed guards for capital. As "Lost Cause" nostalgia settled into both northern and southern culture by the turn of the century, Pinkerton's radical abolitionism faded from the company's advertising.[14] So too did references to Pinkerton's youthful radical Chartism drop away. The agency was so successful in crafting their brand that for years they almost alone provided such services, yet the Pinkerton name also came to represent all the abuses of the system. They were responsible for "Pinkertonism"; other detective companies were held to far less public scrutiny. While the word of Pinkerton agents seemed to carry the weight of law, few were sure whether that made their statements true. Despite the company's best efforts, it was unclear whether the word of Allan Pinkerton and his detectives (including James McParlan during the Molly Maguire trials and Andrew Johnson during the Haymarket trials) could really be trusted. Yet the counternarratives of Pinkerton exploits came from equally unreliable narrators; the hagiographies of the James brothers, for instance, were also filled with convoluted facts, wishful thinking, and blatant falsehoods.

Despite the mythology and falsehoods (or perhaps because of them), the agency was both player and pawn in the epic narrative of industrial expansion in the Gilded Age. Jesse James became an outlaw hero of the unrepentant south, with Pinkerton agents as his northern foil; dime novelists would later transform James into a western bandit, with Pinkerton as the muscle of the railroad. Irish miners in Pennsylvania became either criminal conspirators or labor martyrs, depending on the teller of the tale. Both cheap publications and detective novels alternately glorified or ridiculed the agents' actions and sensationalized their role as detectives and thugs. Progressive exposés eviscerated the company's reputation, congressional investigations challenged the company's legal standing, and American workers rallied against the actions of the "Pinks." When Americans spoke of the Pinkertons (and Pinkertonism), they were exploring the new realities of an industrial society.

The result of the interplay between the agency's actions on behalf of capital-ists and their cultural infamy gave the agency a political resonance. Pinkerton's National Detective Agency emerged in the liberal nineteenth century because so many older institutions of control, deference, and communal oversight did not survive the age of revolutions at the end of the eighteenth century. Further-more, the Industrial Revolution and market expansion helped to create new paradigms of economic and interpersonal relationships, as well as cultural fears of banditry, embezzlement, theft, and disorder. Because the aristocracy, the Crown, and the church were no longer able to provide order, and the state was not yet willing, private firms arose to fill that need. Yet at the same time, the responses to and outrage toward the Pinkertons helped to crystalize the concept of plutocracy and spur the empowerment of the liberal nation-state. Through the advent of weekly magazines, dime novels, and exposés, Americans in the Gilded Age were a people hungry for information and quick to outrage. While the nineteenth-century state often exercised its power through the Pinkerton agency, by the end of the century increasing numbers of people demanded that the modern state had to actively protect liberal individualism within the market-place by both curbing the concentrated power of monopoly and crushing the threats from communism and anarchism. To do so, the modern state had to both confront and co-opt the power and reputation of the Pinkertons.

FOR THESE reasons, a cultural history of the Pinkerton agency reshapes our understandings of nineteenth-century American capitalism and the rise of the nation-state. Largely focusing on the biographies of leading industrialists or the lost artisanal traditions of workers, scholars have long shown how managers within new corporations changed the rules of the game in their favor; they be-came the "visible hands" of the market.[15] Newer explorations into the history of capitalism have given us a broader sense of how a market economy that com-modified every exchange and dislocated older communities rose in the nineteenth century. Managers, tramps, national guards, debtors, farmers, freaks of fortune, and immigrants were all part of what economic historian Karl Polanyi termed the "catastrophic dislocation of the lives of common people."[16] Recent studies have shown us a great deal about how older institutional webs of obligation and interaction came undone in the nineteenth century. Less clear is what rose to replace those broken webs. "What of the arrival of a class of industrial capitalists ready to take labor on, break its associations and subject it to the discipline of the machine, the clock, and the factory?" asks cultural historian Jean-Christophe

Agnew of the new history of capitalism. "What of the active resistance . . . and what of the courts, the National Guard, and the deputized private police forces of the Gilded Age—state actors dedicated to enforcing the new concepts of property embodied in corporate chapters?" If we are looking for the action of capitalism and the enforcement of its new logic, that story runs through the Pinkerton agency. If corporate managers were the "visible hand" of the market, the Pinkertons were the market's visible fist; they were the shock troops of industrial order.[17]

Like other manifestations of the market economy, the Pinkerton agency as both an arm of industrial capital and a distinct form of state power developed slowly over time. American history and memory have long portrayed the nineteenth century as a time of laissez-faire economics and a nonactive state; indeed, both modern conservatives who pine for such deregulation and modern liberals who warn against it have taken the lack of Gilded Age governance as a given. Robber baron power and the excesses of the Pinkertons were long thought to be a product of the state's weakness.[18] Yet new scholarship has drawn into question these assumptions. Through various agencies the state did take an active (though not always visible) role in shaping economic and expansionist policies long before the Progressive Era. Because of their unique role as subcontractors with the Postal Service, the Treasury, and other governmental agencies, the Pinkertons were as much a visible hand of the state as they were of capital. The power of the Pinkerton agent in the Gilded Age does not suggest a weak state but rather shows a powerful but pragmatic state that demanded order but delegated its authority. Even as court rulings such as *United States v. Cruikshank* (92 U.S. 542 [1875]) or the Slaughterhouse Cases (83 U.S. 36 [1873]) seemed to limit governmental intervention and codify the rights of property, the political legitimacy granted to the Pinkerton detective demonstrates a state willing to enforce the new rules of market and actively protect the "property" of capital. In many important ways the anti-Pinkerton laws of the Progressive Era and the civil liberties investigations of the New Deal come to be seen less as radical breaks with a laissez-faire past than as moments when the state took back the authority it had granted the agency. In first legitimizing and then delegitimizing the Pinkertons, the modern state claimed, as Max Weber suggested, a monopoly on the legitimate use of violence.[19]

At the same time, the issues at play within the histories of the Pinkertons, such as the enforcement of industrial order, the creation of a national police, or the romantic banditry of traditional communities, were hardly unique to the

United States. The formation of the national police in France, for instance, served to override the authority and identities of the various regions of France and impose a national order and identity.[20] Great Britain, always desperate to juxtapose itself against France, developed no such national police, yet by 1882 the Metropolitan Police of London had added the Special Irish Branch to deal with Fenians and anarchists.[21] In Mexico, President Porfirio Diaz's federal police force (the *fuerzas rurales*) patrolled and enforced law in the countryside, thereby denying power to local landholding caudillos and deepening the authority of the central state; the elimination of the *rurales* would be one of the principle reforms of the Mexican Revolution. In Central America, the secret police of Luis Borgan's Honduras (led by a former Pinkerton) and the various caudillo armies and national guards of other nations represented different ways that nations dealt with modernization, unrest, and traditional communities. All suggest that behind the late nineteenth-century mantras of "modernity and progress" lay a desire to impose industrial order and new rules of the market. One answer was to empower landowners, private corporations, and mines to raise their own security forces. Other nations chose to embolden the nation-state by forming a professional and uniformed national police.

Uniquely, the United States seems to be one of the few nations to empower private firms to raise their own forces and then vest those same forces with the authority and power of the state. The American republic in the nineteenth century did not have a centralized police agency; local police, sheriffs, and poorly trained marshals constituted law enforcement. Government agencies such as the Treasury or the Postal Service had even less authority. Instead, the Pinkertons patrolled the newly created spaces of the middle border, the west, immigrant and mining towns, and urban rail yards. Tales about the Pinkertons were police stories, yet the official status of the Pinkerton agent was unclear. They could be both agents of the state and enforcers of corporate power. If citizens invented nationalism through notions of "imagined communities," then Americans imagined their nation-state either around or in juxtaposition to the Pinkertons.[22]

Just as the infamy of the Pinkertons came to define law and power in the Gilded Age, globalization and neoliberal privatization at the turn of the twentieth century demonstrate the reemergent problems of Pinkertonism as the meaning of nation-states and "official" actors blurs. The first two decades of the twenty-first century have been defined by transnational migrations, mass internment in private prisons, austerity programs imposed by the International Monetary Fund, and the disruptive power of non-state actors such as Al-Qaeda and ISIS. At the same time, the withdrawal of official actors representing the nation-state from law enforcement, prisons, protection, security, and warfare has resulted in a return of private companies to which these tasks can be outsourced. Perhaps the most infamous of these enterprises, and certainly the one that has drawn the most direct comparisons to the Pinkertons, is Blackwater USA, whose government contracts included security work in Iraq through the State Department, military intelligence through the Central Intelligence Agency (CIA), border security through the Department of Homeland Security, and domestic order and protection in post-Katrina New Orleans through the Federal Emergency Management Agency. Blackwater and the dozens of similar companies that have emerged since 2001 reconfirm the lessons learned about the Gilded Age Pinkertons; it is problematic for the state to privatize the authority to kill.[23]

So HOW do we begin to make sense of both the realities and mythologies of the Pinkertons? In his study of antebellum slave markets, Walter Johnson shows how slave pens and auctions were the peculiar institution at its most commodified, most cruel, and most public. This was where the "invisible" hand of slavery economics became visible for both its proponents and its critics.[24] We might think about the Pinkertons in much the same way; between 1870 and 1937, they were the most visible element of capital's transformation and domination. They were the power and violence of capitalism at its most naked. If there were a single "chattel principle" to nineteenth-century industrialization, it would be this: industrialists had the power to kill their workers. Dangerous working conditions, starvation wages, the testimony of detectives, or the force of hired gunmen were all symbols of this power. This is why the quote so often attributed to Jay Gould, who had hired the Pinkertons to break the 1885 Southwest strike, that he could "hire one half of the working class to kill the other half" resonated so clearly in the nineteenth and twentieth centuries.[25] As the hired guns of capital, the Pinkertons became and remained for American society the focal point of a public discourse on industrial violence. At the same time, the Pinkerton detective, the strikebreaker, and the mercenary all became romantic figures within industrial folklore. The significance of the Pinkertons lies in the intersections of their political and cultural roles.

Journalist Charles Francis Bourke understood this contradiction of the Pinkerton detective when he launched his agency-approved "history" of the Pinkertons in 1905. Instead of Lincoln's inauguration train, the coal mines of Pennsylvania, or any of the other hallmarks of Pinkerton lore, Bourke opened his story with a parody of an absurd dime novel detective. He wrote of "Old Hunks," the stage driver, who "sprang suddenly to his feet." With one hand he threw off his disguise and with the other hand "he drew four revolvers from his belt, and covered the now terror-stricken bandits." Only then did the desperadoes realize that they were facing "DEMON DICK, the BOY DETECTIVE!" who had come to teach the villains that "Uncle Sam's mail coach has the right of way." For all that intentional absurdity, however, Bourke was certain that for his readers, "providing you were a normal and healthy-minded boy, it is a perfectly safe guess that at some time in your career you were tremendously interested in the thrilling exploits of DEMON DICK, or some of his colleagues," because somewhere deep down we all like detective stories. "But why need we take them with a fictional coating?" he asked. "Here—as in every other walk of life—truth is far the stranger."[26]

For Bourke, as for many in the Gilded Age, and indeed for us in the twenty-first century, that was the appeal of the Pinkerton detective. Stories of the Pinkertons wove together the true, the imagined, the politically charged, and the deeply romantic into a parable of the age. The Pinkertons, as an agency, as heroes and villains of American folklore, and as a metonym of industrialization, existed in many cultural forms, and their meaning was debated by an eccentric collection of characters, each constructing their own legends and meanings. Each tale offered a different version of industrial modernity and the nation-state. My tale of the Pinkertons, which is both a history of the agency and a deconstruction of Pinkerton stories, is no different. Is what follows a tragedy, comedy, satire, or romance? I am not sure. Am I a reliable narrator? I won't say. But as we turn to the tales, exploits, and debated meanings of the Pinkerton agency, we might as well follow Bourke's advice from 1905: "See then the sinister figure of the outlaw slinking across the background of these photographs from life,—watched always by 'the eye that never sleeps', and listen to these true stories from the annals of the Pinkerton Detective Agency."

CHAPTER ONE

In which Allan Pinkerton creates his agency

W HEN GENERAL George McClellan began to build the intelligence capabilities of the Army of the Ohio in the first years of the American Civil War, he looked first to his friend Allan Pinkerton. The two had met in 1860 when McClellan had been president of the Ohio and Mississippi Railroad and Pinkerton's private firm, the North West Police Agency, had made a name for itself by "testing" the employees of midwestern railroads for theft and embezzlement. Accepting McClellan's invitation, Pinkerton relocated from Chicago to Cincinnati to work with the general. He soon began to send agents into western Virginia and Kentucky to gauge sentiments and estimate troop strengths, information that helped McClellan control the rail lines of western Virginia and sweep Confederate forces from Philippi. When McClellan took command of the Army of the Potomac in 1861, Pinkerton followed him to Washington, DC. There Pinkerton's tasks included surveillance of Washington's potentially disloyal population and the oversight of spies sent into the Confederacy. In memoirs written after the war, Pinkerton spoke of his arrival in the nation's capital. It was necessary, he thought, to assume a pseudonym (he called himself Major E. J. Allen) not only because of the secretive nature of his work but also because, he assumed, the name Pinkerton was "so well known that it had become a sort of synonym for detective."[1]

For Pinkerton to declare that in 1861 his name was synonymous with "detective" was undoubtedly hubris, but when Pinkerton wrote his memoirs of the war in 1883, that claim was probably closer to true. In that time, Pinkerton had carefully constructed his business, his personal reputation, and his firm's public image. In 1872, the Herring Safe and Lock Company confirmed this reputation by evoking the name of Pinkerton in its advertisements. "The well-known and vigilant moral guardian, Allan Pinkerton, spies out 'cases' as quickly and as correctly as the sharpest of the lynx-eyed fraternity of which he is the acknowledged head and king," read the text. Allan Pinkerton used Herring's safes, it said, because he "is as keen at detecting true merit as he is criminality."[2]

This reputation was neither happenstance nor coincidence. Between 1855 and

1872, Allan Pinkerton crafted a business and a brand to respond to the times. Beginning first with the need for currency control against counterfeiters in frontier Chicago, then expanding into employee oversight along rail lines and express routes, and eventually building an organization capable of chasing professional criminals, Pinkerton's agency filled a perceived void in law enforcement. To maintain this role, Pinkerton had to closely control the cultural perception and reputation of his agency. In 1850s Chicago, Pinkerton's agents offered reliability and trustworthiness to railroads leery of the city's newly created and politically unstable police force. During the Civil War, Pinkerton promised loyalty to McClellan and the Union. After 1865, Pinkerton seized on the memory of Lincoln and the postwar emergence of the nation-state to craft a national agency without jurisdictional limits which could bring order to a seemingly disordered industrial and territorial expansion. In an age of rapid business expansion and monopolization, Allan Pinkerton identified a business niche, tailored his reputation to fit this niche, and helped to create and dominate the new industry of the national detective.

To craft this image, Pinkerton had to balance several different cultural tropes. By the middle of the century, much of Victorian society assumed that there were two different and competing notions of masculinity: a "rough" masculinity of violence and vice, and "gentlemen" who were capable of controlling themselves and encouraging the morality of others.[3] Modern detectives were expected to play at being roughs while secretly maintaining their virtue. Moreover, while Victorian respectability may have brought order to the home, grave concerns remained about how they might transfer the domestic morality of the "proper" home to the seemingly lawless immorality of modern society. Market exchanges between strangers seemed to encourage fraud and theft. Indeed, the self-promoting hucksterism of P. T. Barnum and other midcentury "peddlers" seemed to encourage fraud.[4] If moral suasion had its limits, then organized and professional police forces seemed necessary. By adding uniforms, crime prevention, and investigation to their repertoire over the course of the nineteenth century, urban police transitioned from riot control of immigrant neighborhoods and youth gangs to institutional control over criminal classes. While these police forces were supposed to impose order on a disordered urban landscape, the political struggle to control the police often made this system highly contentious and unstable.[5] Hence, private police firms (often known as "independents") provided an extra sense of security and order for those willing to pay, especially in cities where police lacked investigators for criminal detection.

Allan Pinkerton balanced these different worlds of institutional order, Victo-

rian sensibility, and firm management. His work chasing criminals, testing railroad employees, and spotting counterfeiters shifted seamlessly from official (as
agent of the Treasury and sheriff's deputy) to independent. He carefully crafted
a business, including both private detectives and protective patrols, to fit new
needs. He shamelessly self-promoted through a series of books, but he tried to
avoid the veneer of charlatanism which had defined earlier advertisers. For
Pinkerton, his business and reputation had to be both closely aligned with the
newly emergent powers of capital and the state and within the Victorian ideals
of the gentleman detective. By changing his name and mixing seamlessly into
Washington society, Pinkerton was playing both modern detective and flâneur.[6]
The Victorian gentleman, largely owing to his breeding and manners, could
often move throughout the different subcultures of modern society. While the
flâneur used this ability to sample the many different entertainments and vices
that modern cities had to offer, detectives such as Pinkerton utilized this skill to
ferret out information on treason, corruption, and loyalty. Moreover, the modern detective could, like a stage actor or a confidence man, manipulate his appearance to pass as someone he was not. Pinkerton's image, name, reputation,
and brand seemingly were his to control.

The making of Allan Pinkerton

For a man who would come to embody so many of the Victorian ideals of the
nineteenth century, Allan Pinkerton's early life and politics were far from Victorian. Pinkerton was born in 1819 in Glasgow, Scotland, and came of age in the
notorious Gorbals district. As a young man, he embraced Chartism and became
a vocal leader of the movement in Scotland. An outgrowth of worker protest in
the industrial cities of northern England and southern Scotland, the Chartists
demanded electoral reform and votes for working men. Critics, however, suspected continental-style radicalism. Fearful of the movement, British authorities began to crack down on Chartist leadership and rallies. While Pinkerton's
political loyalties were clear, the extent of his radical activities remains less certain, yet Pinkerton left Scotland in 1842 in the midst of the violent crackdown
against Chartist leadership. Allan and his wife, Joan, landed in Canada and made
their way west to Chicago. Picking up the coopering trade, Pinkerton moved
northwest of the city to the Scottish settlement of Dundee and began to ply his
trade along the Fox River. Still infused with reform ideals, Pinkerton became a
dedicated abolitionist, served as a state representative to Illinois's Liberty Party
convention in 1848, and helped raise money to fund John Brown.[7]

Pinkerton arrived in Illinois just in time for the radical transformation of Chicago. A frontier outpost in the early 1840s, Chicago quickly became a booming metropolis by the 1850s, driven largely by westward expansion and railroad construction. Because of its railroad connections, Chicago's commercial reach was considerable, and the city quickly grew. Independent bank notes, or "wildcat money," often served as official tender, yet these notes were easily forged, faked, and traded in an underground economy, giving rise to both counterfeiters and detectives who caught them. In 1847, Pinkerton was exploring an island in the Fox River, looking for wood for his barrels, when he encountered a suspicious-looking camp that turned out to be a hiding spot for counterfeiters. He returned with the county sheriff to make the arrests and claim the reward. Soon, other businessmen in Dundee contracted with Pinkerton to investigate similar counterfeiters.

A year later, Pinkerton gained fame for his arrest of counterfeiter John Craig. "The country being new, and great sensations scarce, the affair was in everybody's mouth, and I suddenly found myself called upon, from every quarter, to undertake matters requiring the detective skill," Pinkerton would later write, "until I was soon actually forced to relinquish the honorable though not over-profitable occupation of a cooper, for that of a professional detective."[8] Soon after, Kane County sheriff Luther Dearborn appointed Pinkerton as a sheriff's deputy. In 1852, Cook County sheriff William Church hired Pinkerton to track two kidnapped Michigan girls who had traveled through Chicago. The following year, disillusioned by Dundee's increasing anti-abolitionism, Pinkerton relocated to Chicago, where he served as a sheriff's deputy under both Church and Cyrus Bradley. In early 1855, Pinkerton also became a special agent for the US Postal Service to investigate counterfeiting and mail fraud. In 1855 the *New York Times* recognized the fine work of "special mail agent" Allan Pinkerton in capturing mail clerk Theodore Denniston in what it called "the most important arrest in the annuals of Post Office depredations ever brought to light in this country." "To Allan Pinkerton is due all the credit of the detection," praised the paper. "For three weeks Mr. Pinkerton has scarcely seen repose in the devotion with which he has followed up the criminal"; however, he "redoubled his vigilance until his body and brain were nearly exhausted" until he caught his man. "As a detective and police officer, Mr. Pinkerton has no superior," the paper concluded, "and we doubt if he has any equals in this country."[9] At the same time, Pinkerton worked for the Southern Michigan Railroad. In 1855 he contracted with six local rail lines to provide security and oversight of employees. To do so, he formed, along with Chicago attorney Edward Rucker, the North West Police Agency (the forerunner of Pinkerton's National Detective Agency) and began "testing" station agents and conductors to prevent embezzlement and theft.[10]

Pinkerton's career as both a law enforcement official of the state and an independent agent for Illinois railroads mirrored the contentious rise of urban police and private police firms in Chicago. By 1850 Chicago still functioned under an older system of the night watch, but the city had also grown rapidly in terms of geography and population in the preceding decade. Chicago was already a popular destination for European immigrants, which brought nativist and ethnic politics into the mix of urban policing. In 1855, Levi Boone of the new anti-immigrant American Party (more commonly known as the "Know-Nothings") became mayor of Chicago and dismissed all members of the night watch who were of "foreign birth." After riots in April of 1855, Boone eliminated the night watch completely and promised to create a "new police" composed of officers who were all of American birth. His choice for police chief was former Cook County sheriff Cyrus Bradley. Boone's and Bradley's terms were short-lived, but the contentious politics of urban policing remained. In particular, Republican mayor John Wentworth battled with Bradley for political control of the force. The uncertainty of the status of "official" police forces led to a boom in "independent" private forces such as the "Merchant's Police" and Cyrus Bradley's own "Chicago Detecting and Collecting Police Agency." Critics often questioned the integrity and oversight of such private firms and called for either stricter governance or their outright banning. Some feared that such firms operated outside the jurisdiction of the mayor; others felt that corrupt mayors held too much control over the police and that oversight should exist at the state level. In defense, the Chicago *Daily Tribune* called for the raising of money so that private firms such as Bradley's could be hired to clean up the city. Still others were convinced that firms not only oversold the threat of crime but imported criminals into the city or committed thefts and arsons themselves in order to create business. In 1857 the Illinois legislature considered a bill to "suppress police agencies of a private nature." In 1861 the state of Illinois resolved the question of oversight by creating a three-man commission, appointed by the state, to oversee and run urban police departments. The first chairman of this commission was former police chief, and former employer of Pinkerton, Cyrus Bradley.[11]

Although he did submit an affidavit against the proposed legislative ban, Pinkerton was reluctant to wade into the political battles of private police. He did create a new division called Pinkerton's Protective Patrol to provide uniformed security guards within the city of Chicago, yet he preferred to focus his attention on his railroad clients, especially the expanding need for protection for express companies that transferred large amounts of money over vast stretches of territory. William Harden opened the first express company in 1839, followed soon after by Alvin Adams and P. B. Burke, who formed the Adams Express Company in 1840. In 1850 Henry Wells, along with partners Johnston Livingston, William Fargo, and John Butterfield, formed the American Express Company. By 1852, owing mostly to the flow of money into and out of the gold fields of California, Wells and Fargo spun off a separate company, which they named after themselves, that specialized in transcontinental transfers. Like so many of the other products of the west, including lumber, grain, and cattle, the money of the west flowed through Chicago.

With money moving from station to station, the potential for embezzlement and theft increased as well. Railroad companies had long worried about the loyalty of their employees and had hired firms such as the North West Police Agency to test their conductors and stationmasters and ferret out those who pocketed fares or underreported ridership. However, theft from the express line left the company responsible for the money that it had guaranteed. Thus, the interests of the express companies lay in both catching the suspected thief and reclaiming the missing money. Pinkerton's introduction to this line of work came in 1858, when the president of the Adams Express Company, John Bingham, hired Pinkerton to investigate missing funds from the Montgomery, Alabama, station of the company. By shadowing the suspect with a series of agents, Pinkerton was able to provide proof of guilt and locate the stolen money. Following the well-publicized success of the Adams Express case, Pinkerton changed the name of his company to reflect both its new reach and its founder's burgeoning fame. The North West Police Agency became Pinkerton's National Police Agency.[12]

Allan Pinkerton goes to war

By 1860, even railroad companies were becoming increasingly intertwined in the growing sectional crisis. Among those concerned was Samuel Morse Felton of the Philadelphia, Wilmington and Baltimore Railroad, who also happened to be a close friend of John Bingham of the Adams Express Company and was thus familiar with the details of Pinkerton's case. Felton contracted with Pinkerton to provide both security and intelligence for the railroad, as Felton feared that southern agents and sympathizers would sabotage the railroad, especially its ferry crossing of the Susquehanna River. With such sabotage, many feared, the capital of Washington would be cut off from the rest of the north and federal troops would not be able to arrive to protect the city. Employing the same tactics he used in Alabama, Pinkerton assigned agents in Baltimore and the surrounding communities to gain the trust of southern sympathizers and conspirators. As part of this investigation, Pinkerton claimed to have unearthed a broader conspiracy to assassinate president-elect Abraham Lincoln as he passed through Baltimore. According to Pinkerton, a conspiracy of twenty members met on February 8 to plan the assassination. The ambush was to take place in the Calvert Street station, where Lincoln would arrive on February 21. Baltimore chief of police George P. Kane, who had southern sympathies, would ensure that the police presence on the train platform would be minimal. A few "street toughs" were to start a fight down the platform, which would draw attention away from Lincoln and create the chaos necessary for the assassin to approach the president-elect. Toward this end, the conspirators on February 8 drew cards from a box to determine the assassin. The holder of the single red card was to keep his identity secret to everyone else. To make sure of the success of such a plan, eight red cards were placed in the box.[13]

Pinkerton, through Samuel Felton, brought the news to Lincoln. Despite learning of the plot, Lincoln refused to change his schedule and traveled on to Harrisburg, Pennsylvania, as planned. However, when Frederick Seward brought news of a rumored assassination plot from New York police detective John A. Kennedy, who had been hired by William Seward and Winfield Scott, Lincoln acquiesced to Pinkerton's plans. After a dinner with the Pennsylvania governor, Lincoln declared that he was retiring to his room. Instead, agents ushered him into a waiting carriage and rushed him to the train station, where a special car awaited. From Harrisburg the train carried Lincoln back to Philadelphia, where he awaited another car to carry him through Baltimore into Washington. To prevent news of Lincoln's early departure from Harrisburg, Pinkerton arranged with the American Telegraph Company to suspend communications into Baltimore; his agents also sabotaged the telegraph lines of the Northern Central Railway. With Pinkerton's agents posted all along the route looking for potential sabotage or delays and Allan Pinkerton and agent Kate Warne accompanying the president-elect, Lincoln's train sneaked its way into the capital city.[14]

Over the next week, as Lincoln prepared for his inauguration, speculation swirled about the events in Baltimore. Some assumed that secessionist sentiment and general unruliness in Baltimore explained the night. Others thought that radical elements within the Republican Party were responsible for the unrest in

the city. Lincoln bypassed the city, as the argument went, to avoid any association with these folk. For its part, the *New York Times* told both tales. Its Washington correspondent argued that "Mr. Lincoln's coup d'état and rapid passage
through Baltimore have been condemned here by some who do not know the
facts." A set of "unscrupulous political knaves," he reported, had planned to use
Lincoln's arrival as a pretext for a political demonstration. Instead of letting
these radical rowdies usurp Lincoln, the president-elect was "advised by telegraph to pass on to Washington without stopping which he did. This advice
came from gentlemen who had the good name of Baltimore chiefly at heart."
George Kane confirmed this story in a letter sent to the *Times*, in which he argued that Lincoln had sped through the city to avoid "an intended Republican
display . . . offensive to the masses of our people." However, in the very same
edition, the *Times* correspondent traveling with Lincoln's party to Harrisburg
offered a very different interpretation. "On Thursday night after he had retired,
Mr. Lincoln was aroused and informed that a stranger desired to see him on a
matter of life and death," he reported. Lincoln initially declined to see the stranger
without first learning his name, yet "such prestige did the name carry that while
Mr. Lincoln was yet disrobed he granted an interview to the caller." This stranger
(still unidentified for the newspaper reader) laid out the assassination plot, and
the "list of names of the conspirators presented a most astonishing array of persons high in Southern confidence . . . statesmen laid the plan, Bankers endorsed
it, and adventurers were to carry it into effect." This meeting convinced Lincoln
to change his plans.[15]

In presenting both interpretations, the paper admitted that "as to the motive
which induced this departure, there seems to be some discrepancy in the accounts thus far received." The plot described by the correspondent in Harrisburg "comes with so much detail as to leave no room to doubt that it was the
prevailing belief of those connected with the Presidential party." Yet the Washington correspondent "gives us an explanation which seems much more likely to
be well founded." Most likely, the paper concluded, Baltimore was just an unruly
city that "has been specially disgraced by its political clubs." However, by February 27 even the *New York Times* had become convinced. "In regard to the recent alleged conspiracy," it concluded, "we have no doubt of its existence." A
"secret agent of the Government" had supplied General Scott with information.
The plot was then confirmed by "one of the principal officers in Adams' Express
Company," the information "having been procured incidentally by an experienced and skillful detective in their service." "The subsequent development

leaves no doubt at all that the course pursued by Mr. Lincoln," the paper decided, "was eminently prudent and judicious." This did not stop others, however, from criticizing Lincoln and publishing cartoons depicting a frazzled and fearful Lincoln arriving in Washington in disguise.[16]

In later memoirs Pinkerton claimed that both Lincoln and Seward asked him to stay in Washington and form a "secret service." Pinkerton, however, chose to return to his private firm in Chicago. Instead, Lincoln and the War Department formed two separate intelligence organizations, a short-lived firm headed by William Parsons and another firm led by Lafayette Baker. Pinkerton would join the war at the behest of McClellan and began his work estimating troop strength in western Virginia. Pinkerton returned to the capital when McClellan was promoted in the aftermath of Bull Run.[17] While in Washington, Pinkerton, as a private contractor employed by McClellan, organized a service to provide both intelligence and counterespionage, especially investigating the loyalty of high-profile socialites within the city. One such case involved Rose O'Neal Greenhow, a popular Washington socialite who, in entertaining many of the leading politicians and officers of the city, had learned a great deal about Union mobilizations and troop movements, which she then passed to Richmond. Pinkerton, after having Greenhow's residence carefully watched, first placed Greenhow under house arrest and then had her jailed in the Old Capitol Prison. Greenhow was convicted of espionage and deported to Richmond. She soon left Richmond to travel to Europe as a diplomatic emissary of the Confederacy; while in Europe, she would write and publish an account of her "imprisonment and the first year of abolition rule" in Washington. Throughout her narrative, she spoke of the way that Pinkerton (whom she called E. J. Allen) and his fellow detectives affronted not only her honor but that of others as well, including a vivid description of Pinkerton dragging Stonewall Jackson's elderly mother up a flight of stairs. To explain the actions and demeanor of Pinkerton and his fellow "evil spirits," Greenhow offered a peculiar answer. "Detective Allen was a German Jew," she concluded, "and possessed all the national instincts of his race in an exaggerated degree, besides having these inherent characteristics sharpened by Yankee association." While trying to run the blockade back into Richmond, her ship broke apart, and Greenhow, probably weighed down by contraband gold hidden in her dress, drowned. In Richmond Greenhow was mourned with a military funeral, yet in Washington Pinkerton had established a quiet reputation for counterintelligence.[18]

At the same time, McClellan also asked Pinkerton to provide positive intelligence about southern troop strength and movement.[19] Pinkerton, using the tactics he had honed as a railroad detective, sent a handful of undercover agents, including Timothy Webster, into the city of Richmond to pose as transient but outspoken secessionists and infiltrate rebel societies. A Pinkerton agent in Baltimore before the war, Webster, along with fellow agent Hattie Lawton, transitioned easily into Richmond society, and they often served as Confederate couriers between the cities of Richmond, Washington, and Baltimore. Pinkerton agent Pryce Lewis, who had traveled the Virginia countryside in the guise of an English gentleman to gather information before Philippi, also returned to Virginia. Pro-Confederate exiles in Richmond, however, recognized Lewis from his counterintelligence work in Washington. Arrested for espionage, Lewis would spend much of the war in Confederate prisons. Southern authorities, who had grown suspicious of how easily Webster and Lawton had crossed from Baltimore to Richmond, used the information gleaned from Lewis and fellow captured Pinkerton agent John Scully to arrest the pair.[20] Webster, who had been tasked with carrying confidential messages to Baltimore for the Confederates, was convicted of treason and hanged. Several times over the next twenty years, Pinkerton would write glowingly of Webster, and after the war, he paid to have Webster's remains moved from Richmond to the Pinkerton family plot in Chicago. Lewis, after his release, was largely ignored by the agency.

Other agents (about whom Pinkerton would not write after the war) proved less successful at infiltrating Confederate circles. One clearly took the opportunity to swindle the War Department, while another was probably actively spying for the Confederacy. One Pinkerton agent and an agent of Lafayette Baker's spy service spent several weeks shadowing each other. In sum, while Pinkerton focused on Washington parlor intrigues, he was able to provide little quality information out of Richmond. Not until later in the war, long after Pinkerton had left the service, did Union intelligence make contact with a Unionist underground in the Confederate capital. Instead of cultivating pro-Union sources, Pinkerton agents in Richmond relied on infiltrating pro-secessionist circles. The information gleaned from these sources led to Pinkerton's notorious overestimates of Confederate troop strength in and around Richmond, which in turn exacerbated McClellan's caution and his own overestimations. Nor was Pinkerton able to provide for McClellan the far more immediate and useful battlefield reconnaissance and scouting; such intelligence would only emerge later in the war. During the buildup to the Peninsula Campaign, Pinkerton's agency numbered about twenty-four agents, only five of whom were in the south. During Lee's

Maryland Campaign, which would lead to Antietam, Pinkerton's number was about half that. Given the lack of intelligence in both campaigns, McClellan became convinced that he was fighting superior numbers whose location he could not determine.[21] Disgruntled with the general's caution, Lincoln twice replaced McClellan as commander. Fiercely loyal to McClellan and still an independent contractor, Pinkerton and his agents left the Army of the Potomac after McClellan's post-Antietam removal, taking all of their files on Confederate troop strength and intelligence agents with them.[22]

Over the next three years, Pinkerton would contract off and on with the federal government to investigate quartermaster supplies and abuses of governmental contracts. Pinkerton agents would spend some time in occupied territory such as New Orleans to gather information on guerilla bands and Confederate resistance. One quartermaster became convinced that General Grant had used Pinkerton against him as part of a political vendetta.[23] For the most part, however, Pinkerton turned his attention to his private firm and opened new branch offices in New York and Philadelphia. As the war went on, armies continued to rely heavily on informal and decentralized secret services; generals who could find extra money funded their own spy networks. Only much later in the war would any semblance of a centralized and organized intelligence be built, ironically perhaps by former Pinkerton spy John Babcock. Yet no other agency would establish itself as firmly as the Pinkerton agency, nor would any agency consume such a large percentage of secret service monies. Pinkerton not only made his reputation during the war but also made a great deal of money. Indeed, while Pinkerton served McClellan, he sent invoices to the War Department, but he refused to list the names or identities of his agents. Much to his chagrin, Secretary of War Edwin Stanton found himself paying the salaries of unnamed sources. The decentralized nature of the work, however, did not prevent both Pinkerton and Lafayette Baker from claiming, in separate postwar memoirs, the title of "Chief of the Secret Service."[24]

This reputation would not go unchallenged, however. In 1866, in a rush of memorials to the war and Lincoln, Benson Lossing wrote the first comprehensive history of the war, including both the Baltimore plot and the political fallout that followed. "This movement gave life and currency to many absurd theories," he declared. "It was asserted that Mr. Lincoln had assumed all sorts of disguises to prevent recognition—that he was muffled in a long military cloak and wore a Scotch cap—that he was wrapped in the shaggy dress of a hunter, et caetora; and for awhile his political opponents made merry at his expense, and the pencils of the caricaturists supplied fun for the public. . . . It was properly felt to be a national disgrace." Yet Lossing felt that the time had come to change these perceptions, because he felt that "the occurrence was not so humiliating as represented by the politicians, the satirists, and caricaturists." To make his case, Lossing quoted Lincoln's own memories (as told to Lossing) of the night. "Mr. Pinkerton, a skillful police detective . . . who had been employed for some days in Baltimore watching or searching for suspicious persons there," Lincoln recalled, "informed me that a plan had been laid for my assassination." This led Lossing to believe that while "there has never been a public legal investigation concerning the alleged plot to assassinate the President-elect at the time . . . sufficient facts have been made known through the testimony of detectives to justify the historian in assuming that such a plot was formed."[25]

Almost immediately, John Kennedy, the former superintendent of the New York Metropolitan Police, complained about the lack of coverage of his role and an overemphasis on Pinkerton. He sent a letter to Lossing, which the author included in the second volume of his Civil War history, stating that "it furnishes interesting additions to the history of Mr. Lincoln's journey." Not only did Kennedy claim to have uncovered the plot in Baltimore, but "the note I wrote was what Mr. Frederick Seward carried to Mr. Lincoln in Philadelphia. Mr. Lincoln has stated that it was this note which induced him to change his journey as he did." Moreover, Kennedy claimed, "I know nothing of any connection of Mr. Pinkerton in the matter." This letter prompted Samuel Felton to write to Lossing to defend the role and prestige of Pinkerton, a rebuttal that found its way into the third volume of Lossing's history.[26] Pinkerton himself responded to Kennedy's accusations by penning his own account of the Baltimore plot against Lincoln, entitled *History and Evidence of the Passage of Abraham Lincoln from Harrisburg, Pa., to Washington, D.C., on the 22d and 23d of February, 1861.* At this point *Harper's New Monthly Magazine* picked up the story. In an 1868 article the magazine claimed that while "the veil of mystery has never yet been lifted from the evidence disclosing the plot to assassinate Abraham Lincoln," his subsequent assassination by John Wilkes Booth and the conspiracy trial that followed had "removed any doubt in regard to the real existence of the plot." Lincoln was probably always in danger, the magazine concluded, and thus his safety was due to "a man by the name of Allan Pinkerton, one of the boldest, most shrewd and skillful detectives of any country."[27]

Others would argue that Pinkerton overestimated loose talk and fragmentary evidence. Still others claimed that no such conspiracy ever existed and that Pinkerton invented the plot to ingratiate himself to Lincoln and lobby for a placement in any wartime espionage. Ward Hill Lamon, Lincoln's longtime bodyguard who accompanied the president-elect on his inaugural train ride, was particularly scathing in his summary of Pinkerton (whom he called E. J. Allen) and the Baltimore plot. Samuel Felton, he recalled, had "engaged with a private detective discussing the details of an alleged conspiracy to murder." After these discussions, "the detective went about his business with the zeal which necessarily marks his peculiar profession." Although everyone already knew that Baltimore was hostile to Lincoln, still the private detectives pursued their cause. "Whether they detected any plan to burn bridges or not, the chief detective does not relate," concluded Lamon, "but it appears that he soon deserted that inquiry, and got, or pretended to get, upon a scent that promised a heavier reward. Being intensely ambitious to shine in the professional way, and something of a politician besides, it struck him that it would be a particularly fine thing to discover a dreadful plot to assassinate the President elect; and he discovered it accordingly." Suggesting a plot was easy; however, "to furnish tangible proof of an imaginary conspiracy was a more difficult matter." To refresh his memory, Lamon read through the reports that Pinkerton submitted to Felton and Lincoln, yet he found them "neither edifying nor useful: they prove nothing but the baseness of the vocation which gave them existence." This realization struck Lamon, who had dedicated years of his life to protecting Lincoln, very hard.

> For ten years the author implicitly believed in the reality of the atrocious plot which these spies were supposed to have detected and thwarted . . . and for ten years he has pleased himself with the reflection that he also had done something to defeat the bloody purpose of the assassins. It was a conviction which could scarcely have been overthrown by evidence less powerful than the detective's weak and contradictory account of his own case. In that account there is literally nothing to sustain the accusation, and much to rebut it. It is perfectly manifest that there was no conspiracy —no conspiracy of a hundred, of fifty, of twenty, of three; no definite purpose in the heart of even one man to murder Mr. Lincoln at Baltimore.

To Lamon's reading, the only thing that Pinkerton's reports demonstrated was a "secret combination between hireling spies and paid informers" to fabricate treasonous statements. "No disinterested person would believe the story upon such evidence . . . it is probably mere fiction," he concluded. The fact that no one was pursued, arrested, or charged only confirmed for Lamon the fabrication of the plot. "The detectives are cautious not to include in the supposed plot to murder any person of eminence, power or influence," he pointed out. "Their game is all of a smaller sort." Even Lincoln "soon learned to regret the midnight ride . . . he was convinced that he had committed a grave mistake in yielding to the solicitations of a professional spy . . . he saw that he had fled from a danger purely imaginary." If John Kennedy threatened Pinkerton's public reputation by claiming the discovery of the plot for himself, Lamon's critique cut deeper in suggesting that the plot never existed.[28]

Crafting the Pinkerton detective

Within this debate, two different but interconnected things were at stake. Ties to the now beloved ex-president and a reputation as a top detective both had important financial repercussions. Most city leaders and many businesses feared the return of soldiers who had been exposed to all kinds of vices. Many assumed that a surge in crime and a corresponding surge in detective work were imminent. Whoever could claim the reputation as top detective stood to make a great deal of money. It was a public relations coup for Allan Pinkerton when a bio from *Harper's* in 1873 reminded readers that it was Pinkerton "whose exploit in safely conducting President Lincoln through the sanguinary rebel gauntlet at Baltimore previous to his first inauguration is a matter of historical record." The *Harper's* piece not only detailed Pinkerton's war record but also lauded his status as America's most famous detective. The magazine described Pinkerton as "probably the most skillful, persevering, and successful organizer and leader of individual detective enterprise." While such a figure might strike fear into the hearts of *Harper's* readers, the author was so surprised by Pinkerton's "grave and dignified manner" and his conservative black dress that he thought that Pinkerton had "more the appearance of a country parson than of a man thoroughly cognizant of all the arts, wiles, and iniquities of a demoralized age."[29]

To make sense of Allan Pinkerton, however, *Harper's* first tried to make sense of exactly what a detective was. "The rapid and progressive expansion of organizations for the detection, pursuit, and apprehension of malefactors within the last decade has doubtless been commensurate with, and a necessary sequent of, the great augmentation of the criminal record in this country," the article began. "Twenty years ago such a personage as a professional police detective was rarely met with or heard of out of Paris or London; but now nearly every town of magnitude in the United States has its corps of police experts who find continued calls upon their services, and receive ample compensation." Despite this desperate need for qualified detectives, "many corporation police agents who have received appointments through political influences possess but few if any of the qualifications essential to an astute craftsman," the magazine lamented. A modern detective must "intuitively, as it were, possess the ability to read at a glance the complex workings of the human mind in all its phases, and the skill to decipher the infinite variety of emotional permutations of the facial muscles, which often reveal secrets that are understood only by the initiated, and afford a key to the incentive as well as the effect of action," it continued. "Besides these, courage, energy, and activity, as well as discretion and patience, are equally indispensible." But, the paper warned, "as these requisites are rarely found united in one individual, experts in this profession are scarce."[30]

Alone among the population, the detective, with his keen sense of observation, modern detachment, and clinical gaze, could see through facades and reveal the criminal. Yet the "detective" was as much a literary invention as social reality. Beginning in 1841, Edgar Allan Poe gave American literature one of the first criminal detectives. In his series of books *The Murders in the Rue Morgue, The Mystery of Marie Roget,* and *The Purloined Letter,* Poe introduced readers to Auguste Dupin, the detective mastermind. Other references to both criminal detection and detectives slowly began to follow. Charles Dickens talked of detectives and inspectors in *Bleak House* (1853). So too did Wilkie Collins, in *The Moonstone,* popularize the plotlines of mysteries solved by superior intellects and close examination. In France the memoirs of François-Eugène Vidocq and the novels of Emile Gaboriau (especially the exploits of Monsieur LeCoq) helped to craft a similar mythology. Vidocq in particular popularized the idea of the former criminal who used his knowledge to enforce the law. After a brief career of crime, Vidocq became part of the *Sûreté Nationale,* a national police and investigative force. Gaboriau's Monsieur LeCoq was not officially part of the *Sûreté Nationale* but rather freelanced with them whenever they needed assistance with difficult cases. In the United States, Anna Katherine Green in her 1878 novel *The Leavenworth Case* created the first recognizable private detective tale. Beginning in 1887 with *A Study of Scarlet,* Arthur Conan Doyle created the consummate intellectual detective in Sherlock Holmes—a character who would come to define the idea of the all-knowing gentleman detective.

In crafting his own mythology of the detective and advertising for business, Pinkerton built on this emerging idea of mystery, crime, and detection. His detective was an interested but dispassionate professional who utilized powers of keen observation. In interviews and company press, Pinkerton tried to distance himself from the fame and reputation of France's Vidocq, the criminal who could catch other criminals. Although he was often referred to as "America's Vidocq," Pinkerton continually stressed that his agents were of the highest moral fiber. The 1873 *Harper's* biography broached the topic of Vidocq with Pinkerton. "In the course of conversation one day I remarked to him that I took for granted that most of his subordinates were selected from the most debased classes of society," the author said. "Not at all," responded Pinkerton; "on the contrary, I have seldom taken into my service a man whom I did not believe to be thoroughly honest and reliable. Moreover, I do not endorse the old adage of 'set a rouge to catch a rogue' for my experience has shown me that an honest man who possesses the other requisites makes a more efficient detective operator than a villain."[31]

In order to maintain his standards, Pinkerton drafted a series of rules and regulations. The agency published the first version of *General Principles and Rules of Pinkerton's National Police Agency* in 1867. "The character of the Detective must be above reproach," the principles began, "and none but those untainted with crime, of strict moral principles and good habits will be permitted to enter the service." "Under no circumstances will the Detective of the Agencies endeavor to induce any parties upon whom they may be operating to the commission of crime," they continued, and agents were strictly forbidden to work for rewards. Instead, Pinkerton agents earned on a per diem basis and kept meticulous records filed for expenses. Pinkerton updated the principles in 1869 and again in 1873, this time for a rechristened Pinkerton's National Detective Agency. While the basic rules and regulations remained the same, the 1873 principles delved deeply into the detective mythology and reputation of the agency. "The character of the Detective is comparatively new," the principles announced.

> It is true that, from the earliest ages, there have been officers of some kind for the detection and arrest of criminals, and the bringing of them to justice; but the manner and style of these operations were entirely different from those of the modern detective. . . . All his acts should be surrounded with secrecy. . . . The Mouchards of Paris, the old Bow Street Runners of London, and the "Shadows" as they were termed, of the American Police, have passed away before the enlightened intelligence of modern times, and the means and appliances which it has been found necessary to bring into operation, in order to circumvent and checkmate criminals.[32]

The purpose of the detective had changed because "crime, itself, has become more scientific . . . many men have entered upon a course of crime powerful of mind and strong of will who if they had devoted themselves to honest pursuits would undoubtedly have become honorable members of society." Such crime, however, was unnatural: "This agency . . . holds as its cardinal principle that Crime is as foreign to the human mind as a poisonous mineral substance is to the body, and that the Criminal, by his criminal act, weakens the whole fortress of his strength, both mental and moral, by receiving therein an enemy which will be always on the watch to betray him. . . . His crime haunts him perpetually and torments him to reveal it." "Crime can and must be detected," Pinkerton wrote, "by the pure and honest mind obtaining a controlling power over that of the criminal." The detective, the principles concluded, "must be a man of consider- able intellectual power . . . he must have a keen analytical mind . . . he must possess also the player's faculty of assuming any character that his case may require. . . . His movements should be quietly conducted; his manner should be unobtrusive, and his address agreeable. He should be able to adapt himself to all persons, in all the various grades of society." But if people worried about the potential for abuse and corruption, Pinkerton reassured readers that "only such business will be undertaken as is strictly legitimate and right, and then only, for the purpose of furthering the ends of justice and bringing criminals to punishment."[33]

As an additional part of his effort to promote the agency, Pinkerton also began to publish his own tales of detection and criminality. Each of these books, detailing the exploits of himself, his sons, and his detectives, was emblazoned with the name of the agency, its logo of the wide-awake eye, and its slogan of "we never sleep." They were an exercise in self-promotion. The first of these tales was Pinkerton's summary of his pursuit of Nathan Maroney during the Adams Express case of 1858. Published in 1874, the book was, according to Pinkerton, "a narration of some of the most interesting" occurrences of his career. He as- sured the reader, however, that the tales "are all true stories, transcribed from the Records in my offices." "If the incidents seem to the reader at all marvelous or improbable," he concluded, "I can but remind him, in the words of the old adage, that 'truth is stranger than fiction.'" Local officials had already charged Maroney, the agent for the Montgomery, Alabama, station of the Adams Ex- press, with stealing from the company's secured bags. However, as his trial ap- proached, company agents and local detectives could find little evidence of the money. The vice president of the company, according to Pinkerton, "freely ad- mitted his inability to fathom the mystery surrounding the loss of the money." "He said he knew of only one man who could bring out the robbery and he was living in Chicago," said Pinkerton by way of self-introduction; "Pinkerton was the name of the man he referred to." Taking on the case in order to win the re- spect and business of the Adams Express, Pinkerton quickly dispatched agents into the south. Pinkerton noted that he could not pursue the case himself because he had "always been a man somewhat after the John Brown stamp, aiding slaves to escape, or keeping them employed, and cunning them into Canada when in danger," and he feared that his abolitionist politics would give him away in the south. The Adams Express Company clearly "wanted a man who could at least affiliate readily with the inhabitants of the South." "But what class was he to mix with?" Pinkerton wondered. "Did he want a man to mix with the rough element, or to pass among gentleman?" Regardless, Pinkerton could "select from my force any class of man he could wish."[34]

What unfolds in the rest of *The Expressman and the Detective* is a cat-and-mouse game between the wily Maroney and the equally adept agents charged with following him. Recounting his belief that criminals always confess their crimes to someone, Pinkerton suspected that Maroney would "eventually seek someone in whom he thought he could confide and to whom he would entrust the secret." Pinkerton first placed an agent within the sporting culture of Montgomery; his task was to play cards, drink, and gamble his way into Maroney's circle of friends. Another agent donned disguises to shadow Maroney as he traveled throughout the south. In his telling, Pinkerton treated Maroney with the highest regard; he seemed a criminal worthy of Pinkerton's chase. "I found I had to cope with no ordinary man," he wrote of Maroney, "while I was a poor nameless individual with a profession which most people were inclined to look down upon with contempt." Maroney was "an uncommonly shrewd man and had formed a pretty good opinion of detectives and his ability to outwit them." Although Maroney "had seen the best detectives from New York, New Orleans, and other places completely baffled," Pinkerton's agents were cleverly disguised. Maroney "expected to be followed by a gentlemanly appearing man, who would drink and smoke occasionally, wear a heavy gold watch chain and have plenty of money to spend," Pinkerton wrote, "but the idea of being followed by a poor old Dutchman never entered his mind."[35]

While agents followed Maroney, they also shadowed his wife, to whom Pinkerton's account was less kind. After detailing her upbringing in polite society and her descent into the "fast" lifestyle of New Orleans, Pinkerton declared that the best way to shadow such a woman is to provide her with potential lovers, because "a woman of Mrs. Maroney's stamp, while separated from her husband, would most likely desire gentlemen's company." The young agent assigned to this duty quickly fell under the charms of Mrs. Maroney and declared his love for her, only to be advised by Pinkerton that "the woman might be very beautiful but still be a serpent!" Luckily for Pinkerton, he had assigned other, more clear-headed agents to shadow the suspect, including Kate Werne, who posed as a southern belle hiding a scandalous marriage. Werne, according to Pinkerton, was "above the medium height, slender, graceful in her movements, and perfectly self-possessed in her manner." She seemed the model of Victorian femininity except that "she seemed possessed of the masculine attributes of firmness and decision but to have brought all her faculties under control"; in essence, she was able to rise above her gender. Pinkerton congratulated himself on such a cunning hire. "At this time female detectives were unheard of," he wrote. "True it was the first experiment of the sort that had ever been tried; but we live in a progressive age and in a progressive country."[36]

Pinkerton's account is very much the novel of Victorian propriety. Maroney and his wife were living a life of crime and deceit. Eventually, they would expose their true character and lack of respectability. One of the key plot points of the book is the discovery that while living as husband and wife in Montgomery, the Maroneys were not married; they only married later while in the north as a safeguard against having to testify against each other. When news of this impropriety spread, the Maroneys' network of friends in Montgomery dissolved and the couple had to lean more heavily on planted Pinkerton confidants. Eventually, Maroney detailed his crimes and the location of the money to his cellmate confidant, who happened to be a Pinkerton agent. Pinkerton's book also included many of the key attributes of the modern detective story, including a moment when Pinkerton, having become acquainted with new information about Maroney, actually exclaims, "The plot thickens!" But more than anything else, *The Expressman and the Detective*, much like Pinkerton's earlier book on the Baltimore plot, was advertising for the agency. In addition to the company's logo emblazoned on the cover of the book, Pinkerton reminded his readers in the text that "the eye of the detective never sleeps."[37]

Such self-aggrandizement did not go unnoticed or unmocked, however. Critics, such as Mark Twain, saw the persona of the private detective as a fraud. In his sardonic 1882 short story "The Stolen White Elephant," Twain lampooned this kind of charlatanism. Inspector Blunt, who is searching for a missing elephant, quickly fills the newspapers with tales of his investigation and theories of the crime. "There were eleven of these theories and they covered all the possibilities; and this single fact shows what independent thinkers detectives are," remarked the narrator. "No two theories were alike, or even much resembled each other." When asked how such information made it to the press, Inspector

Blunt explained that "fame, reputation, constant public mention—these are the detective's bread and butter. He must publish his facts, else he will be supposed to have none; he must publish his theory, for nothing is so strange or striking as a detective's theory. We must constantly show the public what we are doing, or they will believe we are doing nothing." But alas, for all of Blunt's self-promotion, the trail had grown cold. "Now that the detectives were in adversity, the newspapers turned upon them," the narrator noted, including the creation of "all sorts of ridiculous pictures of the detective badge—you have seen that badge printed in gold on the back of detective novels, no doubt—it is a wide-staring eye, with the legend, 'WE NEVER SLEEP.'" Bartenders would mock the detectives by offering them eye-openers. The air, the narrator noted, was "thick with sarcasms." Still, the master detective remained convinced that the case could be solved. Once he had brokered a "compromise" with the assumed thieves using $100,000 of the narrator's money (half of which went to the detectives as reward) and charging the narrator $42,000 more in fees, the master detective literally stumbled across the rotting carcass of the dead elephant in the detective's sleeping quarters. With the case solved, Inspector Blunt was once again the toast of the newspapers and master of his profession. The detective had invented a façade of order.[38]

Conclusion: A detective mythology

After the publication of *The Expressman and the Detective* in 1875, Pinkerton spent much of the next ten years writing (or having ghostwritten for him) books that both chronicled and lauded the work of his detectives and his agency. Between 1875 and 1884 Pinkerton published seventeen books, most of them following the same formula of short tales of detective work.[39] Exceptions included *Strikers, Communists, Tramps and Detectives*, which was Pinkerton's attempt to write the history of the Great Railway Strike of 1877, *Thirty Years a Detective*, a memoir, and *Spy of the Rebellion*, a history of Pinkerton's spy network during the Civil War. However, all of the books served the same purpose: they were advertisement pieces for the agency. It was part of a larger effort by Pinkerton to distinguish his agency as professional detectives, not independent private police.

The popularity of Pinkerton's books and the notoriety of the Pinkerton agency grew in direct proportion to the popularity of the detective novel and the mystery narrative. The notion of a highly intelligent agent skilled in disguises captured the imagination of a public alternately intrigued and horrified by the other side of modern life. Exposés of New York alone, such as Edward Winslow Martin's *Secrets of the Great City*, Matthew Hale Smith's *Sunshine and Shadow in*

New York, James McCabb's *Lights and Shadows of New York Life,* Edward Crapsey's *Nether Side of New York,* and George Foster's *New York by Gas-Light and Other Urban Sketches,* offered readers tantalizing glimpses into the netherworlds of the city. Likewise, penny presses and flash presses published sensational stories of crime, sex, murder, and violence. The detective who could not only solve such crimes but also survive the dangers of such corrupted streets quickly became a staple of the dime novel genre as well. One of the first such detectives, the "Old Sleuth" created by Harlan Halsey, made his first appearance in *Fireside Companion* in 1872. The Old Sleuth was a young man who, because he had mastered the art of disguise, could pass as an unthreatening old man. A similar detective, Nick Carter, first appeared in the *New York Weekly* in 1886. Many, including Pinkerton himself, assumed that such dime novel detectives were based on Allan Pinkerton. The line between journalism and dime novels blurred in the 1870s, and many sensationalist presses closely followed the career of Pinkerton and his agents. One in particular, the *National Police Gazette,* which was an early sensationalist magazine specializing in rowdy masculine sports, bloody crimes, dashing detectives, and scantily clad women, seemed to revel in both the heroic exploits of the Pinkerton detective and his "merry men" and the sordid details of the crimes.[40] In all, the *National Police Gazette,* along with the exploits of Old Sleuth and Nick Carter, had made detection a popular and romantic profession.

In writing his books, Pinkerton tried (perhaps disingenuously) to distance the "realities" of detective work from the literary constructions of the detective novel and the dime publication. Writing about "bogus and would-be detectives," Pinkerton lamented the existence of "a class which have risen directly from the worldwide reputation which has been secured for my agencies and my method of detection." His books tried to set the record straight on detection.

> Many unthinking people have come to believe that there is something mysterious, wonderful and awful about the detective. . . . All my life, and in every manner in my power, I have endeavored to break down this popular superstition, but it would seem that it could not be done. Many persons seem to desire to believe that a detective hold some supernatural power, or yet is possessed of some finer instinct of keener perception than other mortals; and hence the bogus detective has the elements of success as a swindler when he makes the shabbiest pretense of being a detective.

A "real" detective, Pinkerton declared seemingly without irony, was not a swindler but rather a product of rigorous methods of detection. "This foolish fancy as to the power of the detective comes, I am aware, from that element nearly akin to fear in all of us, for anything mysterious or unexplainable," he concluded. "But I have always contended that the criminal could not best be brought to justice by the criminal, but by the clean, honest mind, using clean, healthy, honest methods, and those persistently and unceasingly." Victorian sanity, propriety, and persistence, not sensationalism and mystery, Pinkerton told his audience, made his detectives successful, even though it was precisely this kind of mystery, sensationalism, and self-promotion that had made him and his agency famous.[41]

The connections not only to dime novel detectives but also, more importantly, to the nation-state represented by Abraham Lincoln were essential parts of this reputation. Benson Lossing had given credit to Allan Pinkerton for uncovering the Baltimore plot, credit that both established Pinkerton's national stature and triggered a controversy about the plot's validity. So tenuous was Pinkerton's reputation that few early biographies of Lincoln (of which there were many) gave much time to Baltimore, and even fewer mention Pinkerton; some mention only a "detective of great expertise and skill." By 1895, however, when Lamon's family republished his recollections of Lincoln, Allan Pinkerton had clearly won the struggle to control his image and the debate over the memory and meaning of the Baltimore plot. All of Lamon's challenges to Pinkerton had been removed, and instead Lamon's daughter, who edited the papers, declared that "it is now an acknowledged fact that there never was a moment from the day [Lincoln] crossed the Maryland line, up to the time of his assassination, that he was not in danger of death by violence, and that his life was spared . . . only through the ceaseless and watchful care of the guards thrown around him," including her father. Yet even still, the family did not mention Pinkerton by name.[42] Other turn-of-the-century biographies were perfectly willing to cite Pinkerton by name and declare him the "most important of the informants" and "one of the most famous detectives in the world." These new biographies gave Pinkerton full credit for Lincoln's journey through Baltimore even as they pointed out that Lincoln came to doubt whether such plots existed.[43] In her history of Lincoln, Ida Tarbell went further and included a picture of Lincoln and Pinkerton at Antietam, a photo that had long been a key part of Pinkerton lore, had graced every National Detective Agency office, and was sent to prospective clients and friends when, as company memos pointed out, it "could be used to a great advantage."[44] Pinkerton had made sure that his name remained closely connected to the now beloved ex-president; indeed, his carefully constructed reputation as the nation's foremost detective relied on it.

In which Pinkerton men become
the antiheroes of the middle west

I n *The Confidence-Man*, his novel of deceit, corruption, naïveté, and treachery, Herman Melville placed a cross section of the American west aboard a Mississippi riverboat. "Here reigned the dashing and all-fusing spirit of the West, whose type is the Mississippi itself," he wrote, "which, uniting the streams of the most distant and opposite zones, pours them along, helter-skelter, in one cosmopolitan and confident tide."[1] In his novelizations of case files, Allan Pinkerton would take a similar view of the American middle west. "Everything contributed to make these places typical of Babelic confusion or Paudemoniac contention," wrote Pinkerton. Migrants, clerks, travelers, "foreigners," veterans "who had been on the wrong side during the late irritation," and all kinds of others came to the west seeking their fortune. In addition to these folk, Pinkerton added "the forger, the bruiser, the counterfeiter, the gambler, the garroter, the prostitute, the robber and the murderer." Because of this influx of criminality, "the few respectable people quickly became discouraged and fell into the general looseness of habits that the loose life engendered, and gradually grew reckless as the most reckless, or quickly acquiesced in the wild orgies or startling crimes which were of common occurrence."[2]

To Pinkerton lawlessness in the west was a disease that spread quickly and needed to be stopped forcefully. Like any disease that continues to corrupt "until arrested by a gradual purification of the whole body or by some severe treatment," so too would lawlessness continue to spread. "From every portion of the country flowed these streams of morally corrupt people," he concluded, "until nearly every town west of the Missouri, or east of the mountains along these lines became a terror to honest people." Surveillance and trained detection alone would not bring order to such places and to such criminals; swift and severe punishment had to be part of the bargain. "Intelligent minds must be trained to battle criminals with their own weapons," he argued, "and these two questions of speedy detection of crime and swift punishment of criminals will be found quite as essential to a preservation of law and society as lofty arguments or high moral dissertations on the right or wrong of the expediencies necessary to bring wrong-doers to immediate and certain justice." Pinkerton offered his readers two choices for order in the west. Either Pinkerton agents could establish law and morality, or the citizens of the west would have to establish order themselves through vigilante justice. While Pinkerton clearly preferred the former, he understood how such lawlessness, if unchecked, would provoke an "irresistible conflict" and a "moral revulsion, sometimes so sweeping and violent as to cause an application of that unwritten though often exceedingly just law, the execution of which leaves offenders dangling to limbs of trees, lamp-posts, and other convenient points of suspension." Order, Pinkerton promised, would be brought to the west one way or another.

By the mid- to late 1870s, Pinkerton's detective work shifted from uncovering embezzlement to imposing order in the middle west, especially the pursuit of train robbers at the behest of express companies. These were the very kinds of spaces where, Pinkerton had warned, moral revulsion would lead to an irresistible conflict. Residents of the middle border, however, often resented and resisted incursions by Pinkerton agents. Local communities often viewed bandits as heroes who defended the honor and position of the community by stealing back from the railroad. Within this version, Pinkerton agents were tools of railroad power and were often derided as the company's "paid assassins." The complicated milieus of frontiers, middle borders, and the west into which Pinkerton and his agents entered were spaces that functioned, both politically and culturally, far differently than the Victorian cities of the mid-nineteenth century. Nor was the "west" a rugged space carved out of the wilderness by a frontiersman and his axe, as Jacksonian politics had imagined in the first half of the century. Instead, the nineteenth-century west was shaped by the interconnected nature of eastern markets, railroads, and government agents. Representatives of the state, such as Indian agents, scouts, sheriffs, marshals, and hired political muscle, existed in a liminal space between official and unofficial; their role and legitimacy were unclear. In the newly settled west there were very real struggles, and often very violent struggles, for power. Pinkerton agents were at the very center of these struggles.[3]

At the same time, the "west" was also a cultural construction of ideologies and assumptions. Myths of rugged frontiersmen such as Daniel Boone gave way to romantic visions of outlaws, lawmen, Indians, and desperadoes.[4] For a modern society faced with the new realities of industrial society, the imagined west allowed for reinvention and regeneration through masculine violence. This west was created as much in eastern cities through dime novels and pulp fiction as it was in dusty western streets. The west was a site of sensationalism and popular culture and reflected Americans' understanding of the Civil War and their fears and fantasies of class conflict in industrial cities; all were part of the same gun-fighter mythology.[5] The line between outlaw and marshal was not clear, nor did it need to be. This frontier was a place of lawlessness, struggle, violence, chivalry, romance, and banditry, and the Pinkerton agent as both hero and villain was a key player in this world. As banking and railroad interests pushed their way into new markets, these companies (along with the federal and local governments) turned to the Pinkertons to enforce order. Business boomed for the Pinkerton agency in the opening of the west. Yet it also meant that the agency, which was still in a formative period, faced new challenges in maintaining a consistent image and suppressing criticism. In order to negotiate the politics and cultures of west-ern and industrial frontiers, the Pinkertons, as a family and a business, developed closer ties with wealthy and "respectable" elements of society; however, this very movement confirmed their new cultural role as the hired guns of capital. The history of the Pinkertons in the west demonstrates just how quickly myths could be made and unmade.

Mississippi outlaws

"The southern and border states, since the close of the war of the rebellion, have been frequent scenes of extensive and audacious robberies," Pinkerton wrote in his 1879 book *The Mississippi Outlaws and the Detectives*. While the "disorder and lawlessness generated by the war" triggered new temptations, the Mississippi River valley had long "been infested by a class of men who never would try to get an honest living, but would prey upon their neighbors or attack the property of southern railroads and express companies."[6] Pinkerton thought that the peo-ple of the middle west, the "larger portion" of whom "may be classified as 'poor whites,'" were predisposed to violence and constituted a "peculiar variety of the human species." He wrote of the local population that

> in their sober moods, they are frank, rough, and courageous. . . . When full of bad whisky, however, they are apt to become quarrelsome and brutal, so that no man can feel sure of his safety in their company. An affront, real or imaginary, will then be apt to cause bloodshed, even if the insulted party has to bushwhack his enemy from a secure covert on the roadside as he is returning to his home. Every man goes armed, and, though fair fights in broad daylight are rare, cold-blooded mur-ders are not infrequent.

"The law is seldom invoked to settle private differences," concluded Pinkerton, "and, in fact, the functions of the legal officials are practically very limited in their influence."

This was, to Pinkerton's mind, a very different world demanding new kinds of detection and new kinds of justice. The criminality of the middle border, it seemed, was far different from professional criminals and confidence men who lurked beneath the surface of modern civilized society. Pinkerton considered Nathan Maroney, for instance, a sophisticated embezzler who was able to move within the finest society circles until his arrest by Pinkerton agents. Such a professional criminal craved companionship, and his guilt would eventually drive him to confide in someone. The bandits and outlaws of the middle border, however, derived from an inferior cultural and biological bloodline and resided in a broad milieu of criminality and lawlessness. Whole families and communities, including local authorities and lawmen, were all part of this degraded world, and, to Pinkerton's mind, none could be trusted. While an undercover agent might infiltrate this world or perhaps find an informant, ultimately a strong outside arm had to impose authority. In such lawless regions, Pinkerton's agency was that arm of authority.

The Pinkertons first entered this world of "western" banditry in pursuit of the Reno brothers. Residents of the southern Indiana community of Seymour, the Reno brothers were bounty jumpers throughout the Civil War. When the war, as well as the ability to acquire more enlistment bounty, ended, the Reno brothers moved into robbery of county treasurers and express companies. In October of 1866 the four brothers (John, Frank, Simeon, and William), along with several other gang members, stopped the Ohio and Mississippi Railroad and relieved the Adams Express Company courier of his treasure.[7] Just as it had earlier, the Adams Express Company turned to Allan Pinkerton and his agency to recover the lost money and punish the robbers. Pinkerton began his investigation by placing several agents within Seymour. Meanwhile, the Reno brothers continued their robberies, including the holdup of the county treasurer in Gallatin, Missouri. Unable to arrest John Reno in Seymour and unwilling to attempt extradition, Allan Pinkerton arranged for the sheriff of Davies County, Missouri, and a posse to depart Cincinnati with an arrest warrant. Their train was to stop in Seymour at the very time that a Pinkerton informant was to lure John Reno to the train station. When the train arrived, the posse emerged from the train, grabbed the unsuspecting Reno, forced him onto the leaving train, and whisked him out of the state. Once the train crossed into Missouri, they arrested the already bound and shackled Reno. He was subsequently tried, convicted, and sentenced to twenty-five years' imprisonment.[8]

Despite John's arrest, the gang continued to rob both express trains and county treasuries across Indiana, Illinois, and Iowa. In 1868, agents traced the gang to Council Bluffs, Iowa, and arrested several gang members, yet all escaped from the county jail. Two months later, the gang robbed the express train in Marshfield, Indiana, killing the expressman. Soon after the Marshfield robbery, Pinkerton agents arrested three members of the Reno gang; however, as agents brought the prisoners into Seymour, a vigilance committee, all masked men, seized the three gang members and hanged them from a nearby tree.[9] Several days later, the vigilance committee lynched three more gang members in a similar fashion from the same tree. Pinkerton's prediction of a "moral revulsion, sometimes so sweeping and violent as to cause an application of that unwritten though often exceedingly just law, the execution of which leaves offenders dangling to limbs of trees, lamp-posts, and other convenient points of suspension," had come true in Seymour.[10]

Within a couple of weeks of the lynchings, Pinkerton agents captured Simeon and William Reno in Indianapolis and detained them in New Albany. Pinkerton agents also apprehended Frank Reno, along with gang member Charles Anderson, in Windsor, Canada. However, if Pinkerton had worried about the logistics of extraditing John Reno out of Indiana, the case against Frank was even more complex. Pinkerton immediately penned a letter to Secretary of State William Seward, using Adams Express Company letterhead, asking him to begin extradition proceedings with the Canadian authorities. Acting Secretary of State William Hunter wrote to Edward Thornton, the British minister to the United States, who in turn wrote to Viscount Monck, the governor general of Canada. However, significant legal and political hurdles to the procedure existed. The Webster–Ashburton Treaty of 1842 established extradition between British Canada and the United States, but several border incidents involving counterfeiters, bandits, raids on Vermont from Confederate rebels, and raids on Canada from Irish-American Fenians had strained the relationship. Moreover, the proclamation of 1867 which created the independent Dominion of Canada meant that all treaties, including extradition, needed to be renegotiated. The queen did not ratify the new extradition treaty until August 8, 1868, several days after the initial arrest of Frank Reno and Charlie Anderson.

The extradition of Reno and Anderson became one of the first tests of Canadian sovereignty. Canadian authorities arrested, released, and then rearrested

Reno and Anderson. They also arrested Pinkerton on a charge of perjury and libel. Assassins twice tried to kill Allan Pinkerton. An attempt was also made on the life of stipendiary magistrate Gilbert McMicken, who was in charge of the proceedings. As a result of these attempts, Assistant Secretary of State Frederick Seward, who had befriended Pinkerton during the war, sent American gunboats into the Detroit River for ten days as a show of force. People on both sides of the case warned of violence and retribution. William Wood, head of the US Secret Service (created by Congress in 1865), argued that his agency and the US federal government could not ensure the prisoners' safety. In an even stranger twist, Dick Barry, the man accused of trying to shoot Pinkerton in Detroit, would claim during his trial that it was Wood who asked for Pinkerton's assassination.

Finally, after rounds of bureaucratic paperwork and an unsuccessful attempt by Reno to bribe McMicken's son, the Canadian courts agreed to turn over the suspects. Into whose custody the prisoners would be released, however, remained an important question. In a letter to Secretary Hunter, Seward confirmed Pinkerton's official status. "Pinkerton telegraphs, that under the treaty or statutes seven days must elapse before the prisoners can be delivered to the custody of the agent of the United States," he wrote, but first his office had to produce a paper "stating that the said authority is received and is conferred by the direction of the President of the United States." "You have all the information necessary to prepare a paper," he concluded, "directing the agents to receive, on behalf of the United States, under the treaty, the persons of the prisoners." In this tense diplomatic battle over extradition, Canadian sovereignty, and the authority of federal officials, Allan Pinkerton, working as a hired agent of the Adams Express Company, had the full authority of the president and the State Department to take charge of the prisoners.[11]

Once the Canadian officials turned over Reno and Anderson to Pinkerton, Canada and Great Britain no longer considered themselves responsible for their fate, yet the US government, while it had taken possession of the prisoners through Pinkerton, had never guaranteed their protection. Instead, it was the governor of Indiana and the Adams Express Company who swore to Canadian officials that the extradited prisoners would stand trial. After an adventurous journey across Lake Erie (during which a passing ship sliced their tug in half), Pinkerton and his agents brought Reno and Anderson to New Albany, where they joined William and Simeon. Shortly after their arrival, however, a special train arrived carrying fifty masked vigilantes. When they reached the jail, the group shot the jailer, forced their way into the cells, and proceeded to hang all three

Reno brothers, as well as Charlie Anderson. The masked vigilantes then proceeded back to the train station and left in the same train. Later it was discovered that the telegraph lines going into New Albany had been cut, severing communication between the town and the rest of the state. The vigilante action in Indiana had been well planned and well funded.[12]

The lynchings in New Albany brought an end to the Reno gang. Despite threats of retaliation from surviving gang members and promises of further lynchings from vigilantes, little violence occurred after the hangings in New Albany. To his mind, Pinkerton considered the case a success; the power of the gang had been forcibly broken. The lynchings, however, triggered an international uproar. Furious British and Canadian authorities opened their own investigations into the extradition proceedings and process, and William Seward offered apologies on behalf of the State Department. Within a matter of days after the lynchings, Congress passed a new law declaring that "whenever any person shall have been delivered by any foreign government to an agent or agents of the United States for the purpose of being brought within the United States . . . the President shall have the power to take all necessary measures for the transportation and safe-keeping of such accused person, and for his security against lawless violence." The bill also stipulated that "any person duly appointed as agent to receive in behalf of the United States the delivery of a foreign government of any person accused of a crime . . . shall be, and hereby is, vested with all the powers of a marshal of the United States . . . so far as such power is requisite for [the prisoners'] safe-keeping." Because Pinkerton's role as both railroad agent and government official led to ambiguity and uncertainty, the bill tried to clarify the emerging role of the federal government in defining sovereignty and borders.[13]

Although Pinkerton denied that his agents had anything to do with the lynchings, a decade later, when dealing with the Molly Maguires in the Pennsylvania coalfields, Allan Pinkerton would write to George Bangs, who ran the New York office, suggesting that what was needed in the region was a vigilance committee similar in form to the one in Seymour. To Pinkerton's mind such drastic measures were sometimes necessary in an effort to impose order on such disordered spaces. As Allan's son William would write years later, once "the people in the vicinity of Seymour became aroused to the fact that war had actively commenced against the Reno brothers, and, as they had been terrorized by these men for years, they were willing to take a hand in exterminating them." Because of such action, he wrote, "for years after that, and in fact up to the present time, Seymour, Indiana, has been noted as a model, flourishing city, and I do not recall a single case of train robbing in southern Indiana." The establishment of law and order was only possible, it seemed to Pinkerton, because the detectives had "actively commenced" war against bandits. Such swift punishments also followed the Pinkerton pursuit of train robbers Levi and Hillary Farrington in western Kentucky. While trying to escape, Hillary first shot William Pinkerton and then plunged to his death off the steamboat they were riding. Levi was later lynched in Tennessee for the killing of a marshal and a deputy sheriff. A pattern of Pinkerton pursuit of train robbers seemed to have been set.

The outlaw Jesse James

The Pinkertons would bring the same methods to the lawlessness of postwar Missouri. The James–Younger gang was already notorious in Missouri for a series of bank and fair robberies dating from 1866, including the 1869 robbery of a bank in Gallatin, Missouri, where Jesse James shot and killed bank clerk John Sheets. In 1871, the band of former Confederate guerrillas robbed a bank in Corydon, Iowa. Bank officials contacted Pinkerton, who sent his son Robert to investigate. Robert joined the sheriff's posse tracking the gang to the border and followed the trail to the James farm in Missouri, but there the investigation stalled. In 1873, the gang began robbing trains; during these robberies, the gang, convinced that Allan Pinkerton was still after them, searched the railcars for the Chicago detective. For the most part, the railroad companies were willing to overlook these losses, but the Adams Express Company was not. When its property was stolen at Gads Hill in 1874, the company contracted with Pinkerton to find the James gang.

Pinkerton quickly dispatched agents into Missouri, including Joseph Whicher, who, upon arriving in Liberty, Missouri, checked in with the local sheriff and then approached the James farm disguised as an itinerant farmhand. Suspicious of Whicher's motives and outsider status, the James gang captured and executed Whicher. Shortly thereafter, gang members confronted undercover Pinkerton agents on a country road; a shootout would leave Pinkerton agent Louis Lull, local official Edwin Daniels, and gang member John Younger dead. Outraged and embarrassed, Allan Pinkerton now considered the pursuit of Jesse James a personal vendetta. Even as Adams Express withdrew its employment, Pinkerton vowed to crush the gang on his own. "I know that the James and the Youngers are desperate men, and that when we meet it must be the death of one or both of us," he wrote to superintendent George Bangs. "My blood was spilt and they must pay. There is no use talking, they must die."[14] Pinkerton sent new agents into the field, including L. E. Angell, who was charged with retrieving Whicher's body. In Saint Louis Angell vented his frustration to the local press. Not only did he suspect that the local sheriff had tipped off the gang to Whicher's presence, but "the people there are of a kind that admire men who ride through town flourishing revolvers and the James boys have established a sort of terrorism throughout the country." The gang not only used violence against its enemies but also cultivated its own popularity. "But they have a great many friends," he continued; "they have established the reputation of robbing the rich to give to the poor and when they have money they fling it around generously." Rooting out the James gang, it seemed, would be harder than finding the Renos.[15]

What Allan Pinkerton and his agents failed to understand, however, was that postwar Indiana and postwar Missouri were profoundly different places. The appeal and fear of the James gang had little to do with notions of law, order, terror, or criminality. Instead, this was a conflict deeply defined by the animosities of the Civil War, animosities that had their origins back in early settlement and statehood battles. Among the early settlers was Robert James, a preacher and farmer from Kentucky who moved to Missouri with his young bride, Zerelda, early in the century. Born in 1843, Alexander Franklin James was the oldest child. His younger brother Jesse Woodson James was born four years later in 1847. James was a slave owner and certainly thought of himself as a slave master and a southerner. By 1819, Missouri's rapid growth made it eligible for statehood, and it quickly became a test case of territorial expansion and slavery politics. Even after the Missouri Compromise, which established it as a slave state, Missouri remained a hotbed of both abolitionism and fierce proslavery advocacy. When Stephen Douglas pushed through the Kansas–Nebraska Act in 1854, which opened up both territories to popular sovereignty, proslavery Missourians, known as the Border Ruffians, poured across the state line, determined to make Kansas a slave state. Abolitionist forces, including Allan Pinkerton's friend John Brown, also came to the territory, sparking a series of violent confrontations known as "Bleeding Kansas." In 1857, when the Supreme Court sought to weigh in on the legality of slave restriction and territorial expansion, it took up the case of Dred Scott, the Missouri slave who sued for his freedom in a Saint Louis court.[16]

By the time of Abraham Lincoln's election and the onset of the Civil War, Missouri was no stranger to the contentious politics of slavery and the bitter guerrilla battles and familial feuds that defined the conflict in the middle border. Roving bands of guerrillas attacked each others' homes, supply routes, and towns. Violence, terror, destruction, and theft were an important part of this war.

The most notable guerrillas of this theater were William Quantrill, with whom rode Frank James and several of the Younger brothers, and "Bloody" Bill Anderson, who counted among his raiders a teenaged Jesse James. Both James boys took part in the ever-increasing brutality of the guerilla war.

The end of the war brought major political changes to Missouri. While not placed under military rule like the southern states that had seceded, pro-Union Republicans did take control of Missouri politics. Much like Reconstruction politics in the southern states, Confederate forces were barred from voting or holding office. And, again much like the rest of the south, pro-Confederate forces responded with campaigns of political resistance, violence, and terror. Secret bands based on the Ku Klux Klan, the White Liners, and other postwar vigilante groups began to exact political violence against Republican state officials in Missouri. The James brothers and the Youngers were certainly part of this movement. The Jameses were never shy about declaring their allegiance to the Confederate cause, nor were they reluctant about declaring the political purpose of their violence. State officials, pro-Union Republicans, and eastern banking and railroad interests were all part of the legacy of the war. James shot and killed clerk John Sheets in Gallatin because he thought Sheets was Samuel Cox, the man responsible for the death of Bill Anderson. After the Corydon, Iowa, robbery, the gang taunted townspeople as "Yankee cowards." During their train robberies, the James–Younger gang donned masks of the Ku Klux Klan. The James brothers and Youngers saw themselves as unrepentant rebels who were part of the southern effort at resisting Reconstruction and taking back power, or "redeeming" the south. Newspaper editor and unrepentant secessionist John Newman Edwards, who had already written glowingly of Confederate guerrilla Jo Shelby's refusal to surrender, took up the cause of the James gang. In a series of articles, published along with a letter from Jesse, Edwards proclaimed the James gang's innocence (they were being unfairly hounded by Unionists) while also suggesting that any crimes were justified. Newman provided a way for southern secessionists to live vicariously through Jesse James.[17]

As Southern Democrats came back into power, the political romanticization of the James gang (and the demonization of outside and northern interests who hunted them) grew. Most railroad and bank companies seemed to recognize this conundrum and dropped their pursuits. Allan Pinkerton, however, was not so forgiving. Instead, following the death of his agents, Pinkerton had begun to mobilize his forces to crush the gang. As part of this effort, he began to recruit local farmers, including Daniel Askew, who owned the farm next to the Jameses, and to send heavily armed agents into Missouri. The plan was to catch the James brothers at home and trap them in their farmhouse. In last-minute instructions, Pinkerton laid out the plans and reminded his agents to be sure that the Jameses were home; he instructed them, "above all else destroy the house, wipe it from the face of the earth."[18]

On January 25, 1875, Pinkerton agents launched their raid. They quickly surrounded the house in the dead of night and threw into the home a specially made incendiary device. Consisting of a cast-iron shell filled with flammable liquid and a cotton wick, the device was designed to illuminate the interior of the home. Panicked members of the James family, however, pushed the sphere into the fireplace, where it overheated and exploded. The shrapnel from the explosion killed the Jameses' young stepbrother and took off the right arm of Zerelda Samuels; neither Frank nor Jesse was home. A local investigation that followed the fire claimed to have found a pistol outside the home with an insignia that suggested that the Pinkertons were under the employment of the federal government.[19] Pinkerton denied any federal connection, but he never tried to hide his company's role in the raid on the Jameses' farmhouse. Public outrage was loud and vehement; indeed, the Pinkerton raid turned the James brothers into folk heroes embraced across the Missouri political spectrum. The Missouri legislature (filled with pro-Confederate politicians who could once again vote and hold office) narrowly failed in passing legislation praising the James brothers and offering amnesty. It did succeed in limiting the monetary amount the governor could offer for rewards. For a short while Pinkerton worried that Missouri officials would try to indict him and his agents. Even more worried were the local farmers who had supported the Pinkerton investigation and raid. Shortly after the failed raid, an armed band rode up to Daniel Askew on his property and shot him to death. The best Allan Pinkerton could do was offer his condolences to Abbie Askew and her children and admit that he had been beaten. Pinkerton called off his pursuit of James.

For his part, James kept seeking the admiration of Missourians and the redemption of southern pride, an admiration increasingly hard to come by as Confederates had come back into power and no longer needed the outlawry of James. Pinkerton remained a useful foil for the bandits; during one robbery, James commanded one railroad engineer to "tell Allan Pinkerton and his detectives to look for us in hell." Further, James wrote letters to the press declaring his own innocence and condemning the Pinkerton raid. One such letter to the *Nashville Republican Banner* prompted a response from William Pinkerton, who insisted that he was in Chicago at the time of the raid and could not be held responsible. The next week James took up the challenge and again condemned the agency in the press. "They [*sic*] is no doubt about Pinkerton's force committing the crime & it is the duty of the press to denounce him," he wrote; "Pinkerton has gained great notoriety as a Detective, but we have so easily baffled him. & he has got his best men killed by him sending them after us." Such declarations not only cut into Pinkerton's carefully crafted reputation but also reinforced the Civil War backdrop of the Missouri conflict.

> As to Pinkerton proveing [*sic*] he was in Chicago at the time he committed the outrage at mothers I do not doubt. . . . Pinkerton can prove in Chicago that Black is white and white is Blac [*sic*] so can Gen Wm T Sherman prove in Chicago that Jeff Davisse [*sic*] had Lincoln assassinated & that the brave and gallant Gen Wade Hampton burnt Columbia S.C. all this can be proven in Chicago, if people in the South didn't know that Chicago was the home of Phil Sheridan and filled with Shermans Bummers it might have some effect for Pinkerton to say what he can prove in Chicago.

This first foray into defending the agency against the James gang's legend would be the Pinkerton family's last. Instead, Allan turned his attention to the agency's more successful pursuit of the Farrington brothers. William's capture of the gang was covered in Allan's 1879 book *Mississippi Outlaws*. Unlike earlier books that focused on the urban crimes of professional criminals, *Mississippi Outlaws* was a western tale. William Pinkerton and his fellow agents were clearly outsiders in a strange land of kinship and lawlessness. Instead of careful investigation and months of shadowing, *Mississippi Outlaws* had fast pursuits, raging gun battles, treacherous kin networks, and dramatic escapes. It was also, along with chapters of *Model Town*, the only western tale that Allan Pinkerton would write; he would not write about Jesse James.[20]

Wild bandits of the border

If Allan Pinkerton was reluctant to write about the James gang, few others felt the same way.[21] The legend and myth of Jesse James would continue to twist and turn over the next ten years. In September of 1876, the gang attempted to rob a bank in Northfield, Minnesota (because one of the prominent residents of Northfield was Del Ames, the former Union general and reconstructionist governor of Mississippi), only to be pursued doggedly by large posses of Minnesotans. Several raiders were captured, Frank was severely wounded, and the James–

Younger gang was crushed. Both Jesse and Frank went into hiding. During this respite, John Newman Edwards wrote *Noted Guerrillas; or, The Warfare of the Border*, a history of the guerrilla wars in Missouri from Quantrill through Bill Anderson to the robberies of the James–Younger gang. Edwards placed the actions of the James brothers in a direct line with Civil War–era political violence and resistance. Edwards also actively cultivated the image of Pinkerton agents as the paid assassins of outside interests. "This great Chicago bugaboo had been worsted in every encounter with those of the border whom it was his especial and self-imposed mission to slay or entrap, and he grew morbidly desirous of striking a blow that had vengeance in it," Edwards declared. Although "only vague rumor or sensational journalism had connected" the gang to any crimes, "nevertheless, according to the theory of Pinkerton and Pinkerton's paid assassins, they were to be shot down as so many horses with the glanders or so many dogs with the hydrophobia." The ill-fated raid confirmed Pinkerton's bloodlust. While the family slept peacefully, "the cowards—how many is not accurately known, probably a dozen—crept close to this house through the midnight, surrounded it, found its inmates asleep, and threw into the kitchen . . . a lighted hand-grenade, wrapped about with flannel saturated with turpentine." The bombing, Edwards concluded, "had been a tragedy performed by men calling themselves civilized, in the midst of a peaceful community and upon a helpless family of women and children that would have disgraced Nero or made some of the monstrous murders of Diocletian as white is to black. Yet Pinkerton's paid assassins did this because his paid assassins knew better how to kill women and children than armed men in open combat." In contrast, Edwards declared that the James gang only killed out of necessity. Given the ruthlessness of the Pinkertons, "what else could Jesse James have done?" Edwards concluded,

> In those evil days bad men in bands were doing bad things continually in the name of law, order and vigilance committees. He had been a desperate Guerrilla; he had fought under a black flag; he had made a name for terrible prowess along the border . . . hence the wanton war waged upon Jesse and Frank James, and hence the reasons why to-day they are outlaws, and hence the reasons also that—outlaws as they are and proscribed in county, or State, or territory—they have more friends than the officers who hunt them, and more defenders than the armed men who seek to secure their bodies, dead or alive. Since 1865 it has been pretty much one eternal ambush for these two men—one unbroken and eternal hunt *twelve years long*. They have been followed, trailed, surrounded, shot at, wounded, ambushed,

surprised, watched, betrayed, proscribed, outlawed, driven from State to State, made the objective points of infallible detectives, and they have triumphed.[22]

This story line about the James brothers and the Pinkertons became a myth repeated in many other publications, even after the governor of Missouri offered a substantial bounty on Jesse's head and new gang members Charlie and Robert Ford killed him in his own home in 1882. "Frank and Jesse James, outlaws as they are, and exiles under kindlier suns than their native land afforded them have illustrated the American virtues of personal bravery and devotion to friends and to principle," wrote R. T. Bradley in an 1882 book entitled *Outlaws of the Border; or, The Lives of Frank and Jesse James*. After the war, the "James boys made a new attempt to adapt themselves to the arts of peace, and to build and beautify their wasted homes." Yet "unseen enemies destroyed their crops and their cabins, and sought their lives by stealthy hunt and by ambuscade." When "they turned upon the invaders of their peace with a terrible fury . . . their excesses made them outlaws." Thus, the violence was not political in nature but rather personal. They had tried peaceful living before "a malignant destiny thrust itself in their path and filled them with a lust for vengeance and for blood." For Bradley the James brothers were "hunted lions." Such a mythology also necessitated a twist of chronology; in the new version the James brothers were law abiding until they were hounded into lives of crime.[23]

After the train robbery at Gads Hill, the story went, the railroads launched an even larger hunt for the outlaws: "the men selected for the work, were not particular whether they brought them in dead or alive; in fact, it would seem they preferred to kill them first, thinking that the safer plan." Yet paid assassins were no match for the men of the middle border. Much like Edwards, Bradley detailed the Pinkerton raid on the Jameses' farm as a "cowardly expedition." "The baffled and chagrined detectives, now perpetrated an act that disgraces our civilization, and for which most of them afterward paid a heavy penalty," he declared. Indeed, the entire campaign from Pinkerton was marked by cowardice and failure. "Detectives had grown weary of trying to track a banditti that vanished at their approach and that rose again to overwhelm and destroy them," Bradley surmised; "Pinkerton had lost the boldest and most crafty of his men, and was himself afraid to travel in the Southwest except under disguise which he believed could not be penetrated."[24] By making the James brothers heroes of the middle border, Bradley shifted the geography of the tale from the postwar south to the American west. So too did Joseph Dacus's *Life and Adventure of Frank and*

Jesse James: The Noted Western Outlaws place the Jameses within a western milieu. As a western bandit and hounded Robin Hood, Jesse James would slip into American folklore. His assassination by members of his own gang would only reinforce this cultural resonance. After the Ford brothers claimed the reward and were pardoned by the governor, they tried to capitalize on their newfound fame by writing and performing a stage show about James's death. Yet Robert Ford would go into American memory as "that dirty little coward" who shot James in the back. Frank James turned himself in to Missouri authorities on the understanding that he would not be extradited to Minnesota. Acquitted on all charges in local Missouri courts, Frank settled into a law-abiding life. Yet much like the Ford brothers before him, James would briefly turn to the theater, touring the United States as part of a wild west show.

As the publishing market grew rapidly in eastern markets at the end of the nineteenth century, books that specialized in lurid tales of western outlaws, bandits, and detectives grew more popular. The exploits of Jesse James, most of which were completely fabricated, became a staple of this dime novel genre. James starred in titles such as *Wild Bandits of the Border, a Thrilling Story of the Adventures and Exploits*, which was an unidentified reprint of Dacus's book. He was also the hero of adventures such as *Jesse James, Knight-Errant; or, The Rescue of the Queen of the Prairies, Jesse James in Chicago, The Complete and Authentic Life of Jesse James*, and other fanciful tales. Some of these adventures also reimagined the roles of additional Pinkerton agents, such as *Jesse James Foiled; or, The Pinkerton's Best Play, The James Boys and Pinkertons; or, Frank and Jesse as Detectives*, and *Jesse James' Nemesis; or, The Pinkerton Oath, a Brave Detective Meets a Cruel Death.*[25]

These dime novels dealt with the Pinkerton agents in a variety of ways. At times they were worthy foils for Frank and Jesse, sometimes they were heroic protagonists, and at still other times they were played for fools by the James–Younger gang. Sometimes the coverage of agents varied within a dime novel, such as William B. Lawson's *Jesse James, the Outlaw*, the first in a series entitled *Jesse James Stories: Original Narratives of the James Boys*. Told in the first person, Larson's dime novel follows his own imagined efforts to track down the James–Younger gang for the reward money. The gunshots that open the story come from Pinkerton agents. "I knew them instantly, though, very fortunately, they didn't know me in the disguise," Lawson wrote. "They were three daring Chicago detectives in the disguise of horse-traders. . . . They were on the lookout for Jesse and Frank James, the noted train robbers and bandits, and had just visited old Mrs. James' farmhouse, in the hope of finding the dreaded outlaws there, and worming themselves into their confidence, with a view to their ultimate capture." Although Lawson was on the same case, he "didn't admire their mode of procedure, and proposed to go about the dangerous job in my own way." No sooner do the Pinkerton agents ride up to Lawson than the James brothers appear; the exchange ends in the deaths of all but one of the detectives. "I reckon those Chicago detectives, at all events, will give the James boys a wide berth in the future," the dime novel James proclaims. Later, after Lawson has worked his way into the gang, James captures another man. "To my secret horror and commiseration, I recognized in this man, Langman, the fifth Chicago detective," Lawson confides. "I tracked him to the telegraph office in the town, Jess," declares a member of the gang. "He sent off two dispatches to Chicago, one to the name you said to be on the lookout for."

Unlike the agents met earlier, this Pinkerton agent faced his impending death with bravery and honor. "In this position the wretch faced the whole party with eyes that were wide and haggard, but in whose hopeless depths, I am happy to say, there seemed not an atom of cowardly fear," wrote Lawson. Later in the story, however, Lawson meets the "sole remaining Chicago detective" as he is leaving town. "The decidedly demoralized detective meandered off," wrote Lawson, "looking this way and that, as if he dreaded to see a James brother sprout out of every gate post." Overall the Pinkertons prove incapable of catching Jesse James. "Hasn't the fate of Pinkerton's Chicagoans proved the futility of private action against the Jameses and their devil's crew?" one character opined. "Three were killed, and Jewell, the sole survivor, slunk homeward yesterday, half scared out of his senses, though naturally a man of steady nerve." Once again, and repeatedly in dime novels into the twentieth century, Jesse James triumphed over the Pinkertons.[26]

Conclusion: Highwaymen of the railroad

When William Pinkerton wrote his brief history of what he called "the highwaymen of the railroad" in 1893, he lumped the train robberies of Jesse and Frank James together with the robberies by the Reno brothers, the Farrington brothers, Sam Bass in Texas, Jim and Rube Barrow, Fred Whitlock of Kansas, and Bill Dalton and his gang in Indian territory. Within this history, he acknowledged the vigilante violence that had, on separate occasions, ended the lives of the Renos and Levi Farrington. Pinkerton also admitted that after the death of Whicher in Missouri the agency's pursuit of the James gang " became a war of extinction." Pinkerton offered no apology for the agency's aggressive tactics to tame the lawlessness of the west. However, while Pinkerton's essay on railroad thefts tied his agency to the romantic history of the west, he wrote the piece to advocate for new legislation making train robbery a federal crime. If train robbery were a federal crime, the "robbers are not likely to be able to control United States officials as they control the local authorities," he argued. "The latter will frequently drop pursuit at the state or county lines, claiming they have no further authority to go further. A state or county line would not act as a barrier for a United States officer." Pinkerton also laid blame for the newest wave of western banditry at the feet of pulp novels. "One of the reasons for the recent epidemic of train robberies may be found in the general business depression," he wrote. "It is, however, also largely due, in my opinion, to the reading of yellow-covered novels. Country lads get their minds inflamed with this class of literature. Professional thieves or designing men find among this class many who are willing to go into their schemes."[27]

So too would Cleveland Moffett, a chronicler of Pinkerton exploits at the turn of the century, attribute the killing of US Express Company agent Kellogg Nichols to the romantic ideals of the dime novel. On March 12, 1886, the Rock Island Express departed Chicago for Davenport carrying two express cars. By the time the train reached Morris, Illinois, Nichols was dead. William Pinkerton's investigation quickly centered on brakeman Harry Schwartz and expressman Newton Watt, the latter of whom claimed that two men in masks entered the top of the car and robbed him at gunpoint. Although Pinkerton suspected Schwartz and assigned agents to shadow the man, he pretended to take Schwartz into his confidence and asked the brakeman to follow Watt. Agreeing to play detective, Schwartz returned with reports that Watt had "met a man who wore a slouch hat, had unkempt hair, and in general looked like a border ruffian." "Schwartz had a sort of Jesse James theory (which he seemed anxious to have accepted)," reported Moffett, "that the crime had been committed by a gang of Western desperadoes." However, Pinkerton's investigation revealed that Schwartz and Watt conspired to rob the express cars and had concocted the desperado tale. After their convictions, Schwartz's wife acknowledged that "her husband's mind had been inflamed by the constant reading of sensationalist literature of the dime novel order; and that under this evil influence he had planned the robbery." In addition to sullying the reputation of the agency, dime novels, it seemed, had begun to corrupt American youth and encourage lawless behavior.[28]

Such publications were certainly a sore spot for the image-conscious Pinkerton agency. Allan Pinkerton had carefully constructed a detective mythology to surround his agents. The failure to capture the James gang and the popularity of pulp novels that romanticized the bandit outlaw complicated this mythology. Indeed, by the late 1880s the agency had lost a great deal of control over their name. Not only did accounts of Jesse James document the Pinkertons' failed raid, but dime novels invented new Pinkerton agents and new Pinkerton adventures. While some of these were kind to the agency and others less so, it was no longer an image that the agency controlled. One such author (or perhaps a series of authors) wrote under the pseudonyms Allan F. Pinkerton and A. Frank Pinkerton. Although no relation to the family, Frank Pinkerton wrote several tales stolen either from Allan's books or from famous agency cases, such as *Jim Cumming; or, the Great Adams Express Robbery*, *Dyke Darrell the Railroad detective; or, The Crime of the Midnight Express*, and *Five Thousand Dollars Reward*. Frank Pinkerton also wrote other tales outside of the company case files, such as *The Whitechapel Murders; or, An American Detective in London*. The books formed the basis of a detective series published by Laird and Lee of Chicago under the name "The Pinkerton Detective Series." While only some of these traced actual Pinkerton cases, the dime novels tried to present an aura of authenticity by having some of their books written by "Frank Pinkerton" and others anonymously written by "one of America's most famous detectives." At least as far as dime novels were concerned, the Pinkertons had lost control of their image. Even when they were presented as heroes, their name and reputation were no longer theirs to shape and control.[29]

CHAPTER THREE

In which Pinkerton agents infiltrate secret societies

THROUGHOUT MUCH of his early career, Allan Pinkerton investigated crimes, especially acts of embezzlement, for railroad and express companies. Petty crimes and riot control were, to Pinkerton's mind, affairs for the city police, not professional detectives. But brand-new towns with little established order were a very different matter. These towns, including new farming communities along rail lines in the midwest, mining towns throughout the coal regions of Pennsylvania, and new industrial mill towns, not only lacked proper law and authority but also tended to be filled with shiftless migrants looking for easy crime. These places needed different attention. "The history of all places which have had a rapid growth is full of startling incidents of crime," Pinkerton wrote in 1875. "Particularly has this been the case in the western country," he concluded, "where the incoming population has been of such a mixed character, and opportunities for criminal deeds so numerous, as to sometimes create an epidemic of wrong doing." Such places were not the lawless frontiers of Missouri, where local bandits threatened railroad interests, but rather they were new towns that temporarily lacked law and morality. "Almost every community has known one or more periods when the dissolute elements of the place have seemed to be unusually active, and the majesty of the law so little regarded and feared as to cause a perfect carnival of crime," he claimed. "Under such circumstances, the honest portion of the population become bewildered and disenchanted, and the rogues apparently take charge of affairs, until some sudden discovery brings to punishment a number of the guilty men, and then order returns."[1]

One such town was Mariola, Illinois, just outside of Chicago, which Pinkerton described as "a very pleasant and thriving inland place, the law-abiding people far outnumbering the law-breakers; yet previous to the time when my services were engaged there was a period of almost total disregard of law and authority in the place." Once Pinkerton dispatched several operatives, "in a few weeks my detectives were successful in identifying the ringleaders of all the evil-doers of the town. ... From the moment it was revealed that Pinkerton's detectives were at work in the town, the orderly character of the place was assured for an indefinite length of time." Pinkerton committed himself and his agency to Mariola to prove a point about fears of vast conspiracies and criminal undergrounds. The residents of Mariola had become convinced that "a 'gang' or society of desperate criminals existed in and about the city, which was sworn to act in concert and to create a reign of terror in the county," but Pinkerton was convinced that no such society could exist. The idea of criminal conspiracies, he claimed, "has been carefully cultivated by some writers of fiction for the purpose of adding color, life, and romantic interest to their tales . . . [but] criminals as a rule are selfish, cowardly, and revengeful." Mariola's criminals acted out of self-ishness and were driven by opportunity; once Pinkerton detectives arrived, this once seemingly lawless city became a "model town."[2]

Despite Pinkerton's efforts to dispel theories of vast conspiracies, by 1878 many Americans believed that a number of criminal conspiracies existed, ranging from secret labor societies to radical political ideologies to vast networks of intimidation, extortion, and murder. Ironically, it was Pinkerton who would help popularize these fears. In 1876, at the request of railroad and mining interests in Pennsylvania, Pinkerton agent James McParlan (or McParland) infiltrated and exposed a secret society of Irish miners called the Molly Maguires.[3] In 1877, a railroad strike against the Baltimore and Ohio, which began in Wheeling, West Virginia, quickly became a bloody general strike that involved open warfare in the streets. After the conflict, Allan Pinkerton took it upon himself to write the definitive history of the Great Strike of 1877 by using his case files and trumpeting his agents' role in infiltrating the unions and societies responsible for the violence. In so doing, Pinkerton not only came to believe in the existence of criminal conspiracies but also positioned his agency as a key tool in battling these sinister forces. By the Haymarket bombing of 1886 much of the nation believed that radical anarchists involved in a vast conspiracy were probably behind the violence. Industrialization had changed the method, purpose, and culture of sleuthing. Pinkerton detectives no longer just shadowed professional criminals and tracked down gangs of "bad men" in the middle border; they also infiltrated and unearthed secret societies and criminal conspiracies.[4]

Secret societies were largely considered anathema to the political ideologies of the early republic because within a political system based on virtuous and independent citizens who sublimated their own desires for the common good, secrecy itself seemed corrupting and self-serving. Yet by the end of the nineteenth century, the *North American Review* would declare the last third of the century the "golden age of fraternity" because of the vast popularity of secret societies and fraternal organizations. Such fraternal organizations offered tangible business benefits to its members, including contacts, networks, ready credit sources, and homosocial spaces of close interaction. National societies offered stability and familiarity and cultivated social networks in what had become a largely impersonal world of rapid urbanization and mobility. The rituals and rites of the Victorian fraternal society helped create a pathway to masculinity for Victorian men at a time when middle-class parlor culture was becoming increasingly feminized.[5] Yet secret societies in the nineteenth century could be more than mere social clubs or islands of familiarity in a newly confusing world. Many fraternities served as political organizations that used secrecy as protection and anonymity. Immigration and industrial expansion also prompted new forms of labor and immigrant societies that offered mutual insurance, community solidarity, and ethnic identity, along with the important element of protection through secrecy. Despite the popularity of the fraternal society in the late nineteenth century, the politicization of worker and immigrant societies deeply worried many. Such secret organizations were not merely criminal abnormalities at the fringes of civilized society but a threat to the very existence of industrial order. These societies, the thinking went, had to be infiltrated, exposed, and crushed; such times seemed to call for the use of Pinkerton agents. Yet once again, for every piece that declared the Pinkerton spy a force for good, another decried the spy as an agent provocateur responsible for much of the violence.

This transition from a quasi-official arm of the state chasing criminals and bandits to a tool that capitalists used to infiltrate and crush worker resistance could not have been easy for Allan Pinkerton. After all, he was a former Chartist and antebellum abolitionist who was no stranger to radical politics. How and why, then, did Pinkerton make this important shift in the purpose of his agency? Part of the answer lies in hindsight; while we know how this story will end, Allan Pinkerton probably did not envision his agents becoming the private army of capital. Another part of the answer probably comes out of sheer pragmatism. In the wake of the Civil War, as federal troops withdrew from occupied areas (which included Missouri, Kentucky, southern Indiana, and central Pennsylvania), there was a vacuum of power. Pinkerton's voracious defense of his role in protecting Lincoln was in part about claiming some of the postwar business of providing order. His high-profile pursuit of Jesse James, however, had ended in an embarrassing failure. In 1876, the agency was in dire financial straits and desperate for another chance to redeem its reputation and public standing. At the same time, it should not surprise us that the Glasgow Scot might not have held a high regard for immigrant Irish workers. In his descriptions of Pennsylvania, Pinkerton's understanding of the region insinuated a clear connection between criminality and Irishness. But perhaps most interestingly, Pinkerton explained his agency's actions in Pennsylvania and later in Chicago in terms of free labor ideologies. The criminal conspiracies of radical Irishmen and anarchists, to his mind, undercut the independence and autonomy of the honest workman. By working for American industrialists, Allan Pinkerton did not believe that he was helping capital to crush workers, but rather that he was helping to liberate and protect free labor. By the 1880s, however, as control of the agency was passing from Allan to his sons, this justification and indeed free labor ideology in general were becoming harder to maintain.

A noxious weed of Ireland

In 1873 Allan Pinkerton received an urgent request of "business of importance" from Franklin Gowen, president of both the Philadelphia and Reading Railway and the Philadelphia and Reading Coal and Iron Company. "The coal regions are infested by a most desperate class of men, banded together for the worst purposes—called, by some, the Buckshots, by others the Mollie Maguires—and they are making sad havoc with the country," relayed the railroad president, according to Pinkerton's recollections. Gowen asked Pinkerton to investigate this "mysterious order" and expose its "evil transactions." Local sheriffs and the "usual run of detectives" had proven ineffective. The secrecy of the organization had rendered the state powerless. "Now, if you cannot disperse the murderous crew, or give us grounds upon which to base prosecutions," Gowen pleaded with Pinkerton, "then I shall believe that it never will be effected."[6]

After his plea caught the detective's attention, Gowen explained the society's origin: "As far as we can learn, the society is of foreign birth, a noxious weed which has been transplanted from its native soil—that of Ireland—to the United States, sometime within the last twenty years. It lived and prospered in the old country considerably earlier." Gowen continued, "The same minds, the same combinations, are to be encountered here. The Mollies rule our people with a rod of iron." Regarding the extermination of this weed, Gowen believed that "the State cannot attain these things; she has repeatedly tried, and tried in vain." But he said to Pinkerton, "you can do it. I have seen you tested on other occasions and in other matters, and know your ability to conduct the business." To do so would not be easy, both Pinkerton and Gowen agreed. The Mollies seemed an "impenetrable ring," which made it hard for anyone to "turn to the light the hidden aide of this dark and cruel body, to probe to its core this festering sore upon the body politic, which is rapidly gnawing into the vitals and sapping the life of the community."[7]

While Pinkerton understood the importance of the task, he also knew that this would require a new role for his agents. Instead of a detective testing conductor loyalty, shadowing suspected embezzlers, or tracking outlaws in the middle west, this kind of detective work meant the slow and careful infiltration of a close-knit community. While there were "many able and trustworthy men in my force . . . it is no ordinary man that I need in this matter," he concluded. "He must be an Irishman, and a Catholic, as only this class of persons can find admission to the Mollie Maguires," Pinkerton declared. "My detective should become, to all intents and purposes, one of the Order, and continue so while he remains in the case before us." Pinkerton insisted that the identity of his detective had to stay secret; no reference to the agency or the presence of the detective could be uttered for as long as the investigation was under way. Furthermore, Pinkerton asked that "whatever may be the result of the examination, no person in my employ—unless the circumstances are greatly changed and I demand it—shall ever be required to appear and give testimony upon the witness stand."[8]

Pinkerton worried whether he had an agent "who held sufficiently broad and deeply-grounded notions of the real duty of a true Irishman to his country and his fellow-countrymen to intrust with this great mission." Such an Irishman would earn repudiation from the Catholic Church. His public reputation would be destroyed, and "for an indefinite period he was to be as one dead and buried in the grave—dead to his family and friends." Pinkerton understood that "my man must become, really and truly, a Mollie of the hardest character, attend their meetings, and possibly be charged with direct participation in certain of their crimes." An Irish detective in the coal regions had the potential not only to solve crimes and exact justice "but to wipe off a dark blot which had fallen upon the escutcheon of Ireland, and which clouded the fair fame of every Irishman in America." In so doing, however, the agent would be ostracized by the very community he was saving. Could anyone within the famed agency handle such a case, and how would Pinkerton choose his man? "Surely here was a task for me, in the very outset," he concluded, "the fellow of which I had not encountered since the war of the rebellion." Pinkerton found his agent in James McParlan, a twenty-nine-year-old detective who had emigrated from Ulster, Ireland, in 1844, but an Irishman whom Pinkerton determined to be a "fine specimen of the better class of immigrants to this country." McParlan had "earned a reputation for honesty, a peculiar tact and shrewdness, skill and perseverance," which would be invaluable in the Pennsylvania coalfields. Just as Kate Warne proved capable of rising above the limits of her gender to become a successful detective, Pinkerton assumed the same about McParlan and the limits of his ethnicity.[9]

Both Gowen and Pinkerton assumed that the Molly Maguires emerged out of the rural traditions of Ireland. Vigilante organizations that took the names of the "Ribbonmen," the "Whiteboys," the "Defenders," and the "Molly Maguires" existed in rural Ireland. However, the label of "Molly Maguire" first emerged in Pennsylvania in 1857 as a way for political adversaries to lump together various different crimes and conspiracies under a single name. Attributing violence to a secret society called the Molly Maguires was a politically expedient act of cultural invention. Violence did occur in the coalfields of Pennsylvania, and Irish miners of the region did respond to ethnic conflict, labor strife, and the growing power of the Reading Railroad by reaching into rural Irish traditions of vigilante violence and secret societies. Benjamin Brannen, a staunch Whig and advocate for coal mine owners, first used the epitaph of "Molly Maguire" in 1857 to describe a political conspiracy imported from Boston to assist local Democrats. The first "coffin notices," or threats of retaliatory violence, came out of the strike violence of 1858. The death of Frank Landon in 1862 marked the first death later attributed to "Molly Maguires." Antiwar and pro-southern (or "Copperhead") sentiment ran strong throughout southern Pennsylvania, as did pro-Union condemnation of such sympathies. The politics of the Civil War, especially the implementation of drafts, prompted a series of riots and street protests. Violence between 1862 and 1868 would later be classified as the first wave of Molly Maguire actions. Even ten years after the war, people would still cast the threat of the Mollies in terms of Copperhead sentiments and political treason. The postwar collapse in coal prices and the return of war veterans to the coalfields only increased this tension and anxiety. In 1865, railroad corporations convinced the state legislature to create a special "railroad police" to patrol these industrial districts. Railroad companies hired and paid these forces, yet they were uniformed and vested in the authority of the state. In 1866 the legislature expanded this authority to other industries, including coal mines; the railroad police became the infamous Coal and Iron Police. In Pennsylvania during the 1870s, the fear of conspiracy, the concentrated power of the Reading Railroad, and lingering ethnic animosities meant that Franklin Gowen and the Pinkertons had almost carte blanche to pursue the Molly Maguires.

Between 1873 and 1876, McParlan infiltrated the world of the Molly Maguires, becoming, he would later claim, a full member of first the Ancient Order of the Hibernians and then the Molly Maguires. During this time, McParlan took part in several secret meetings where the Molly Maguires planned ambushes, murders, and other forms of intimidation. Once the Mollies learned that a spy was working within their organization, McParlan fled the region, returning only to testify in the various trials of accused Mollies. Despite being the president of the Reading Railroad and the direct employer of James McParlan, Gowen, as a former district attorney for Schulykill County, argued several of the key cases. Other trials were argued by Charles Albright, who was officially a lawyer for the Reading Coal Company but had served as a general in the Civil War and arrived to trial in full military attire.

In his closing arguments, Gowen reinforced for the jury the vast conspiratorial nature of the organization. "It is frequently customary for lawyers, in opening a cause, to refer to it as one of great importance," he told one jury. "I am sure that you will bear with me, when I say that I do not exaggerate the merits of this case in stating that it is perhaps one of the most momentous trials that has ever been submitted to a jury in this country." "For the first time, after struggling under a reign of terror that has extended over twenty years," he continued, "we are placed front to front with the inner workings of a secret association, whose members, acting under oaths, have perpetrated crime in this county with impunity." It was this conspiratorial nature, Gowen argued, that not only gave the jury the opportunity to disregard alibis but also explained Gowen's unique position as attorney, industrialist, and employer of McParlan. "It was when I was District Attorney of this county," Gowen declared, "that for the first time I made up my mind from what I had seen, in innumerable instances, that there then existed in this county a secret organization, banded together for the commission of crime."[10]

Once he became president of the Reading, or, as he described it, "when the time came that I became so much interested in the prosperity of this county, and in the development of its mineral wealth," Gowen became convinced that the battle against the Molly Maguires was a "struggle between the good citizen and the bad citizen as to which should obtain the supremacy." It was then, he claimed, that he dedicated himself to the task of exposing the Mollies. Furthermore, Gowen "knew that it could only be done by secret detectives, and I had had enough experience, both as a lawyer, and as the head of a very large corporation, to know that the public municipal detectives, employed by the police authorities of the cities, who operate only for rewards, are the last persons to whom you could trust a mission and an enterprise such as this." His time with the railroad introduced him to detectives whom he could trust. "I knew, for I had had experience before, of the National Detective Agency of Allan Pinkerton, of Chicago, which was established by an intelligent and broad-minded Scotchman, established upon the only basis on which a successful detective agency can be established," he stated, "and I applied to Mr. Pinkerton."[11]

Gowen then established the reputation of the Pinkertons and of McParlan to counter the defense attorney's efforts to depict the detective as an accomplice and agent provocateur. "I have adverted to the case of an accomplice; but remember that McParlan is not an accomplice," Gowen reminded the jury. "McParlan is a detective, engaged in the performance of a professional duty, who enters upon his quest with the avowed purpose of trying to make all those with whom he was brought in contact believe that he is one of them." Furthermore, the county had been made safe by the mass arrests of Molly Maguires. "And to whom are we indebted for this security, of which I now boast? To whom do we owe all this?" asked Gowen. "We owe this safety to James McParlan, and if there ever was a man to whom the people of this county should erect a monument, it is James McParlan, the detective." The power of the Pinkerton agency, Gowen assured the jury, would break the conspiracy. "It is simply a question between the Mollie Maguires on the one side and Pinkerton's Detective Agency on the other, and I know too well that Pinkerton's Detective Agency will win," he claimed. "There is not a place on the habitable globe where these men can find refuge and in which they will not be tracked down." Even those Mollies who had not yet faced trials were not safe. "The cat that holds the mouse in her grasp sometimes lets it go for a little while to play: but she knows well that at her will she will again have it secure within her claws," Gowen explained, "and Pinkerton's Agency may sometimes permit a man to believe that he is free who does not know that he may be travelling five thousand miles in the company of those whose vigilance never slumbers and whose eyes are never closed in sleep."[12]

In his condemnation, Gowen stressed that although the accused were Irish and the organization of the Mollies was "identical with that of the Ribbonmen in Ireland, who have terrorized over the Irish people to so great an extent," the prosecution did not target the accused because of their ethnicity or religion. The condemnation of the Catholic Church and the excommunication of suspected Mollies proved that the miners in no way represented any kind of genuine Catholicism. Even more importantly for Gowen, the political motives of the Molly Maguire violence were not connected with labor relations. Gowen claimed that he hired the Pinkertons out of a resolve formed during his frustrating years as district attorney, not out of any economic interest as president of the railroad. Echoing the principles of free labor ideology, Gowen reminded the jury that "if there is anything which should be accorded to a member of a free government, if there is any right which the humblest man in this country should possess, it is the right to labor for the support of his family, without hindrance or molestation from any one." While the defense might suggest that the trial pitted capital against labor, "on behalf of every honest laboring man in this county," declared Gowen, "I protest with indignation against the assumption that these men are the representatives of labor." Instead, he insisted that the jury consider the Mollies a criminal conspiracy. "Do this, gentlemen," he concluded, "and I am sure that linked together with that of McParlan and of others who have aided in this glorious crusade, your names will be enshrined for long coming years in the grateful recollections of an enfranchised and redeemed people." McParlan's testimony about the crimes of the Molly Maguires led to the execution of twenty miners, all convicted of different crimes. Although the courts could never prove that the organization of the Molly Maguires actually existed, most juries assumed the connection between these various crimes.[13] To further this connection, the state executed the first ten Molly Maguires on the same day in 1877.[14]

Among the assassins!

Missing from Gowen's account of criminal immigrant conspiracies was the economic transformation of the coalfields after the war. Between 1865 and 1875 the Reading Railroad was consolidating its control over the southern coalfields of Pennsylvania. While other companies operating out of New York had already monopolized the northern fields, small mines and independent operators still dotted the southern fields. Gowen, who became president of the Reading Railroad in 1869, vowed to change that. He first consolidated the shipment of coal throughout the region. As the Reading came to dominate rail rates, it also began to purchase, through shadow companies, its own coal mines. Once it controlled the majority of both coal production and shipment in rural Pennsylvania, it then opened coal yards in Philadelphia to cut out the coal sellers of the city. By 1870, the Reading Railroad controlled much of the production of coal in eastern Pennsylvania from mine to market. The only obstacle left in Gowen's plan was the newly created Workingmen's Benevolent Association (WBA). Formed in 1868, the WBA was the first region-wide trade union that unified workers of different locations and different ethnicities in a single organization that sought to control the amount of coal produced by its members. Although a series of strikes had weakened some of its strength, the WBA was a major player in the economics of coal production when Gowen hired Pinkerton in 1873. As Mc-Parlan entered the coalfields to infiltrate the Molly Maguires, fellow Pinkerton agent P. M. Cummings worked his way into the WBA.

The long-brewing conflict between Gowen and the WBA over pay scales and control over work exploded into a massive strike in January of 1875. The so-called Long Strike lasted until June. Unable to force the Reading to negotiate and unable to provide adequate food to its hungry membership, the WBA collapsed, and workers returned to the mine under the complete authority and oversight of the Reading Railroad. By July of 1875 industrial order had been firmly established in the southern coal regions. The Long Strike was not without its bitterness and violence, however. Supplied with information from Cummings and McParlan, the Coal and Iron Police formed flying squads to break up strike meetings and intimidate miners. Pinkerton agents not only supplied information to the Coal and Iron Police but also served in their ranks. Robert Linden, for instance, served as both a Pinkerton operative and a captain in the police. To make matters even more confusing, a number of secret vigilante groups formed out of both the Pinkertons and the Coal and Iron Police. In a letter to George Bangs, Allan Pinkerton advocated for extralegal rough justice. "If Linden can get up vigilance committee that can be relied upon, do so," Pinkerton wrote. "When M.M.'s meet, then surround and deal summarily with them. Get off quickly. All should be securely masked."[15] Such sentiments culminated in the vigilante attack at Wiggans Patch on December 10, 1875. Months after the strike had ended, a band of thirty masked men forcibly entered the home of Mrs. O'Donnell, the mother of suspected Molly Maguires James and Charles O'Donnell and mother-in-law to Charles McAllister and John Kehoe. The vigilantes pistol-whipped Mrs. O'Donnell and shot and killed her daughter Ellen McAllister. After abusing and threatening several of the paying guests in O'Donnell's boarding house, the vigilantes dragged into the street Charles and James O'Donnell, as well as Charles McAllister's brother James. McAllister and James O'Donnell escaped, but the vigilantes shot Charles O'Donnell fifteen times. He died in the street. Both James O'Donnell and John Kehoe were later executed as "Mollies."[16]

The context of the Long Strike should have shaped the meaning of violence in the coal regions. Yet the trials and subsequent histories and fictionalizations attributed the violence solely to the ethnic animosities of the Molly Maguires. Because of its detail of the case and because of its source, Pinkerton's account quickly became the standard history. Several different histories of the battle in the coalfields, including Ernst Lucy's *The Molly Maguires of Pennsylvania; or, Ireland in America* (1877) and Francis Dewes's *The Molly Maguires: The Origin, Growth and Character of the Organization* (1877), borrow heavily from Pinkerton's text. Indeed, Lucy admits that much of his history comes directly from Pinkerton's book. Moreover, these works and most of the coverage of the trials from the popular press assumed the same thing about the Molly Maguires which Pinkerton laid out in his introduction—this was a criminal society brought directly from the shores of Ireland and transplanted into Pennsylvania. Little mention is made of the history of labor strife, including the bitter Long Strike of early 1875, the end of which prompted the second wave of violence attributed to the Molly Maguires. Instead, in these works, modern society was pitted against the ancient ways of uncivilized tribes. While such violence had been stomped out in rural Ireland, the fight had moved to America. "As to myself, I am not a political partisan, unless it be partisanship to support the cause of Great Britain and of civilization," claimed Lucy in his introduction, "for secret murder and lawless outrage are crimes against civil society all the world over."[17] Other publications, such as *Among the Assassins! The Molly Maguires and Their Victims* (1876), *Lives and Crimes of the Molly Maguires: A Full Account* (1877), and *The Molly Maguires: A Thrilling Narrative of the Rise, Progress, and Fall of the Most Noted Band of Cut Throats of Modern Times* (1876), continued to assume that the miners were part of a larger criminal conspiracy imported from Ireland.[18]

The popular press and sensationalist dime novels borrowed the same narrative of criminal conspiracies and valiant detectives. In the wake of the trials, the *Fireside Companion* began serializing "The Molly Maguires; or, the Black Diamond of Hazelton," and the *New York Weekly Storyteller* printed "The Molly Maguire, the Terror of the Coal Fields." Other presses, such as New York Detective Library, printed *The Molly Maguire Detective; or, A Vidocq's Adventures Among the Miners*, written by a "US Detective." Likewise, a fictional Sergeant O'Donnell penned *Coal-Mine Tom; or, Fighting the Molly Maguires* for the Five Cent Wide Awake Library. Yet the novelizations of the Molly Maguires differed from those of James and other outlaws. While the James brothers were dashing bandits who were as often the heroes of their dime novels as villains, the dime novels about the Mollies never painted them sympathetically. The *National Police Gazette* categorized the miners as "Coal Region Thugs."[19]

Sympathy for the Molly Maguires came from different places. Local folklore alone portrayed the violence and trials as part of the struggle between local miners and the increasingly powerful Reading Railroad. Many within the region criticized the cooperation of witnesses, who it was claimed testified against suspected Mollies to ensure their own freedom. Others tried to carefully distinguish between the actions of the legitimate WBA and the Mollies. Still others complained that the railroad company had fabricated the Molly Maguires in an effort to extend its monopoly. Local critics accused McParlan and other Pinkertons of being agents provocateur who at best allowed crimes to happen and at worst commissioned crimes to help make their case. As evidence, these critics pointed to the fact that violence attributed to the Molly Maguires began to spike only after McParlan entered the region. In particular, there was local outrage about the vigilante raid at Wiggans Patch. Others pointed to the role that Pinkerton agents and officers of the Coal and Iron Police played in planning and directing the raid. Yet this outrage remained local. Despite the similarities of the raid on Wiggans Patch to the Pinkerton's ill-fated raid on the Jameses' home in Missouri, public perceptions were very different. Broad sympathy for the Molly Maguires was slow to emerge.

Strikers, communists, tramps, and detectives

One of the few sympathetic writers on the Molly Maguires was E. H. Heywood, who saw both strikers on the Baltimore and Ohio line and the Molly Maguires as martyrs in a larger struggle between labor and capital. The Great Railroad Strike of 1877, he argued, originated with "the tyrannous extortion of the railway masters and the execution of eleven labor reformers called 'Mollie Maguires'" and culminated in the "burning of corporation property" during the strike. The strike began in Martinsburg, West Virginia, on July 16 as railroad employees seized the rail line as part of a protest against the Baltimore and Ohio's reduction of wages. When local police proved unwilling to forcibly break the strike, officials of the B&O turned first to the governor of Pennsylvania and the state militia and then to the president. Declaring the workers' seizure of the rail lines and their refusal to let trains pass an "insurrection," President Rutherford Hayes ordered federal troops into Martinsburg to reopen the line. The arrival of heavily armed federal troops in Martinsburg meant that trains, staffed by strikebreakers, began to move out of the depot. However, railroad workers and those sympathetic to the strike attacked locomotives and railroad bridges across Pennsylvania, thereby continuing to prevent the movement of trains. Given the broad reach of railroad monopolies and the growing animosities toward the power of the railroad, what had begun as a spontaneous strike in Martinsburg soon spread into a series of general strikes and violent confrontations. Residents of Baltimore clashed with federal troops in the city's streets, and workers in Pittsburgh trapped the state militia in the depot roundhouse. General strikes began in Cincinnati, Louisville, Saint Louis, and Chicago, and in each of these cities workers clashed with urban police, private security guards, and, in the case of Chicago, vigilante groups formed by the mayor as "special police." After forty-five days and the intervention of the US Army in several different cities, the strike and its violence burned out.

In the aftermath of the strike, urban elites began construction of heavily fortified urban armories and raised state militias and state police. The Citizens' Association, a reform organization of leading Chicago businessmen which had formed in 1874 to exact the "moral purgation of the city," shifted its attention away from electoral reform and sanitation and instead began to purchase and store large numbers of arms and ammunition for "the maintenance of public order" and "city defense." Not a militia themselves, the members placed these arms into "hands of the civil and military authorities," yet the arms remained the "property of and subject to the control of the contributors." The Citizens' Association also began to hire Pinkerton detectives to infiltrate suspected societies of anarchists, communists, and trade unionists within the city.[20]

At the same time, Americans also looked for ways to explain why the conflict had taken place. Increasingly, the answer assumed a conspiratorial cabal of communists who had tapped into and corrupted the vast populations of shiftless tramps and immigrant labor. In 1878, Allan Pinkerton published his own account of the great strike. For a man who had begun the decade of the 1870s with the firm belief that vast criminal conspiracies could not exist because criminals were too selfish and cowardly, Pinkerton's opinion was very different by the end of the decade. A combination of tramps, radical political communists, and secret society labor unions, he argued, together duped the American working classes into violence. "A good deal has been written and said regarding the causes of our great strike of '77," he wrote in *Strikers, Communists, Tramps, and Detectives.* "To my mind they seem clear and distinct. For years, and without any particular attention on the part of the press or the public, animated by the vicious dictation of the International Society, all manner of labor unions and leagues have been forming. No manufacturing town, nor any city, has escaped this baleful influence." Such labor unions, he argued, secretly adhered to a European communism that called for an "agitation of subjects which would antagonize labor and capital." Thus, when railroad workers who were "under the leadership of designing men" struck, "nearly every other class caught the infection, and by these dangerous communistic leaders were made to believe that the proper time for action had come."[21] To Pinkerton the origin of the violence lay not in wage cuts or discontentment with industrial conditions but rather in the dangerous confluence of permanent tramps and radical politics. This was a disease of criminality; it spread like a contagion and had to be battled like one.

Even honorable men could find themselves on the road in hard times, and Pinkerton claimed to hold no grudge against the temporary tramp. The permanent tramp, however, was rootless, unwilling to work, and part of a secret world of other tramps. On their own these men posed no societal threat. However, the specter of radical politics made tramps more dangerous. With the collapse of their 1871 revolution, European communists were looking elsewhere. "When bloodshed was stopped in Paris, many of that city's Commune sought refuge in the United States," said Pinkerton. "It is certain that their societies have been gradually increasing, and that in the mobocratic spirit, the outrage and pillage of July, 1877, are plainly seen the outcroppings of this foreign-born element," he concluded. This secret organization with "agents always actively at work in Europe and the United States" was the "sworn enemy of all political institutions as they now exist," he concluded. "It is a standing conspiracy against progress, liberty and civilization the world over."[22]

The final piece in this conspiracy for Pinkerton was the growth of secret labor organizations that furthered the goals and ideologies of dangerous European political radicalism. "An organization, called the Knights of Labor, has recently attracted some attention in the coal regions of Pennsylvania," he noted. "It is probably an amalgamation of the Mollie Maguires and the Commune." Other organizations, such as the Universal Brotherhood, the Brotherhood of Locomotive Engineers, and the Trainmen's Union, were also vast and violent secret societies. "Tramps and communists, as classes, both played a prominent part in the great strikes of '77," declared Pinkerton. "Tramps, who had nothing to lose, in their philosophical way entered upon the rioting and plunder because it seemed to be the order of the day." Communists took part in the violence "merely for the purpose of precipitating a condition of things where they might wreak their vengeance on society." One might expect such behavior from communists, "but the great moral responsibility for the strikes and their vast train of disastrous effects," Pinkerton concluded, "is certain to rest upon the Brotherhood of Locomotive Engineers." It was skilled labor, with its European-style communist ideologies, its connection to and influence over tramps and the unskilled masses, and its criminal conspiracies and secrecy, that crafted the chaos and violence of the Great Strike. Only the diligence of Pinkerton and his agents, he claimed, saved American society from foreign radicals, shiftless tramps, and "old socialistic leaders" who had the audacity to eulogize what they called "the martyred Mollie Maguires," but the threat remained. "Citizens of the United States must not forget this constant and increasing danger," he argued, "and must work heartily and unanimously towards its suppression."[23]

Just in case his claims seemed too self-aggrandizing, Pinkerton made clear that his only goal in writing the book was to "present merely the truth . . . and look squarely under the mask and in upon the inner workings of the most important of those labor organizations which invariably result in disaster to their members and ruin to themselves." His role as America's most famous private detective and operator of its most famous agency gave him, he claimed, even greater insight. "My extensive and perfected detective system has made this work easy for me, where it would hardly have been possible to other writers," he bragged. Moreover, "ever since the great strikes of '77, my agencies have been busily employed by great railway, manufacturing and other corporations, for the purpose of bringing the leaders and instigators of the dark deeds of those days to the punishment they so richly deserve." He also tried to deflect criticisms of himself and his agency as the hired muscle of industrial monopoly. "In reciting these facts and considering their lesson, I believe that I of all others have earned the right to say plain things to the countless toilers who were engaged in these strikes," he claimed. "I say I have *earned* this right. I have been all *my* lifetime a working man. I know what it is to strive and grope along." However, by 1878 the image of Pinkerton as a protector of American labor and American society from foreign radicalism and lawlessness was increasingly difficult to sell to American working classes, especially immigrant workers, who tended to see Pinkerton agents and Pinkerton himself as tools of an emerging industrial order.[24]

Conclusion: Anarchists and the detectives

In a later chapter of his history of the Great Strike, Pinkerton noted that eventually "the surgings of trouble reached Chicago, the great inland metropolis of America," and were "fierce and furious while they lasted." Pinkerton admitted that his hometown "undoubtedly contains as pestilential a crew of communists as any city in the world" and that the city had "gradually drawn to her a floating population both vicious and unruly." "It was this class, and no other, that precipitated riot and bloodshed in Chicago," concluded Pinkerton, "and it is a notable fact in connection with these communists, that their viciousness and desperation were largely caused by the rantings of a young American communist named Parsons." Albert Parsons, according to Pinkerton, possessed

> a strange nature in every respect, as he has for several years lived in Chicago with a colored woman, whom he has at least called his wife. He is a young man . . . of flippant tongue, and is capable of making a speech that will tingle the blood of that class of characterless rascals that are always standing ready to grasp society by the throat; and while he can excite his auditors, of this class, to the very verge of riot, has that devilish ingenuity in the use of words which has permitted himself to escape deserving punishment.

"It was more through this man's baleful influence, than from any other cause," wrote Pinkerton, "that the conditions were ripe in Chicago for all manner of excesses."[25]

Nine years later, Pinkerton agents would again target Albert Parsons. Beginning in 1884 and accelerating through 1886, participants in broad general strikes demanded reforms to industrial society, including an eight-hour workday. In early May of 1886 the Chicago police fired into a crowd at a rally outside the McCormick Reaper plant in south Chicago, leaving four dead and many wounded. Labor leaders called for another rally at Haymarket Square for the following day. As the police arrived during the waning hours of the rally, someone from the crowd threw a handmade bomb into the police ranks. The explosion killed seven policemen and triggered chaos. In the aftermath of the Haymarket Square bombing, officials in Chicago raided the offices of labor leaders and political anarchists across the city. The police arrested eight leading anarchists, including Albert Parsons, and charged them with conspiracy and murder. To prove that the defendants were part of a large anarchist conspiracy, the prosecution provided the explosives and dynamite found on the defendants, the testimony of an eyewitness who claimed to have seen one of the defendants light the fuse, and the rhetoric of the defendants' past speeches and anarchist newspapers, especially those that called for violence against officers of law and order, including both Chicago police and Pinkerton detectives.[26]

Pinkerton agent Andrew Johnson, one of several agents hired by the Citizens' Association to infiltrate anarchist organizations, including the "American group" of the worker's militia Lehr und Wehr Verein, connected for the prosecution the anarchists' public rhetoric of violence and the planning of specific acts of violence. In his testimony Johnson spoke of plans for revenge killings, raids on the city's armories, experiments with explosives, and the destruction of the new Board of Trade. "The full force and meaning of the testimony of the Pinkerton men in the Anarchists' trial will hardly be understood until more of it is put in," declared the *New York Times*.[27] "Detective Jansen [Johnson] is only one of five of Pinkerton's oldest officers who were put to work early last Winter to find out how much the Anarchist crowd actually meant by their speeches." The paper lauded the tactics of the agents who "actually penetrated to the Anarchist dens, took part in their most secret conclaves, [and] listened to their instructions to their dupes." Furthermore, the paper argued that "Pinkerton had been employed by a party of the largest property holders in the city to make the investigation and furnish the information obtained as he got it. His men were not employed to accuse or convict anybody." Instead, "they were instructed to report facts simply as they found them, and their testimony is, therefore, not open to the objection which is usually urged with force against a detective's evidence—that it is procured to convict." Even though the agency was a private firm under the employ of leading Chicago industrialists, Pinkerton agents and their testimony should not be doubted, the paper concluded. Much as James McParlan had done a decade before, Johnson gave the public a glimpse into a vast criminal under-world filled with foreign radicals, murderous plots, and general upheaval.[28]

As such, the Haymarket trial represents the pinnacle of Pinkerton agents' reputation as trustworthy detectives and moral guardians, yet the trial also con-tained hints of discontentment and distrust. To prove the violence of anarchist organizations, prosecutors introduced numerous newspaper articles calling for retaliations against Pinkerton detectives. "The working men should arm before the first of May to meet Pinkerton's scoundrels, the Police and the militia," read one editorial in the *Arbeiter-Zeitung*. "All organized working men in this country . . . should engage in a general prosecution of Pinkerton's Secret Police," read another. "No day should pass without a report being heard from one place or another of the finding of a carcass of one of Pinkerton's," it concluded. "This should be kept up until nobody would consent to become the bloodhound of these assassins."[29] Other editorials and speeches referred often to Pinkerton scoundrels, Pinkerton murders, Pinkerton's private army, and Pinkerton's thugs. Still others argued that the discovery of small, poorly designed packets of dyna-mite pointed not to serious anarchists but to agents provocateur. One radical editorial concluded,

To be brief, that tin can, with the explosive and partially burned fuse, was put there by the firm of Pinkerton, a very ordinary business trick of that despicable gang, to give a serious aspect to that attack the end of the fuse was allowed to burn before it was put into the can. . . . The citizens will be excited about this "diabolical" plot, and all means must be engaged to find out the perpetrators. They call on Pinkerton, who at once puts three men at eight dollars a day, at their disposal. Now they have a sure trace of the perpetrator, he cannot fail to fall into their hands, the engagement must be prolonged. To prove that they were not idle, a poor devil is arrested once in a while, etc.

"We want to caution our capitalistic fellow-citizens against this last attack of the Pinkertons upon their pockets," the editorial warned; "at the same time we want to advise them that true dynamiters are not so stupid as to enjoy such child's play. They do not joke in such matters, they do not blast a stone palace with a quarter of a pound of dynamite by laying it on the steps; and if they do undertake something like that, the fuse does not fail." To some, such an article proved that there was indeed a violent world of anarchist bombers against which Pinkerton detectives fought. Others saw Pinkerton and his detectives as agents provocateur who used these fears to drum up more business. Dime novel detectives could always be either hero or villain, but by 1886 so too could real-life detective Johnson.[30]

CHAPTER FOUR

In which the Pinks serve as a private army for capital

W HEN ALLAN Pinkerton first began his private agency, he also created a preventive patrol as a kind of merchant's police. Alongside detectives, businesses could also hire armed guards, or "preventives," to patrol their shops and factories. In the late 1860s and early 1870s, as Pinkerton sought to establish clear guidelines about the practice, morality, and purpose of his detectives, he also laid out clear roles for the preventive patrol in the *General Principles of Pinkerton's National Detective Agency*. "The duties of the Preventive are essentially different from those of the 'Detective,'" the rules pointed out. "The Preventive is required to faithfully patrol his Beat . . . on the other hand it is the duty of the Detective to discover and convict the perpetrator of Crime, after it has been committed." Although the detective's work was secret and involved infiltration, the "preventive should take care to make himself known," the rules stated. An 1873 edition of the rules and principles added that "the preventives are required in every respect to conduct themselves in a civil and courteous manner."[1] Although they were not supposed to be connected to "any Municipal Corporation or Government authority," the preventive patrol did take on official capacities within Chicago. After fire decimated the city in October of 1871, Pinkerton vowed to protect the property of his clients by placing guards in the street and posting declarations to "Thieves & Burglars" that "any person stealing or seeking to steal any of the property in my charge, or attempt to break open the safes, as the men cannot make arrests at the present time, they shall kill the persons by my orders, no mercy shall be shown to them, but death shall be their fate." The response to the Great Chicago Fire showed that the Pinkerton agency was willing to use extreme force to "protect" its clients and their interests.[2]

Even before the fire (and before the 1873 edition of the *General Principles*, which declared that "the sphere of their duties will not extend beyond the city of Chicago"), the Pinkerton Preventive Patrol began strike duties in 1866 protecting coal mines in Braidwood, Illinois. Although advocates claimed that "Pinkerton's success was in a great measure due to his stubborn adherence to several rules he regarded as cardinal," the use of the preventive patrol as strike guards outside the city of Chicago demonstrated that the agency was willing to go outside of its own stated rules in order to stake out a place within the conflict between capital and labor. In his writings, Allan Pinkerton, who had long been both the public face of the agency and the chief architect of its mythology, stressed that he hired educated and moral detectives who pursued the public good (and protected free labor). Upon his death in 1884, much of that changed. When Allan's sons, Robert and William, took over the agency, they quickly expanded the scope of the agency, especially the protective patrol. "Since the death of the elder Pinkerton," one paper summarized, "the organization has increased in strength and efficiency until at present it is recognized as the great private resource by large corporations for the protection of lives and property in times of stress and storm."[3]

The sons, unlike their father, had not experienced the poverty of working-class Glasgow or the free-labor politics of antebellum America, instead growing up as members of the bourgeois class at a time when fraternal association and membership in exclusive clubs provided key business connections while also offering proof of Victorian status.[4] Both had attended the University of Notre Dame before joining the family business, and both sons were accepted members of the elite class. The family's maturation into Chicago high society was symbolized by the marriage of Allan's daughter Joan to William Chalmers, heir to the Chalmers manufacturing business (all despite Allan's stern lack of approval of Joan's marriage). Robert, who had been sent to New York to learn the family trade under the tutelage of George Bangs (while William worked with his father in Chicago), was particularly keen to expand the agency into private guards in order to compete with new agencies offering the same services. Between 1888 and 1893, the agency opened several new field offices, including ones in Boston, Kansas City, Portland, and Saint Paul. Offices in Saint Louis and Denver were opened to directly compete with the rival Thiel Detective Service Company, operated by George Thiel, a former Pinkerton agent, whose disloyalty the Pinkerton family could not forgive.

But to ascribe the shift in Pinkerton policy to only family drama would miss the larger political and cultural shifts taking place at the same time. While Mark Twain and Charles Dudley Warner may have given the Gilded Age both its name and much of its reputation with their satirical novel of political corruption and personal greed, this was an age that belonged to the monopolists of American industry. The robber barons of the immediate postwar period made their wealth through either railroad construction (assisted by the federal Pacific Railway Act) or stock and currency manipulation (or, in the case of the Crédit Mobilier scandal, both). By the late 1870s, however, centralization shifted the focus of the economy away from the railroad barons and toward the captains of industry, who built vast empires of monopolized industrial production. For example, after decades of expanding its control over the Pennsylvania coalfields and hiring Pinkerton agents and Coal and Iron Police to break resistance, Franklin Gowen's Reading Railroad found itself deeply in debt and twice fell into receivership. In 1883, financier John Pierpont Morgan bought the failing railroad and ousted Gowen as president. National monopolies were matters of high finance, which meant efficient production methods and breaking artisanal control over the pace of production.[5] Unlike midcentury ideals of independent free labor, late nineteenth-century battles between capital and labor embraced the power of association. For capitalists this meant organizing themselves into business associations, funding national guards to enforce social order, and hiring private guards and militias such as the Pinkertons. For labor, national organizations, such as the Knights of Labor, arose to battle these business associations. This often placed these unions in direct confrontations with Pinkerton guards; hence, as one historian has suggested, the Pinkertons became the "Knights of Capitalism."[6] Historians have described this as the managerial revolution, and Alfred Chandler named the corporate managers the "visible hand" of the market. But this new order did not happen without struggle, and these managers increasingly relied on the Pinkerton agency.

After 1886, Pinkerton's National Detective Agency became in essence a private army on the side of industrialists. "The Pinkerton agency formed armed bands of ex-convicts and hoodlums," labor leader Mother Jones would write of the Chicago strikes of 1886, "and hired them to capitalists at eight dollars a day, to picket the factories and incite trouble." A state convention of the United Labor Party in early 1887 called upon the governor of New York "to assert his authority and to stamp out the blood-stained gang of murderers and tramps who have dared to establish their headquarters in the Metropolis of American civilization." In a scathing exposé on the power of the Pennsylvania Coal and Iron Police, Henry George took time to note that these forces "should not be confounded, as they sometimes are, with that private army organized by the Pinkertons, and sent hither and thither to the aid of those who will pay for their services." For labor leaders, "Pinkertons" were merely one manifestation of a larger monopolistic enemy. "Against us we find arrayed a host guarded by special privilege, buttressed by legalized trusts, picketed by gangs of legalized 'Pinkertons,'" wrote labor union leader Samuel Gompers.[7] Not only did this transform the roles and national reputations of Pinkerton agents, but it also posed important questions for the role of the state in the Gilded Age. Between 1860 and 1880 expansionist capital's interests were tied directly to the state. With the emergence of monopoly capital after 1880, the state was starting to stand in the way of their integration and power. As the interests of the state and capital began to split, the Pinkerton agency, in the employ of capital and deputized by the state, was caught in between.[8]

The "Pinkerton Force" or detectives on trial

During his Haymarket testimony, Pinkerton agent Andrew Johnson admitted that anarchists regarded the Pinkertons as "a lot of cold blooded murderers, and the worst enemies the workingman has, and they are all in the pay of the capitalists." It was precisely this reputation that the defense used to impeach Johnson's testimony. In cross-examination, the defense tried to pierce the detective's testimony and credibility. Johnson acknowledged that the meetings he attended were public; no one was turned away, and often the press was there to document the speeches. The militia drills, he admitted, were conducted without actual arms, and no specific threats were ever planned by the anarchists. Johnson also could not name others who had overheard the same whispered conversations that he had claimed to hear. Moreover, the defense attorney tried to undermine the standing of Johnson the private detective. First, the defense coyly tried to distinguish Johnson's time as a private detective from time spent in "legitimate business." When Johnson replied that he had worked in a hotel for a spell, the defense asked if he had not been "detailed to go through the hotel and see what you could get listening on the back stairs." When the defense challenged the discrepancies between Johnson's written reports immediately after the meetings and his later testimony, Johnson replied that his testimony was more accurate than his reports. "Your memory is better now after a year and half than it was on the same night?" the defense asked. "Considerable better," countered Johnson; "I get my memory refreshed." "Detective's memory grows better as time goes along," the defense retorted, which drew an objection from the prosecution.[9]

After their convictions, the Haymarket defendants appealed their trial based on the legality of the trial and the credibility of the Pinkerton agents. Albert Parsons, in particular, vociferously condemned the actions of the Pinkertons. "As to the responsibility for the Haymarket tragedy," he wrote from his prison cell, "the Haymarket Tragedy was, undoubtedly the work of a deep-laid monopolistic conspiracy originating in New York City & engineered by the Pinkerton thugs."[10] In particular, Parsons wanted to draw the courts attention "to the way armed men, militiamen and Pinkerton's private army, is used against workingmen, strikers; the way it is used to shoot them, to arrest them, to put up jobs on them and carry them out." After quoting an agency circular that promised industrialists that Pinkerton agents could not only infiltrate labor organizations but also "deal promptly" with them, Parsons declared, "Here is a concern, an institution which organizes a private army. This private army is at the command and control of those who grind the faces of the poor, who keep wages down to the starvation point. This private army can be shipped to the place where they are wanted." Without geographical or jurisdictional limits to its interventions, this army "moves about to and fro all over the country, sneaks into the labor organizations, worms itself into these labor societies, finds out, as it says, who the ring-leaders are and deals promptly with them. 'Promptly,' your honor, 'with them.'" Given the "work for which they receive their pay," the Pinkertons were probably to blame for Haymarket, he concluded. "I say that a Pinkerton man, or a member of the Chicago police force itself, had as much inducement to throw that bomb as I had, and why?" asked Parsons. "Because it would demonstrate the necessity for their existence and result in an increase of their pay and their wages. Are these people any too good to do such a thing? Are they any better than I am? Are their motives any better than my own?"[11] All the alleged speeches and violent plans were, he pointed out, "reported by the Pinkerton detective, Johnson, who was, as the record shows, employed by Lyman J. Gage, vice president of the First National bank, as the agent of the Citizens' association, an organization composed of the millionaire employers of Chicago." He concluded that "it will take corroborative testimony before the American people will credit the statements of such a man engaged for such a purpose . . . and it is well known that supreme courts have decided that the testimony of detectives should be taken with great caution."[12] Undercover agents in the service of Chicago industrialists, it was beginning to seem, could not be unquestionably believed when they claimed to uncover secret conspiracies.

"Pinkerton is neither more nor less than the head of a band of mercenaries"

At the same time that the Pinkerton agency was expanding its system of labor spies (a system that was falling under closer scrutiny), the agency was also undertaking a much more public and controversial role as armed guards and strikebreakers. The agency began its first forays into strikebreaking in 1866, when it sent armed guards to the newly discovered coal region south of Chicago, which would become Braidwood, Illinois. Agents would return to Braidwood in 1874 during another strike. Yet Pinkerton guards earned their first notoriety during the 1884 Hocking Valley Strike in Ohio.[13] After coal miners struck in response to wage cuts, the Columbus and Hocking Coal and Iron Company hired Pinkerton guards to protect company property and ensure that replacement workers could resume work. The arrival of "blackleg" replacements further angered striking miners, resulting in several clashes with Pinkerton guards and the destruction of company property.

The introduction of armed Pinkerton guards into the labor conflict in Illinois changed not only the role of the agency but its public reputation and political resonance as well, because the Pinkerton guards had become a much more visible player in the growing struggle between capital and labor. "The strike of the coal miners in the Hocking Valley region of Ohio has been one of the most important, most extensive, and most costly that the country has ever seen," wrote *Harper's Weekly*, which "only now comes to an end not by the surrender of the strikers but by their replacement by other men, and the complete victory of the operators." Such use of replacement workers to break a strike also meant that the company was "obliged to have them guarded by Pinkerton's detectives, heavily armed."[14] Between 1877 and 1892, the Pinkertons took an active part in at least seventy different strikes. During the 1888 Burlington strike, the company also expanded into providing strikebreakers to companies. In his summary of the labor conflict, C. H. Salmons declared that "Pinkerton bullies with their repeating rifles and their court proceeding" were a constant presence in the conflict. As employees of the Burlington tried to rise up and "undertake to cure this injustice, all the Pinkerton detectives, deputy sheriffs, and state militia are called out to suppress them." The instances of violence, he argues, were triggered by the aggressive behavior of armed Pinkerton guards. While many worried about the violence of striking railroad workers, "no word was spoken against the usurpation of state and municipal authority by the Burlington officials, with the deputy sheriffs and armed force of Pinkertons and scabs."[15] After 1888, in the minds of many, "pinkertons" became shorthand for any armed guards or vigilance committee that intervened on behalf of American industrialists. The "heavily armed Pinkerton" became a problematic symbol of labor strife during the Great Upheaval.

The political role of armed guards became even more contentious when

Pinkerton guards killed. During an 1886 strike in south Chicago, the Lakeshore Railroad Company hired armed Pinkertons to protect its railcars. During one public confrontation, Pinkerton guards fired into a crowd and killed a protestor.[16] The following month, during a stockyards strike, Pinkertons again fired into a Chicago crowd, killing bystander Terence Begley. The coroner's inquest attributed the shooting to Pinkerton guards and declared that "we, the jury, believe that the Pinkerton detective agency has been derelict in keeping and withholding the names of the 123 men on the train where from said shooting took place." Town of Lake officials arrested six Pinkerton operatives.[17] Eyewitness testimony from both protestors and bystanders was consistent in reporting that the crowd taunted the Pinkertons as they passed in a railcar and the guards responded by firing into the crowd. But the passions concerning the Pinkertons clouded the case. Pinkerton supporters claimed that "there was a very general opinion among the better element of Packingtown that the presence of the Pinkerton men there in such force was the only thing that kept the lawless faction as quiet as it was." For their part the Pinkertons were convinced that they "stood between the riotous element and their destructive propensities and hence drew upon themselves the enmity of this crowd." Moreover, the conflict, they believed, was part of a larger radical "scheme . . . to attack us, to force us to retaliate and then bring up their sympathizers to the front with a preponderance of false evidence to the effect that we were the real aggressors." The *Chicago Tribune* concluded that "the difficulties surrounding the discovery of the real facts in connection with the shooting can be readily seen when the intense hatred of all the workmen about the Stock Yards toward the Pinkerton force is considered." Despite the testimony of witnesses in the crowd, the grand jury failed to indict the Pinkertons, and a judge dismissed all charges.[18]

The following year Pinkerton guards shot and killed fifteen-year-old bystander Thomas Hogan during a dockworker strike in Jersey City, New Jersey. This time public outrage came quickly. Local officials condemned Pinkerton forces as an outside agitation. According to the police chief of Jersey City, "it was a wonder that a riot was not incited by the tragedy last evening . . . the striking coal handlers were especially vigorous in their threats against the Pinkerton force." The chief was pleased to announce that after "consultation with the railroad people this morning and as a pacific measure, the Pinkerton specials have been withdrawn from the outskirts of the yards" so that their presence would not foster more violence.[19] Organized labor responded vigorously and publicly to the Jersey City strike. Shortly after the shooting death of Thomas Hogan, the

United Labor Party met in a convention and declared that "a private and irresponsible body of armed men have for several years assumed to exercise throughout the United States functions which essentially belonged to the police of cities, the militia of the States, and the regular Army." Moreover, the practice of swearing in "men of unknown residence and notorious characters in the pay and under the command of private individuals and corporations is a glaring imposture in violation of American liberty and fundamental law." The condemnation went further, stating that "Pinkerton men go from state to state committing murders for which none of them are ever brought to trial."[20] Likewise, the Federation of Organized Trades urged in their August 1887 convention that "united action be taken . . . against the Pinkerton detective system."[21] A State Trades Assembly passed a similar resolution, but with much harsher language. "Whereas it had come to the knowledge of the assembly that in Jersey City there is a section of the mobilized army of Hessian murderers known as the Pinkerton detectives," the resolution declared, "therefore be it resolved that we condemn the employment of irresponsible hirelings by soulless corporations." The assembly suggested that the wealth acquired by those within powerful corporations "had made them so arrogant that it is only a question of a short time when each one of them will become a feudal lord with his own private department of murder."[22]

Terence Powderly, Grand Master Workman of the Knights of Labor, led much of this new criticism. In an interview with the press Powderly declared that "a general experience has shown me that the calling in of armed men is utterly unwarranted. I am opposed to the importation of Pinkerton men, they act on the passions of men just as a red flag acts on a bull." Not only did the presence of Pinkerton agents exacerbate tensions and violence, but he went on to say, "I am positive that the introduction of the Pinkerton detective as an agent in the settlement of disputes is entirely foreign to the letter and spirit of the Constitution of our common country." Powderly also attacked the moral standing of the agents and the judgment of the capitalists who hired them:

> The men who make up the Pinkerton army are gathered in from the gambling dens and slums of our large cities, and are composed of creatures who are outcasts from decent society. Their introduction for the purpose of settling disputes through force of arms is an insult to society everywhere. The employer of labor who calls to his aid a body of hired assassins—and the Pinkerton thugs can be called by no more appropriate name—must have a poor estimate of his own abilities and intelligence when he lets such delicate and important work . . . out to a human brute

devoid of intelligence, manhood, self-respect and decency. If these men came to a community without the badge of the Pinkerton Detective Agency they would be arrested and imprisoned as suspicious and dangerous characters. With the badge of that agency, they are entitled to no more respect than if they did not wear it.

In the same article, Pinkerton director Robert Linden (who had served as a Pinkerton agent, a Coal and Iron Police officer, and a vigilante in Schuylkill County in 1875) responded to Powderly's accusations. The criticisms were unfair and inaccurate, he claimed. "I do not think, but I know, that the Pinkerton men are a necessity in all the cases where they have been called in," he concluded. "The Pinkerton men are the best to call in when it is necessary to control the rioters. They are never driven away."[23] In an editorial a couple of days later the *New York Times* argued that "it is not surprising that General Master workman Powderly does not like detectives or that he should object to having this class of men employed by capitalists to guard their property from the malignant assaults of striking Knights of Labor." Criminals were often indignant, it claimed, when "officers of the law" were prepared to thwart their "criminal designs." Law-abiding men had nothing to fear from the Pinkertons. "Private detectives are employed not to intimidate honest workmen," the editorial argued, "but to prevent the accomplishment of the designs of evil counselors and professional agitators."[24] For labor, the presence of a Pinkerton army represented the most egregious abuse of corporate power. For industrialists, Pinkerton guards were called in not to create disorder but to reestablish order; thus, the blame for any violence lay not with the Pinkertons or their employers, but with labor leaders and "professional agitators" who caused the chaos. For the *New York Times*, the Pinkertons still were the "officers of the law" protecting property from criminal intents.

Others saw the pitched battle between capital and labor as a tragedy in which there was plenty of blame for both. "The unfortunate killing of a boy in Jersey City, by a chance shot from one of Pinkerton's men employed in guarding the coal company's wharves in Jersey City against the strikers," declared the *Nation*, "is exciting a great deal of indignation against this organization among the strikers and their friends." Yet the fault began with local officials who allowed the Pinkerton presence and then condemned their actions. "That disgraceful demagogue, Mayor Cleveland of Jersey City," it wrote, "is particularly loud in his denunciation of them." Yet "a great many good people are asking why an armed body of this sort, which is not under the control of or responsible to any public authority, should be permitted to figure as prominently as it does in these labor troubles." In regard to the Pinkerton Patrol, the magazine was "very glad that people are beginning to ask what it means, and why it exists, because the answer is most instructive." The *Nation*'s own answer was very blunt. "Pinkerton's Men are, we must all admit, the greatest disgrace that has befallen the United States," it concluded. "Its appearance in any other civilized country would fill to-day every man in it with shame and astonishment," the magazine continued. "For it is—let nobody shrink from this plain truth—an unmistakable sign of retrogression towards medieval barbarism. Pinkerton is neither more nor less than the head of a band of mercenaries."[25]

However, following this clear denunciation of Pinkerton's guards, the *Nation* explained why such "medieval barbarism" had resurfaced. "They are called into existence by exactly the same causes now as then—the absence of a public force capable of enforcing the law of the land, and affording security for life and property to the peaceable and well-disposed." When all other routes of "civilization" such as courts, police, or troops prove unable to protect property, industrialists will "hire an army of their own" for their own protection. "Of course, this is anarchy in its first stage," the paper concluded. "The word is not a pleasant one, but it must be used when the occasion calls for it."[26] "The demand for Pinkerton's Men began nearly twenty years ago in the coal regions in Pennsylvania, when the Molly Maguires took possession of them, and superseded the law by a foul and murderous conspiracy," the *Nation* explained. "This conspiracy was then called, as some such things are now called, 'Labor.' Labor overawed the sheriffs, defied the courts, intimidated the juries, and marked out its enemies for assassination literally by the dozen." Because of the condition of "terror and disorder" that the Maguires helped to create, "the corporations owning the property, finding there was no help to be expected from the public force, hired a force of their own, with Pinkerton at its head, and through his exertions Labor was at last brought to justice, and twenty cut-throats righteously hanged." However, "since then the need for a small private army of this sort for the defence of property has not diminished, but on the contrary has increased." In response to this need, "Pinkerton has enlarged and improved his force. It is better armed and drilled every year, and it travels to and fro, all over the United States, a sort of moving shame and disgrace for us all. No American ought to be able to look on it without blushing to the roots of his hair." However disgraceful the Pinkerton army was, the *Nation* reminded its readers, the fault for its creation lay elsewhere. Mayors, sheriffs, and even governors have, either by "the demand of Labor or through the fear of Labor," refused to protect property rights. Instead, they "stand idly by while Labor pursues poor men with brickbats, bludgeons, and pistols to prevent their accepting employment which is offered them." The fault lay in a combination of radical labor and a political state that was unable or unwilling to enforce order and protect free labor. "The poor demagogue who is playing the role of Mayor over in Jersey City ought, however, to be the last to complain of Pinkerton's Men," the paper concluded. While the Pinkertons may be a disgraceful mercenary army patrolling stockyards and warehouses for capital, "if the country should be carried much further on the road to medieval anarchy . . . these private armies would not remain shut up in the yards or warehouses or mansions of their employers." Instead, "they would sally out, medieval fashion, and twist the necks of the Clevelands, and Hills, and Greens, and Oglesbys in very summary fashion." The failure of local politicians had created the monster of the Pinkerton force.[27]

Yet others placed blame with shortsighted capital. In editorial cartoons, *Puck* lampooned the business practice of hiring Pinkerton guards and American business practices in general. In one such instance, a Chairman Foster tells a Chicago manufacturer, "Your factory receipts last year were one hundred thousand dollars, and wages and material come to only fifty thousand dollars. Now, as we have a rather large deficit, you will please shell out." To which the Chicago manufacturer replies, "but my dear sir, think of the cost of the Pinkertons." In another aside a mill owner regrets his current predicament. "We are running behind fast, and as there is no prospect of a reduction of the tariff on raw materials, we will have to reduce wages," he tells his superintendent. The superintendent responds, "That won't do. If we offer a reduction, there will be a big strike, and then we'll have to hire Pinkertons to protect our property. That will provoke rioting and half a dozen or more may get killed." To which the owner replies, "Well I don't want any bloodshed. I'll simply close the mills for repairs." In an article that argued for compulsory arbitration as a cure for labor strife, the *Atlantic Monthly* stated that without labor struggles there would be no need for such private armies. "With arbitration to prevent instead of to settle strikes there will be no riots or acts of violence on the part of hot-headed sympathizers with the men," it concluded, "[and] no employment of Pinkerton 'detectives' by the management, to obscure the real issue and render impartial judgment impossible."[28]

In a similar piece, William Schuyler applied the lessons of Shakespeare to understand the arrogance and power of modern industrialists. Much as Prospero controlled Caliban through threats and violence, so too did corporations hold power over their workers through company stores, blacklists, and "private armies of wicked spirits called 'pinkertons,' conjured up by the magic power of wealth." While Prospero may keep temporary control over Caliban, Schuyler argued that "each time the revolt grows more and more dangerous." "Each new revolt has been more potent than its predecessors because it has been more rational," he concluded, "and deny it as we will, the roar of the coming torrent of revolution is now distinctly audible." Prospero's charms and force over Caliban did not last forever. Perhaps most interesting in Schuyler's article is his choice of forgoing capitalization when talking of the "pinkertons," because in many of these articles the very concept of "pinkertons" had come to mean more than the specific actions of the Pinkerton agency. It had become a kind of shorthand for the general violence and tension that marked the struggle over labor and capital in the Gilded Age. Thus, when the *New Englander and Yale Review* commented on a new book that traced the several rises and falls of "civilization" and argued that man periodically fell back into stone age savagery, the authors commented that "indeed we confess that we rather enjoy contemplating the possibility that man had a long reprieve from some of the miseries of civilization, the wretched life of our mines, the wars of strikes and lockouts, of Pinkertons and brickbats."[29]

The Knights of Labor and the Pinkerton roughs

While religious leaders, editorialists, and commentators saw in the Pinkertons allegories of anarchy, feudalism, and the fate of civilization, for organized labor the effect of armed Pinkertons was far more direct. Labor newspapers and proletarian novels denounced the Pinkertons as tools of capitalist oppression of free and honorable labor. Others saw the Pinkerton guards as instigators of violence and chaos. Especially for the Knights of Labor, who clashed with Pinkerton guards at numerous strikes between 1884 and 1890, the Pinkertons were an immediate threat to their power and legitimacy. Formed in 1869, the Noble and Holy Order of the Knights of Labor was a secret trade union that, like many worker organizations in the mid-nineteenth century, was steeped in ritual. This began to change in 1879 with the ascension of Terence Powderly to the position of Grand Master Workman. Powderly began to institute major reforms, including the elimination of secret rituals, the dropping of "holy order" from the title to appease Catholic bishops, and the rapid expansion of membership. Powderly embraced the concept of "producerism," where all productive members of society create tangible wealth regardless of race, ethnicity, or skill. Such an ideology gave the Knights of Labor a broad appeal and a diverse membership. In 1884 Powderly and the Knights won a major victory in the Wabash strike against Jay Gould, after which the membership of the Knights grew rapidly. This success, Powderly knew, made his organization a target for both railroad companies and Pinkerton agents. In an 1889 memoir entitled *Thirty Years of Labor* (a title tantalizing similar to Allan Pinkerton's own 1884 memoir *Thirty Years a Detective*), Powderly criticized the Pinkerton detective as a "plague spot on American civilization . . . who, in order to earn his salary, added to his treachery the crime of perjury and murder in order to make out a case against his fellow men." Thus, the Knights under Powderly were left with a conundrum; staying a secret organization made them a target of Pinkerton detectives, but expansion and openness, while making the organization more transparent, also made infiltration easier.[30] The fear of labor spies was confirmed in 1885 when suspected Knights were fired from Jay Gould's Southwest Railroad line, prompting another confrontation between Gould and the Knights.

By 1886, the Knights had also grown concerned about the use of Pinkerton guards as armed guards who incited violence and as agents provocateur. Violence during the Great Southwest railroad strike in 1885 turned public sentiment against the Knights and allowed Gould to crush the union in Texas and Missouri.[31] During the 1886 Chicago stockyards strike, district secretary T. B. Barry wrote to Powderly detailing the situation. "The town of Lake is in a state of siege with Pinkerton men in the employ of the packing firms," he wrote. "There are five hundred Pinkertons here and the first and second regiments are under orders at the Armory." Powderly urged caution and restraint, yet he suspected that this would not be enough. "I had had enough experience to believe that if the men did remain absolutely quiet and sober," he would later write, "some agent of the Packers or Pinkerton's could be depended upon to start trouble."[32] Indeed, violence in south Chicago also turned public opinion against the striking packers, and the Knights were dealt another defeat. The fact that the Knights were linked to so many of the strikes that seemingly had led to the Haymarket bombing further put the labor organization into public suspicion and internal turmoil. Later that same year, many skilled trade unions formed their own organization (the American Federation of Labor) to distance themselves from the perceived radicalism of the 1886 strikes.

The 1890 strike against the New York Central Railroad in Albany, New York, became vitally important to the Knights because it represented an opportunity for the Knights to replicate the success of the Gould strike of 1884 and distance themselves from the failures of the strikes of 1886; it became for the Knights a struggle for survival. The strike began on August 8, 1890, with a general walkout and tie-up of the rail lines by the Knights of Labor, in response to the New York Central's dismissal of dozens of employees who were members of the Knights. On August 10, the first squad of Pinkertons arrived; the president of the railroad would later admit that he had contracted with the Pinkertons before the strike occurred.[33] In the city's rail yards and rail crossings, strikers and Pinkerton agents began to clash. As early as August 11, Albany officials worried that "since the arrival of the Pinkerton men the strikers have been restive. The presence of the detectives has had the effect of causing much irritation and little outbreaks between them and the strikers during the night are feared."[34] On August 14 the *New York Times* reported that "Pinkerton Men [were] assaulted at Albany yesterday" by stone-throwing strikers. By the eighteenth, "firearms [were] freely used" by strikers, Pinkertons, and police officials as "the strikers attack Pinkerton detectives [and] shots returned by the officers for the stones thrown." The paper also reported that "trouble was expected all along the line of the Central railroad within the city limits to-day owing to the fact that the Pinkerton men were all known to be armed." In picking up the story, other papers began to refer to the agency as "Pinkerton Roughs."[35]

As in Jersey City, public officials demanded that Pinkerton agents disperse from public crossings in the city "as their presence served to excite the frenzy of the throng of onlookers." Over the next several days, tensions mounted as Pinkerton agents shot several protestors and bystanders, including firing a "fusillade on the crowd" from the top of a railcar. When local officials tried to arrest a Pinkerton guard for one such shooting, fellow Pinkertons "rescued the prisoner and handled the officer roughly." By the end of August "rumors [were] prevalent of assaults upon Pinkerton men coupled now and then with statements that Pinkerton men had been killed . . . bulletins were issued frequently, one of which informed the men that Bob Pinkerton had detailed some of his 'cut throats' to mingle amongst them." Throughout the strike, many assumed the presence of the Pinkertons to be a primary cause of disruption and violence. When engineers found railroad ties stacked across the rails, District Master Workman Edward Lee argued that "the ties were no doubt placed upon the track by Pinkerton Men to throw discredit on the Knights."[36]

Such actions within the 1890 strike gave Powderly a chance to confront the Pinkertons within the court of public opinion, a new tactic against the agency. Early in the strike the Knights sent a circular to strikers suggesting that they stay sober and orderly and avoid conflict with local officials, strikebreakers, and hired guards. "Have no altercations with the Pinkerton men," the circular read; "keep

THIS PORTRAIT of Allan Pinkerton was taken in 1861. By this year, Pinkerton had converted his business connections with American railroad companies, his personal fame as a detective, and his role in (maybe) foiling a (possible) assassination plot against Lincoln into a position as spymaster for the Army of the Potomac. *Library of Congress*

A LLAN PINKERTON and his secret service headquarters after the Battle of Antietam in 1862. As an unofficial head of an unofficial secret service, Pinkerton took on responsibilities for both counterespionage in Washington, for which he was lauded, and positive intelligence in the field. He and his field agents, as seen here, were far less successful in predicting Confederate troop strength. *Library of Congress*

GIVEN PINKERTON's personal fame during the war and the competitive market for law enforcement after the war, Pinkerton's agency and logo underwent several changes. Between 1855 and 1867, the agency once called the North West Police Agency added Pinkerton's name, advertised itself as "National," and replaced "Police" with "Detective." The company logo became the all-seeing and unsleeping eye, which evoked the Masons, the French secret police, and the prewar abolitionist "Wide Awakes." *Library of Congress*

ILLUSTRATION FROM Allan Pinkerton's *Molly Maguires and the Detectives*, a literary telling of Pinkerton agent James McParlan's infiltration and exposure of the dangerous world of Irish miners. To maintain his fame and company brand, Pinkerton "wrote" sensationalist and fictionalized versions of several of his cases. *Library of Congress*

A S CONTROL of the company passed to Allan Pinkerton's sons and company business shifted west, agents had to take on new roles and affectations. Here William A. Pinkerton (*center*) poses with railroad special agents Pat Conwell (*left*) and Sam Finley (*right*), 1886. *Library of Congress*

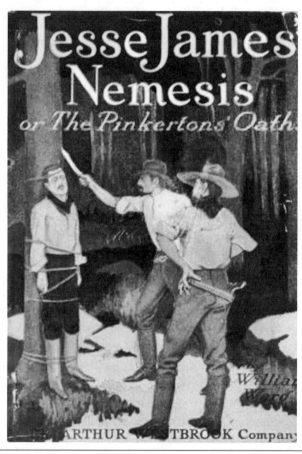

IN THE morally murky and entirely fictionalized world of dime novels, Jesse James and Pinkerton agents could play either heroes or villains, depending on the tale. Shown here is the cover of the dime novel *Jesse James' Nemesis; or, The Pinkerton's Oath* by William Ward, published in 1908. *Carleton College Special Collections*

H*arper's Weekly*, one of the most popular newsmagazines for upper-class audiences in the late nineteenth century, offered its depiction of the chaos that surrounded "The Homestead Riot." *Library of Congress*

T*he National Police Gazette*, a sensationalist newspaper that reveled in stories of box-
ing, crime, detection, and scantily clad women for its largely working-class audience, offered its version of the "Battle of Homestead." *Library of Congress*

BY THE 1890s, the Pinkerton agency tried to distinguish itself on its modern detective work and scientific approach, including tracing serial numbers on currency and printing wanted posters with accurate photos, such as this photo of railroad bandit Will Roberts. Clearly, by the end of the nineteenth century, bandits also did not mind the notoriety and fame that came with such photos. *Library of Congress*

DESPITE BEING supposedly hounded by the Pinkertons, Butch Cassidy and his gang stopped in Fort Worth, Texas, to have a proper Victorian portrait taken. *From left to right*, Henry Longabaugh (the Sundance Kid), Will "News" Carver, Ben Kilpatrick (the Tall Texan), Harvey Logan (Kid Curry), and Butch Cassidy. Ideas about the photo varied: defenders of the bandits understood the photo to be a taunt; the Pinkerton version said that a wily detective noticed the photo in a shop window and used it to hunt the gang. *Wikimedia Commons*

TWO TRAIN ROBBERS KILLED NE
ANDERSON TEX MAR 13 191
PHOTO BY

THE LAST bandit of Butch Cassidy's Wild Bunch, Ben Kilpatrick, and his new partner Ole Hobek were killed while trying to rob the Galveston, Harrisburg and San
Antonio (of the Southern Pacific railroad). Wells Fargo agent David Trousdale killed
both bandits. Although they were not directly involved, the Pinkertons prided themselves on the death of the known bandits and added this photo to their files. *Library of
Congress*

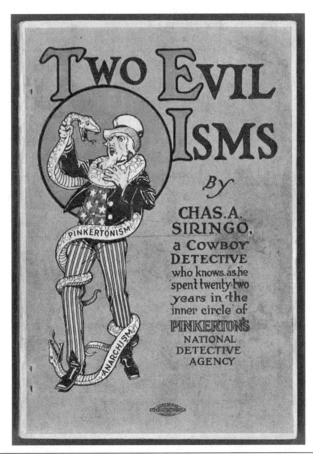

ONE OF the agency's most trusted "cowboy" detectives, Charlie Siringo, wrote *Two Evil Isms*, a scathing exposé of company practices and the firm's employment of killers such as Tom Horn, in 1914. Siringo claimed that he joined the firm in 1886 to battle anarchism but found Pinkertonism to be just as evil.

away from them when there is danger of a rupture . . . remember that every man of you is being watched, your footsteps are being dogged, and even a joking remark may serve to fasten upon you a crime of which you would scorn to be guilty." By avoiding conflict, the strikers could postpone the intervention of the national guard and state police and court public sympathies. "By taking this course you will strengthen our hands," it concluded, "and public opinion, always fickle, will be borne to your aid by the shifting winds."[37] To further this cause, Powderly also took his case against the railroad and the Pinkertons to the public. "We are not the disorderly mob that their papers paint us," he wrote in an open letter. Instead, the "orderly and law abiding conduct" of strikers had won the "admiration of the public." Only the "introduction of an armed force under the command of Robert Pinkerton, a man who holds no commission from the state or nation, to recruit or arm men for military duty," had caused the public outrage. "It was not necessary to call upon them," Powderly argued, "and yet a hireling mob of the worst characters in the land have been quartered upon the people of New York to terrorize citizens, to provoke men to anger and wrath, to shoot down those who asked for the rights to be heard in their own behalf." Powderly also demanded that "it will be well to ask why blank commissions with the Sheriff's name attached are placed at the disposal of Robert Pinkerton to be placed in the hands of ignorant men who believe that under this authority they have the right to shoot citizens to death."[38]

In later testimony about the New York Central strike, Powderly would again return to the violence he saw as inherent within the Pinkerton system. "Where the Pinkertons gain a foothold they incite a riot for the purpose of lengthening their terms of service," he argued. Workers would not destroy corporate property because, as producers, it was not in their interest to do so. "On the contrary, it would be to the interest of the 'watchmen' to start fires, drive away imaginary intruders, and perform other services in order to prejudice the public mind against all strikers," he argued. "This, if you will pardon the expression, is the old game of the regulation Pinkerton 'watchmen.'" William and Robert Pinkerton had created an atmosphere of fear and paranoia by claiming, Powderly quoted, that "all capital so invested is practically at the mercy of secret labor organization, whose tyranny and despotism exceed anything ever known in the history of the world." Powderly not only disagreed with the Pinkertons' summary of labor, but he also argued that the Pinkerton agency victimized organized labor and cheated industrialists. "It is the part of policy for the Pinkerton agency to terrorize timid capital by making it believe that it is at the mercy of labor organizations," he claimed. "It is also to their interest to cause men of wealth to believe that their wealth is not safe while labor organizations exist." This fear mongering was a key part of the detective's job. "Their existence as a detective agency depends upon their detecting something," he concluded. "In order to prevent their occupations from vanishing," detectives "conjure up the imaginary where the real would not answer their purpose." Overall, he concluded that "there exists no necessity whatever for the existence of a wandering army of vagabonds raked together from the four quarters of the earth, to engage in labor disputes. Capital makes a mistake in engaging these vagrants."[39]

Moreover, Powderly tried to deny the Pinkerton agency its self-created mythology as agents of law working always in the cause of justice. "If the Pinkerton detective agency was influenced by the philanthropic motives which its managers would have us attribute to it," he asked, then why were they only employed by capitalists? "Surely workingmen and workingmen's organizations are right once in a while, and, if the cause of right alone attracted the service of the Pinkerton agency," then they would side with workers now and again. Yet, he pointed out, they did not. "It is not philanthropy, it is not a sense of duty, nor is it patriotism that actuates the institution under discussion," he concluded. "To make the record read accurately it must be written that the agency operates for gain, and that cause or object which can command the most money will find the employés of the Pinkerton agency arrayed in its service and in opposition to the interests which are not influential or wealthy." Maybe "if labor organization could command the wealth that employers of labor do at this day, we could hire the services of 'watchmen' from the Pinkerton agency by offering a higher reward for such service," he joked, yet he knew that this was unlikely. Powderly's public campaign to win sympathy for the strike was successful in some circles and less successful in others. Some doubted the authenticity of worker complaints. "You are surely mistaken about that," offered one congressman in response to Powderly's testimony. "Mr. Depew [of the New York Central] has stated publicly that the system had been brought to perfection and was so fairly and justly regulated toward the men, and so entirely satisfactory was their situation, that their position depended entirely upon a proper discharge of their duties," he continued, "and that so universal was their satisfaction that there was absolutely no conflict existing between the employers and the employed. I am surprised at your statements."[40]

For all their successes and failures in courting public opinion, the Knights were never fully able to tie up the rail lines, nor could they convince the local

Brotherhood of Railroad Engineers to join the strike. In late August, while Powderly tried to negotiate an end to the strike, word came from Terre Haute that the Brotherhood of Locomotive Engineers would not join the walkout. Replacement workers continued to fill union jobs, and by the end of August the strike had entered its final days. With the disastrous end to the strike, the Knights suffered a major setback, and by 1893 they ousted Powderly as Grand Master Workman. For those opposed to the use of Pinkertons, however, two very important things emerged out of the Albany strike. First, not only the strikers but also some local officials and observers acknowledged the Pinkerton guards as an interventionist force whose primary goal was to trigger violence and create chaos. Secondly, state officials felt compelled to step in and mediate the conflict between Pinkertons and strikers. In early September of 1890, the newly created State Board of Mediation and Arbitration began an investigation into the New York Central strike. It was during these hearings that officials for the railroad admitted to contracting with the Pinkertons before the onset of the strike. Indeed, investigators bristled when Pinkerton officials refused to answer their questions of not only when arrangements with railroad officials were made but also what those arrangements entailed. Even the state had grown suspicious of the agency.[41]

Conclusion: Anarchists and the detectives

For a company that had long built its reputation and brand on professional detection of crime, this new public role as capital's muscle was very different. The popular press, which had long reveled in the mythology and romance of the detective, began to question many of the Pinkerton methods. Public accusations that Pinkerton agent Johnson exaggerated his testimony in the Haymarket trials, as well as suspicions that detectives may have served as agents provocateur in the violence, gained traction. Stories noted that the Citizens' Association of Chicago continued to bankroll the infiltration of anarchist and other political groups. Sources revealed that Pinkerton detectives were watching many of the high-ranking officials of the Knights of Labor.[42] The assumptions and fears of organized labor about Pinkerton spies were confirmed when a secret circular of the Pinkerton agency became public. It read,

> Corporations or individuals desirous of ascertaining the feeling of their employés and whether they are likely to engage in strikes or are joining any secret labor organizations with a view of compelling terms from corporations or employers can

obtain, on application to the Superintendent of either of the Pinkerton offices, a detective suitable to associate with their employés and obtain this information. It is frequently the case that by taking a matter of this kind in hand in time and discovering the ringleaders and dealing promptly with them serious trouble may be avoided in the future.

The Pinkerton agency had long advertised two different functions (sleuthing and armed guards) performed by different employees. Detectives infiltrated criminal conspiracies, and guards protected industrial property and broke strikes. Increasingly, it seemed, these two functions had become intertwined, calling into question the motives for both.[43]

In June of 1893, Governor John Altgeld of Illinois revisited the trials and events of Haymarket Square. "The meeting was orderly and was attended by the mayor, who remained until the crowd began to disperse and then went away," he concluded. Only after the arrival of Chicago police officers did disorder begin and the bomb was thrown. Altgeld went on:

> The prosecution could not discover who had thrown the bomb and could not bring the really guilty man to justice, and, as some of the men indicted were not at the Haymarket meeting and had nothing to do with it, the prosecution was forced to proceed on the theory that the men indicted were guilty of murder because it was claimed they had at various times in the past uttered and printed incendiary and seditious language, practically advising the killing of policemen, of Pinkerton men and others acting in that capacity, and that they were therefore responsible for the murder of [Chicago policeman] Mathias Degan. The public was greatly excited and after a prolonged trial all of the defendants were found guilty.

Yet the governor found that the trials were filled with legal inconsistencies. In particular, he singled out the brutality and carelessness of Captain John Bonfield of the Chicago Police. His record of breaking up political rallies and worker strikes, along with a general record of violence, created the atmosphere for retaliation. "While some men may tamely submit to being clubbed and seeing their brothers shot down, there are some who will resent it and will nurture a spirit of hatred and seek revenge for themselves, and the occurrences that preceded the Haymarket tragedy indicate that the bomb was thrown by someone who was seeking personal revenge for having been clubbed," the governor concluded, "and that Capt. Bonfield is the man who is really responsible for the death of the police officers." While ultimate fault may have lain with Bonfield and the Chicago Police, Pinkerton detectives shared some of the responsibility for creating this environment of hostility and violence. "Again, it is shown here that the bomb was, in all probability, thrown by some one seeking personal revenge," wrote the governor, and "that a course had been pursued by the authorities which would naturally cause this." In addition to the broad history of labor conflicts, there were also several cases where "laboring people, guilty of no offense, had been shot down in cold blood by Pinkerton men and none of the murderers were brought to justice." There was good reason for animosity toward the agency. Later in his decision Altgeld would return to the role that Pinkerton agents played in Chicago's social unrest. "In 1885 there was a strike at the McCormick Reaper factory on account of a reduction in wages and some Pinkerton men, while on their way there, were hooted at by some people on the street, when they fired into the crowd and fatally wounded several people who had taken no part in any disturbance," explained the governor; "four of the Pinkerton men were indicted for this murder by the grand jury, but the prosecuting officers apparently took no interest in the case . . . and in the end the murderers went free."[44]

Because of what he understood to be the legal inconstancies of the trial and the fact that "much of the evidence given at the trial was a pure fabrication," Governor Altgeld issued pardons for the Haymarket anarchists (although George Engle, Adolph Fischer, Albert Parsons, and August Spies had already been executed and Louis Lingg had committed suicide in his jail cell). The governor had reversed one of the great achievements of the Pinkerton agency. According to Altgeld, the Pinkerton agents and not anarchists were to blame for creating the environment in which bombs would be thrown. Far from protecting private property and maintaining social order, by the early 1890s, the Pinkertons seemed to create disorder and to encourage the destruction of property, and the state was beginning to feel the need to intervene against the Pinkerton force.

CHAPTER FIVE

In which Pinkerton myrmidons invade Homestead

HERE WAS a time, in the days of sturdy old Allen [*sic*] Pinkerton, when the Pinkerton agency was useful and reputable," wrote journalist Myron Stowell in 1892, but that had changed "when another wing was attached to this bird of prey, whose function consisted of spreading death throughout the ranks of laborers having misunderstandings with their employers." By the last decade of the century, the Pinkertons had already earned a reputation as capital's hirelings; Terence Powderly considered himself "the principle opponent of the Pinkerton agency" because of how often the Knights of Labor confronted the agency. But it would be the conflict between striking steelworkers and Pinkerton guards in Homestead, Pennsylvania, that would make the firm infamous and finally signal a crisis of the state. At the onset of a labor conflict with the skilled workers of the Amalgamated Iron and Steel Workers, Andrew Carnegie and Henry Frick locked out the union, fortified the mill, and contracted with Pinkertons to provide three hundred armed guards. On July 6, 1892, when the Pinkerton guards arrived in Homestead by barge, they were met by armed and angry steelworkers. What followed was a long and bloody gun battle that dwarfed the sporadic violence of earlier Pinkerton conflicts. The carnage of the battle caught the public's attention, and descriptions of Homestead filled headlines. "A few days after our return to New York the news was flashed across the country of the slaughter of steelworkers by Pinkertons," political activist Emma Goldman would remember. Frick had fortified the mills, she wrote, and sent for strikebreakers "under heavy protection of heavily armed Pinkerton thugs." Workers arrived on the shore "determined to drive back Frick's hirelings," but once within range, the Pinkertons opened fire into the crowd. Such "wanton murders," Goldman noted, "aroused even the daily papers." For Stowell as well, the events of Homestead represented a breaking point in industrial relations. "The world was shocked at the frightful crimes committed under the pretext that because the body happened to be covered with blue cloth, adorned with brass buttons, it gave the 'guard' a license to club and shoot at will," he declared. "The world not only stood aghast at the spectacle but it entered a protest that ended in what is hoped will effect a final

overthrow of the Pinkerton's power and a complete annihilation of the pernicious system."[1]

Homestead proved to be an important watershed in the histories of the Pinkerton agency, organized labor, and the growing authority of the nation-state. "The
Pinkerton policemen" were, declared the *Social Economist*, "a body of questionable legal status at best, and one whose chief functions have been to intensify
rather than to suppress strife among wage workers." Because the paper believed
that a "system of private mercenary police has no legitimate place in this republic," it suggested that the courts and the state look into the actions of the Pinkertons more than the strikers. "A proposition for the suppression of Pinkertonism,"
it concluded, "is quite as pertinent as trial for treason of workingmen who were
indiscreet enough to resist armed intrusion." So too did the *American Journal of
Politics* question the state's decision to indict strikers for treason. "If they had
fired on state or national troops, or even on a legally organized police force, their
offense might be made to look more like treason," the paper concluded, "but
their war was against the Pinkertons, a body of men collected from all quarters
of the continent, the very mention of whose name rouses a warlike feeling in the
breasts of thousands of law-abiding citizens—a body of men who are not permitted to enter some states in the mob-provoking capacity, under penalty of
law." How could a civil society exist, some asked, where "millionaires are permitted to hire and drill the scum of society to shoot down workers"?[2]

The reputation, discretion, and respectability of the Pinkerton guards were
key issues at the center of popular debate about the meaning of the Homestead
violence. Pittsburgh journalist Arthur Burgoyne made this reputation a pivotal
part of his description of the Homestead conflict. "A sketch of the personnel and
methods of the 'Pinkerton National Detective Agency' as it is styled by its chiefs,
will make clear to the reader the reasons for the hatred and contempt enter-
tained for this body by workingmen everywhere," he wrote; "in recent years the
conversion of the guards into an irresponsible military organization with self-
constituted authority to overawe striking workmen had provoked a feeling of
intense hatred on the part of organized labor toward these soldier-policemen."[3]
To some the agency represented the worst examples of the concentrated power
of capital, while others questioned the morality and standing of the Pinkerton
guards. Still others fretted over the dangerous potential for anarchy and chaos
in industrial districts; however distasteful the agency might seem, the unruly
and violent crowds of strikers seemed worse. And where, many asked, were state
officials during this conflict, and why had they allowed this to occur?

In the wake of Homestead, Congress launched a series of investigations into the employment of the Pinkertons and their effect on labor relations. For his part, Powderly's opinion of the Pinkertons remained the same as it had been for the preceding decade; "if Pinkerton has the right to arm men to engage in strikes," he testified, "the strikers have the right to meet them with arms in their hands, and to such extremities we should not be driven." The key difference was that, by 1892, most congressmen and much of American popular opinion were willing to agree with him. "There is no division of sentiment," stated the committee's chairman at one point of Powderly's testimony, "as to the bad policy that is complained of, and which we decide to remedy . . . while there may be the power to employ these men, we believe it is bad policy, and that such things are liable to bring on trouble." "It is liable to lead to civil war," interjected Powderly. "I agree with you as to that," the Chairman responded.[4] And with that the Victorian sensibilities of moral suasion and the confinement of dangerous elements to industrial peripheries no longer seemed capable of maintaining order. Instead, there were increasing calls for direct and visible state intervention. The Gilded Age state had never been quite as benign or laissez-faire as it liked to appear. While federal courts set increasingly tight limits on social policy and intervention, other actions such as tariffs, taxes, land grants, and use of the army in labor conflicts all benefited the growth of market capitalism. Yet the growing concerns about late nineteenth-century monopoly capitalism, with its interconnected railroad networks, massive immigration of unskilled labor, international finance and securities, labor unrest, public health concerns, and plutocratic armies all seemed to coalesce into larger and more comprehensive threats. What was at stake in Homestead was not simply the role of the state in providing the securities of industrial modernity but the very shape of industrial modernity.

The Great Battle of Homestead

Andrew Carnegie had long been a pioneer in industrial monopolization. His empire included not only the production of steel but also the coal mines and rail lines that made steel production possible. As such, he could control the price he paid for materials and shipping rates. A steel tariff enacted by Congress in 1889 set the price of finished steel. Carnegie's methods also included the control of production costs and efficiencies within the steel mill, including implementing scientific management and the deskilling of artisan labor. Hence, a struggle between Carnegie and the artisanal union for control of the process of steel manufacturing within the mills had been brewing for some time. In 1889, however,

Carnegie thought that the passage of the tariff was more important than a pitched battle with labor. Thus, the company signed a three-year contract with the Amalgamated Association through June of 1892.

By the spring of 1892, Henry Frick, Carnegie's superintendent, was preparing for a significant conflict with the union at Homestead. By the end of June, he had built around the mills a protective twelve-foot fence that included rifle holes, water mains capable of blasting strikers with boiling water, and wires attached to a generator which could be electrified; in response, workers dubbed the mills "Fort Frick." He also began secret negotiations with the Pinkerton agency to provide security and guards beginning in early July. However, workers were aware that Frick had hired Pinkertons to break the Connellsville coal strike the previous year, and many suspected that an arrival of Pinkertons in Homestead was imminent. During a rally on June 19, Burgess John McLuckie chided those in the crowd who had supported Republican candidates in earlier elections. "You men who voted for the Republican ticket for high tariff," he stated, "and you get high fences, Pinkerton detectives, thugs, and militia!" According to Burgoyne, rumors about the arrival of "an army" of Pinkerton detectives quickly gained credence in town. Some speculated that Pinkerton agents were already in the mills preparing the ground for the arrival of the main force. Others said that replacement workers were to arrive, not only under the protection of the Pinkertons but "disguised in the blue uniform of Pinkerton detectives."[5]

On June 25, Frick announced that the company would no longer negotiate with the union but rather only contract with individual employees. In response, 3,000 of the 3,800 workers within the Homestead mills voted to strike, even though the Amalgamated Association, a skilled trade union, represented only seven hundred workers in the mill. Hoping to reopen the works with replacement workers, Frick made plans to import three hundred Pinkerton guards. To the *Pittsburgh Post*, Frick explained that "from past experience, not only with the present sheriff but with all others, we have found that he had been unable to furnish us with a sufficient number of deputies to guard our property." The company had to protect its own workmen and provide watchmen to assist the sheriff, and "we knew of no other source from which to obtain them than from Pinkerton agencies."[6]

The Pinkertons arrived in Pennsylvania by different rail lines, rendezvoused several miles upstream from Homestead, and boarded specially outfitted barges. Workers, however, closely watched the river. On the morning of July 6, strikers met the barges at the water's edge. After a brief exchange of words, shots were fired. In later testimony Pinkerton agents would swear that the first shots came from the crowd, and most later accounts default to the notion that who fired first remains unknown, yet popular accounts that quickly followed from the conflict assigned blame to the Pinkertons. Although the crowd faced off with "an organized and disciplined force of 300 Pinkerton men," reported the *New York Times* the following day, "not a man of the strikers fell back . . . there was a puff from the barrel of a Winchester, a sharp report, and Fey [a worker confronting the landing force] fell dead in his tracks. Instantly the Pinkertons were made to pay for their work." In its analysis, *Harper's Weekly* agreed that during the parley between strikers and agents "someone from the boat fired a Winchester rifle and then a serious battle begun."[7]

This serious battle would last the next fourteen hours. After an initial surge, the Pinkertons were pinned down in their barges. After several hours, the crowd attempted to sink the barges by cannon fire (residents borrowed the cannon that the city used for commemorations). The crowd also sent burning railcars rolling toward the barges and sprayed oil into the river, which they then attempted to light on fire in hopes of burning the Pinkertons out of their barges (the lubricating oil thrown into the water proved impossible to set aflame). According to some on the barges, most of the Pinkerton guards had no idea where they were, for what purpose they had been hired, and what precipitated the conflict. When confronted by the angry crowd, many huddled in dismay and confusion in the boat. Some, it was later claimed, leapt overboard into the river to avoid the gunfire. Others demanded that their superiors surrender. By the time the regular Pinkerton detectives who were leading the expedition decided to surrender, the angry crowd shot down their offer of a white flag. Shortly thereafter, Hugh O'Donnell, one of the leaders of the Amalgamated Association, stepped forward to negotiate a surrender of the Pinkerton barges. Once the guards surrendered, the crowd disarmed the agents and marched them through the city. On this march the Pinkertons walked what was later referred to as a "gauntlet" of angry residents, who assaulted and beat the agents. In total, nine members of the crowd and three Pinkerton agents died in the fight. After the battle and the gauntlet, nearly all of the Pinkertons were wounded. McLuckie held the Pinkertons until they could be shipped out of town by rail.

The sense of victory for the strikers would be short-lived, however. Upon hearing of the conflict, the governor of Pennsylvania ordered the state militia into Homestead. Initially the strikers and residents of Homestead welcomed the arrival of the militia, but the troops soon took up defensive positions in the hills overlooking the city and began escorting locked train cars of strikebreakers into the Homestead mills. The strike ended after four months, with workers returning to the mills without union representation. Carnegie Steel blacklisted strike leaders and broke trade unionism in Pennsylvania. In the aftermath of the Homestead conflict authorities charged O'Donnell, McLuckie, and 160 other strikers with crimes such as murder and treason. While none were convicted, the legal defense of the strikers diminished the already-meager resources of the Amalgamated Association. Many of the Pinkerton agents were also charged with various crimes from Homestead, but these charges also did not result in conviction.

Mr. Frick's hired invaders

Much like the Molly Maguire trials before them, the Homestead riots triggered a local culture of resentment and criticism of Pinkerton men and their tactics. Folk songs lamented that "father was killed by the Pinkerton men" or that "bum detectives come without authority, like thieves at night when decent men were sleeping peacefully."[8] One letter of support to Hugh O'Donnell claimed that "you have put an end for all time to the Pinkertons, and am tempted to say, notwithstanding your sorrow and mourning, that it is worth the cost."[9] Other political radicals also saw in Homestead a common cause. "To many rough fellows, heroic in their way and easily misled by circumstances, it appeared more likely than not, that the killing of those two barge-loads of Pinkerton guards was but the first step in a conflict of national extent, which would wind up in the coming of an industrial millennium," reported Burgoyne. "Hardly a man among them imagined that the law would seek atonement for the death of Mr. Frick's hired invaders."[10] Such radical sympathies led anarchist Alexander Berkman to attempt to assassinate Henry Frick in his Pittsburgh office shortly after the Homestead debacle.

The difference between the Homestead strike and the Molly Maguire trials, however, was in the coverage of the popular press. Nearly every story in the immediate aftermath of the conflict questioned the conduct of the Pinkertons and the wisdom of hiring them. "There have been few great strikes or riots in the United States during the past twenty years in which Pinkerton men have not taken a prominent part," the *New York Times* noted, "and among the laboring classes the name of Pinkerton has for this reason come to be despised." Since governors were reluctant "for political reasons, to call out the militia for the repression of riots," the paper concluded, "the Pinkerton men found a use for their arms, and they have for many years been employed by railroads and other large corporations for such emergencies." Such emergencies, however, called for

large numbers of armed men, and the suspicion was that the agency often recruited men of low moral standing. "The men employed for such work do not,
as a rule, form part of the regular Pinkerton organization of detectives, but are
known as 'reserves,'" the paper reported. "It has been said by more than one
high authority in such matters that these 'reserves' are for the most part members of the class of petty criminals." The Pinkerton office maintained a list of
known criminals, and the paper reported that when numbers of guards were
needed, such petty criminals were "forced to volunteer for such work whenever
called upon." The use of men "who have as a rule shown a recklessness of human
life" presented a very real crisis of state authority and social order. "There is
scarcely a state in the Union in which labor troubles are frequent that there has
not been an attempt to pass laws prohibiting the employment by corporations
of these men," the paper reported, "yet few had been successful owing to the
mysterious influence which the Pinkerton people are said to have when such
laws are in contemplation." Hence, wherever labor conflict arose, the seemingly
ubiquitous "man in citizen's clothes with a Winchester and side arms was also a
prominent factor."[11]

In its initial coverage, *Harper's Weekly* called Homestead "one of the most
serious and disastrous riots that has ever occurred in America." The magazine
also noted that the importation of Frick's hired guards probably provoked the
violence because "a 'Pinkerton' as these men are called, is as unpopular among
laboring-men of the various organizations as a 'scab.'"[12] So too did the *New York
Times* conclude that the troubles at Homestead "were brought about deliber-
ately by the company of which Andrew Carnegie is the head." The company
wanted to break the union, and Frick had previously demonstrated that "a few
lives sacrificed in the struggle between the strikers and his detectives didn't
worry him apparently." The paper documented how "the company had been
preparing for trouble for some time in a quiet way and as soon as open hostilities
had been declared they rushed their arrangements for a protracted fight to a
finish by transforming their plant into a sort of fortress" and concluded that "all
these warlike preparations were made while the works were kept running . . .
naturally such an exhibition increased the bitter feeling of the workmen."[13] The
importation of what many referred to as "Frick's invading army" triggered the
conflict. "The men have conducted themselves peaceably until this attack was
made upon them by the Pinkerton thugs," the paper quoted Samuel Gompers
of the American Federation of Labor, yet "the men who have built up Homestead would not submit to the invasion of their city by an armed band." While

he noted that "it has never been legally settled whether a Pinkerton detective is liable to trial for murder if he shoots down an American citizen," he felt that "the maintenance of an armed force which had neither the dignity nor the Federal authority of a standing army, such a force as these scoundrely private detectives, hired from an agency, is contrary to all American principles and ideas."[14]

At the end of July, *Harper's Weekly* again returned to Homestead, noting that the "lamentable occurrences at Homestead have drawn the attention of the country again to a singular phenomenon in our social development." Pinkerton's agency was a "private enterprise" that made up for "delinquencies of our public service." Companies that "get into trouble with their working-men . . . have fallen into the habit of calling upon a business firm that furnishes to order protection of property in the shape of armed men at wholesale or retail as may be required." While this "arrangement may do credit to American enterprise and invention," the existence of the Pinkertons "throws a singular light upon the state of American civilization." Private detection was a "perfectly legitimate business." However,

> when such an agency . . . also furnishes armed bodies of men for the defence of factories or railroad shops in case of trouble between employers and working-men, it assumes a different character: It becomes, in a large sense, a private military organization, keeping itself in a state of readiness to respond to a call into active service at short notice. It has a standing corps of experienced officers—captains and lieutenants—and a body of trained privates large enough to form the nucleus of a little army.

"In this way an armed force of several hundred men may quickly be set on foot to serve ostensibly as the posse comitatus of some officer of the peace, as deputy sheriffs or deputy marshals, in any part of the country," the paper concluded, "but really being in the pay of some rich man or corporation, to do such watching and marching and fighting as the interests of the employer may require."[15]

The Pinkerton system is a standing menace to order and good government in this country

It was within this political climate that the US Congress took up the issue of the employment of Pinkertons. While both the House of Representatives and the Senate chose to investigate the role of private armies and guards, they asked very different questions. The Judiciary Committee of the House was mainly concerned with the legal ramifications of armed guards. The Pinkerton agency was a private firm hired to protect private property, yet local sheriffs would often deputize the agents, making them officers of the county. For the committee this was the primary concern of their investigation—were the guards deputized, when were they deputized, by whom, and should such guards ever be deputized?[16] The Senate Committee on Labor and Education worried about the effect of Pinkerton agents on labor strife. It wanted to know what conditions precipitated the hiring of Pinkerton agents and "what legislation if any is necessary to prevent further unlawful use of employment of such armed bodies of men for private purposes." In his testimony before the committee, Powderly was far more direct in his critique. "The Pinkerton system," he declared, "is a standing menace to order and good government in this country."[17]

The testimony before the Senate committee largely consisted of three different groups: law enforcement officials weighed in on the use of armed militias and the ethnic makeup of working classes, capitalists explained their need for Pinkerton agents, and workers described their relationship with Pinkerton guards and the foreign populations within their industries. Among law enforcement officials, there was great disagreement about the legitimacy of the Pinkertons. Robert W. McClaughry, general superintendent of police in Chicago, testified that Pinkertons serve "as an irritant rather than having a quieting effect." Public order should be established by the police, he felt, and if they were incapable, then the state militia should be called in. But the Pinkerton Patrol was "an utterly vicious system" that was "responsible for much of the ill-feeling and bad blood displayed by the working classes." Captain Patrick Foley of the Pinkerton Protective Patrol disagreed vehemently. In cases of industrial unrest, he argued, Pinkertons acted "as special police and deputy sheriffs" and as such have often been called upon to confront "hoodlums and toughs." A willingness to use force to reestablish order made the Pinkertons effective because unruly crowds feared "the increased power" of the Pinkerton men. "I will state without fear of contradiction," Foley declared, "that class of people have no respect for the law or law officers. . . . The only law they recognize is the law of might." The Pinkerton guards played an important role in preserving order largely because the state was unwilling or unable to do so. "Now Captain from your long experience in this sort of work," the committee asked Foley, "what reason can you give, that is satisfactory to yourself, why your sort of men here in Chicago should be employed to preserve the peace and suppress riots in other States of the Union?" Foley responded that "the authorities in those States are unable to give protection to the people."

Pinkerton agent Frederick Heinde also testified to the high quality of the Pinkerton agents. "Have you personal knowledge as to the quality and character of the men who were sent from New York City to Homestead?" he was asked. "Yes sir. I was personally acquainted with nearly all of them," he responded. "What have you to say as to their character?" the committee continued. "Very good men, indeed sir," returned Heinde. "Were they, so far as you know, American citizens or aliens?" the committee asked. "Americans," Heinde returned. "Do you know of any exceptions?" "No, sir." US marshal Frank Hitchcock agreed that the Pinkertons filled a void caused by the breakdown of the posse comitatus system, which failed to work when no one was willing to join the posse. Yet Hitchcock tempered his praise for the actions and character of the Pinkertons. While the "system of the Pinkerton National Detective Agency, for its legitimate purposes [by which he meant 'ferreting out crime'], is the best system in the world," he concluded, the Pinkerton Patrol was no substitute for federal or state authority.[18]

William B. Rodgers of the General Steamboat and Coal Business, which had brought the Pinkerton guards to Homestead, described the lawless character of the crowd. To explain why Carnegie Steel needed protection from its own employés, Rodgers explained that "the employés in this case constituted to a large extent the criminal classes . . . these men at that time would have fired at United States troops just as well as they did on us. They didn't know who were in the barges. They fired regardless of who were in there." Most laborers did not resent detectives, he argued; "that feeling only exists among those who have very little regard for law. The majority of laboring men are law-abiding." "What class of men in Homestead or elsewhere have you discovered to be turbulent and not law-abiding?" the committee pressed. "Those who are the most illiterate," said Rodgers. "Are they for the most part unnaturalized foreigners?" asked the committee. "I think it applies to our own people as well as foreigners. Wherever there is the greatest intelligence it makes the best citizens . . . this class of men that work in the mills are drinking men; all of them as a class. Now they would have no fear of a man that was not armed."

Frank Newell, construction superintendent of the Illinois Steel Company, was far more willing to connect lawlessness to foreign birth. "I attributed it to the restless disposition of our employés there, mostly foreign, Polish and Bohemians," he said of another labor conflict involving Pinkerton agents. "I think that 90 per cent of the employés were Polish; naturally restless, and a desire for higher wages led them to combine among themselves for the purpose of enforcing higher wages." The committee pressed Newell for details on the proportion of workers who were unnaturalized foreigners. "When they first come here do they demand as high wages as our folks are getting?" the committee asked. "When they first come here the original demand is made by the emigration companies that bring them here," he answered. "After they have learned a little of the customs of the country they make demands of their own account." When asked a similar question about whether he hired citizens or unnaturalized foreigners, Frick responded in much the same way: "Well, I began business in 1871, we had a certain percentage of foreigners at that time . . . the tendency from that time until the present has been to employ a larger per cent of foreigners from necessity." "When did the labor troubles begin with you in your business, and from which class of labor, that is the native or the foreign labor, did complaints begin and continue?" asked the committee. "The first strike of any importance that I remember occurred in 1886 in the coke region," responded Frick. "Did I understand you to say that the troubles when they originated were on the part of the foreign element that you had in your employ?" asked the committee. "Largely so," Frick replied, "although a certain percentage of American born were troublesome people."

The workers of Homestead disagreed with Frick and other capitalists about both the origins of the conflict and the quality of the character of the Pinkerton agents. "Then you did not find these men whom the Pinkertons employed and sent to Homestead as a very high grade of men, did you?" the committee asked of Robert Bruce. "They were the scum of the earth," he replied. "What is your opinion . . . of the propriety of sending the class of men employed by these agencies into manufacturing and railroad establishments for the purpose of acting the part of spies among laboring men?" the committee asked. "It is very detrimental," returned Bruce, "causes ill-feeling." "In your association with workmen, have you been led to feel that they have a good or bad opinion of the so-called detectives furnished by the agencies in Chicago?" the committee asked Thomas Morgan of the Machinists and Blacksmiths Union. "The English language is inadequate to express the hate of the men in regard to them," he replied. "To the class of men that is hired and shipped in all these large cities we have an objection to them," stated stockyard worker Richard Powers, "first, because we believe that 95 percent of them are not citizens of the United States; secondly, that they are of the criminal classes, and thirdly because they are men who can not be depended upon, and are not to be believed under oath." The implication was that lawlessness was caused not by workers but rather by Pinkertons. "The militia are preservers of the state. They are called into these matters to preserve the peace," concluded Powers; "[workers] look upon the Pinkerton men as being called in to disturb the peace."

"We look upon the hiring of Pinkerton forces as an unjust and unlawful way of forcing us into submission to the will of people who seem disposed at all times to take advantage of us," said William Roberts, a skilled worker at Carnegie Steel. "The reason why we look upon the Pinkertons suspiciously, we may say more than anybody else, is, as we understand it, they generally go around these large cities and, wherever they can, hire what are known among the workmen as 'bums' and loafers," he concluded. "Do you think from your knowledge of the spirit and temper and purpose of workmen, I mean now as a class, that if the so-called Pinkerton organization was out of existence in this country, that property and rights of men who employ labor would be as secure as they are to-day?" the committee asked. "I think a great deal more secure," Roberts replied. "Do you think that if the working people of the country could be made to understand authoritatively that this thing we call 'Pinkertonism' would be wiped out of existence now, that the general feeling between them and the lawful authorities, and also their employers would be very much better?" the committee posed. "The men in our organizations have been just as willing and ready to go out whenever they have been called with the military as we have been to confront the Pinkertons when they came," returned Roberts.

In a written statement read before the committee, Robert Pinkerton tried to restore the name and reputation of his agents. "The men employed by us in this strike work are selected with great care and only after a full investigation of their character and antecedents," he wrote. "Moreover we have seldom permitted our watchmen to carry arms for the purpose of protecting property and life unless they were authorized by the proper legal authorities or sworn in as deputy sheriffs." Pinkerton also disparaged the tactics of the strikers. "It was impossible to attempt to shoot those firing at the barges," he concluded, "because the strikers made a breastwork for themselves by placing women and children in front and firing from behind them. Not a single woman or child was injured by our men." Furthermore, "the acts of the strikers after our men surrendered would be a disgrace to savages. Yet because done in the name of organized American labor, sympathy, if not encouragement, is shown for such deeds by part of the press and by political demagogues," he complained. "Whatever may be the present prejudice against our agency," he declared, "we shall patiently wait the sober reflection of the country in the confidence that the enormity of the wrong and outrage done to our men at Homestead will be ultimately recognized." The effect of not having an agency such as theirs was dangerous, he warned. "If the owners of mills, factories, mines, and railroads and other valuable property can not employ watchmen to protect life and property," concluded Pinkerton, "then all capital so invested is practically at the mercy of secret labor organizations, whose tyranny and despotism exceed anything ever known in the history of the world." Many members of the committee remained unconvinced. When one Pinkerton administrator tried to explain the distinction between "detectives" and "protectives," the questioning senator shot back that the protectives were "sometimes 'destructives' are they not?"

Although far more concerned with the legality of the incursion into Pennsylvania, the House Judiciary Committee also delved into the questions of Pinkerton agent reputations and the nationality of Homestead's workers. "I can understand why the workmen should oppose the introduction of a foreign force armed, and I can understand why they should be so much prejudiced against watchmen or anybody else called Pinkertons," the committee said to William Heine, president of the Amalgamated Association of Iron and Steel Workers. After quizzing Hugh O'Donnell, the chairman of the strikers' advisory committee, on the percentages of native-born and foreign-born populations in Homestead, the committee returned to the arrival of the Pinkertons. "What was the great antipathy of these people to the Pinkertons and what was their object in fighting them and keeping them from landing?" the committee asked. "Of course you know that the laboring class have a natural antipathy to that class of men; I suppose that will about answer that," O'Donnell responded. Asked why "working people generally are so much opposed to them," O'Donnell explained that "in that particular instance, in regard to the Pinkertons leaving the barge—which has been referred to in the newspapers afterwards as running the gauntlet—it might be owing to the fact that in the town there were then lying dead 5 men who had been shot to death and more wounded." He concluded that workers "looked upon the Pinkertons as armed invaders, men who are thoroughly antagonistic to all laboring interests and allies of the capitalists." John McLuckie confirmed O'Donnell's sentiments. "Our people as a general thing think they are a horde of cut throats, thieves, and murderers," he said, "and are in the employ of unscrupulous capital for the oppression of honest labor." Homestead did not represent a war between capital and labor, he concluded, but rather a conflict between laboring men and "these Pinkertons" who were "there under pay and the person who employed that force was safely placed away by the money he had wrung from the sweat of the men employed in that mill, employing in their stead workmen to go there and kill the men who made his money."[19]

In its conclusions, the House Report declared that the Pinkertons constituted a "mercenary private police force," which, especially in their capacity of watchmen for hire, "may properly be characterized as a sort of private military or police force. . . . [Pinkertons] produce irritation among the strikers frequently resulting in hostile demonstrations and bloodshed." Even the minority report of the House declared that the "Pinkertons have grown to undue and in some degree menacing proportions . . . with its officers, corps of drilled men and supply of arms it is the nature of a military force under the control of private individuals to be hired out to whomever may be able and willing to engage it." The best that Congress could say of the Pinkerton agency was that it was "comprised of men of superior courage but doubtful discretion."

The Senate concluded that the Pinkertons may well have filled a perceived need. "In olden times the posse comitatus (the power of the people vested in the sheriff) was relied upon to subdue all violations of good order and peace in a community," the committee stated, " but it is doubtful whether that means can be relied upon at the present time, especially in mining and manufacturing communities." Lawful remedies for strikes did exist and have been "speedily applied and found to be adequate." "Such use of private armed men is an assumption of the state's authority by private citizens," the committee continued; "if the state is incapable of protecting its citizens . . . then anarchy is the result." The character and practices of the Pinkertons were very much in doubt. "It is reasonable to suppose that they are hurriedly assembled to meet an immediate exigency," the committee assumed, as well as that "they are not of the highest moral order or morals or intellect." "This force is composed of a body of men gathered from distant locations and brought, without direction from any local civil authority, into a scene of excitement and disorder," concluded one committee member. "They are not known to the people of the vicinage. They are, generally, not even citizens of the same state. They are simply a private police or militia. Such a force, brought into a community already excited over the real or fancied wrongs . . . inevitably serves to heighten excitement, to increase disorder, and to make outrages upon persons and property more probable." Senator John Palmer of Illinois was blunter in declaring Pinkerton men as "enemies to mankind that ought to be hunted down."[20] Very real dangers to social order and stability did exist, Congress concluded, yet the state had to reestablish authority, not private interests who hired men of dubious morality.

Even with this conclusion, many senators and congressmen were uncertain what authority they held to rein in the Pinkertons. Congress could regulate interstate trade and oversaw immigration and naturalization, but state militias, sheriffs' deputies, and armed guards protecting property seemed to many to be state issues instead of federal concerns. Rejecting broader legislation, Congress instead passed a federal "anti-Pinkerton" bill that prohibited the federal government or the District of Columbia from employing agents from Pinkerton's National Detective Agency or "similar organizations." Very quickly, twenty-three states followed with their own versions of anti-Pinkerton legislation designed to rein in the authority of private detectives. No longer, it seemed, would the state delegate its authority to firms such as the Pinkertons. While most labor organizations rejoiced in these new limits to the authority of the Pinkertons, others were more cautious. One labor periodical thought that the flurry of legislation and the emergence of an interventionist state would have dire consequences for organized labor. "What fools these mortals be: organized labor is congratulating itself over the downfall of Pinkertonism at Homestead, and calls it one of labor's greatest victories," the paper wrote. "Can people not see that the great lesson taught at Homestead is that the militia will abundantly protect the capitalist, and there is no use for the Pinkertons when the state will furnish the militia free?" the paper concluded. "Better to fight Pinkertons, whom all people despise, than to fight the militia with public sympathy on their side."[21]

Conclusion: Pinkerton raiders, the advance guard to Poles and Hungarians

In the Gilded Age the issues of labor and immigration were closely intertwined, which meant that the debates surrounding the Pinkertons and foreign populations were also intertwined. Certainly Samuel Gompers of the American Federation of Labor saw the power of the Pinkertons and the threat of unskilled immigrant labor as part of the same issue. "Pinkerton raiders," he said of the Homestead conflict, "came as the advance guard to the Poles and Hungarians with whom the company would like to replace self-respecting American workmen."[22] In its coverage of the Homestead riots, the *New York Times* offered an incident "specifically worthy of note," which showed "the bravery and coolness of one Pinkerton man." Amid "a shower of stones and missiles of all kinds this man separated himself from the others and begged for a hearing. In the silence which followed he said: 'Fellow Citizens—When I came here I did not understand the situation or I would never have come. I was told that I was to meet and deal with foreigners. I had no idea that I was to fight American citizens.' "[23] The crowd cheered and let him pass. Still other critics, however, questioned the ethnicity and thus loyalty of the rioters and strikers of Homestead. "How many American citizens were engaged in these disorders I do not know," offered one editorial, but "a report of a speech made in congress states that in the crowd which insulted and abused the captive Pinkertons were foreign women and children." As such, the violence in Homestead was first and foremost an immigration problem. "If foreigners come here to break our laws, we had better punish them first and then send them back whence they came," it concluded. "All of those disturbers of the peace, foreign or native, acted in defiance of the law."[24]

For some the conflict in Homestead and in other industrial districts could easily be read as part of a larger immigrant problem connected to the failures of the state. "There had been trouble brewing in an iron and steel manufacturing town in Western Pennsylvania for weeks," summarized H. L. Wayland, president of the Social Science Association; "at last in the early morning it was known that the Pinkertons were coming. You know the rest. . . . This was not a riot. It was a war and the essential state of war continued for ten days." Industrial towns such as Homestead were ripe for chaos and violence, he argued, because of immigration. Mill and mining towns, which had once been pastoral places where sons of Civil War veterans worked in mines to send their children to college, have become "Italian or Polish, filled with ignorant, superstitious anarchists, addicted to assassination." To make matters worse, "every year the immigrants were of a lower grade" and the dangers of disease, crime, vices, and conspiracy deepened. The result was that "a large and rich tract of territory has here become denationalized, and had become a national peril," he concluded. "And the State?" asked Wayland. "The State is so speechless that the silent grave or the voiceless tomb is chattering loquacity in the comparison." "The duty of the government to interfere for the restriction of immigration is all the more pressing," he declared, "from the fact that excessive and indiscriminate immigration is the direct result of measures adopted by the government."[25]

In order to ensure stability within an industrial society, Wayland stated, an active state had to be capable of not only regimenting immigration and foreign populations but also restricting the industrialist who would use "his mill as to dispossess a thousand American citizens, and to create a mob of ignorant, superstitious passionate foreigners, who shall be a curse and a menace to the State, who shall be the raw material of riot, of savagery, of murder, of everything that is threatening to our civilization." Without such a state, he continued, the use of private armies such as the Pinkertons would only increase. "It does not require an extraordinary flight of the imagination," he warned, "to fancy two of our great railroad corporations contesting the control of some district of territory and employing two different private armies to win by force what cannot be won by peaceable means."[26]

One way to avoid such industrial feudalism and the clash of private armies, the argument went, was a federal state willing to regulate the power and control of business. Integral to this notion of social control was an integrated, scientific, and bureaucratic institution, including public schools, penitentiaries and reformatories, mental asylums and hospitals, and modern police departments. The bureaucratic state also took an active role in regulating behavior and economic trade, including the Interstate Commerce Act of 1887, the Sherman Anti-Trust Act of 1890, and a series of immigration acts that placed the oversight of immigration policy under federal control. As Alan Kraut has argued, "the modern version of the bureaucratic state was born in response to challenges too overwhelming for local governments and private charities to handle by themselves. Immigration was foremost among these challenges."[27] Starting with the Page Act of 1875, which first established federal control of immigration through the establishment of Ellis Island in 1892 as a central processing center, the state not only chose to oversee immigration policy but also made the processing of immigrants scientific, bureaucratic, and efficient. At the same time, immigration policy was also connected with other public concerns such as health (symbolized by the medical exams of the uniformed US Marine Hospital Service) and labor. But, of course, the Pinkerton agency was not a part of this new bureaucratic state; instead, it was outside of and thus a threat to the state. In order for the new state to be legitimate, it needed to publicly respond to growing condemnation of the agency by reining in their actions and authority, while also borrowing their methods to control immigrant populations.

{CHAPTER SIX}

In which the disgrace of Pinkertonism
is subjected to public scrutiny

I N THE wake of the disaster that was Homestead, the Pinkerton agency launched a concerted effort to rebuild their reputation and their mythology by drawing attention away from its strikebreaking work and back toward its work in chasing bank robbers. Beginning in the fall of 1894, the agency gave Cleveland Moffett from *McClure's Magazine* access to the Pinkerton company archives, from which he created a series of articles lauding the company's record. The first of these articles was entitled "How Allan Pinkerton Thwarted the First Plot to Assassinate Lincoln: Stories from the Archives of the Pinkerton Detective Agency." The next articles in the series covered "The Overthrow of the Molly Maguires," a series of train robberies in "The Rock Island Express Robbery" and "The Pollock Diamond Robbery," and finally the railroad bandits of "The Destruction of the Reno Gang." After a published confirmation from Colonel A. K. McClure of Pinkerton's service to Lincoln in "The Night at Harrisburg; a Reminiscence of Lincoln's Journey to Washington in 1861," the magazine again picked up Moffett's tale of high-profile Pinkerton cases with "The American Exchange Bank Robbery," "The Great Northampton Bank Robbery," and "The Susquehanna Express Robbery." These were not tales of union busting in Homestead or threats of "Pinkertonism"; rather, this was a detective mythology of agents doggedly pursuing their men.[1]

In a series of articles for *Frank Leslie's Monthly Magazine* in 1905, Charles Francis Bourke would tell much the same story. However, in Bourke's version, Allan Pinkerton ceased to be a Chartist chased from Scotland by his politics. Instead, the key moment in young Allan's life, according to Bourke, was the death of his policeman father at the hands of the "'physical force' men of the revolutionary Chartists of those days."[2] At its very origin, the new mythology read, the Pinkerton agency was a bulwark against radicalism and disorder. The agency also kept a file of press clippings and quickly responded to any bad press. For example, the agency responded to a *Kansas City World* article from November of 1898 that retold the "bombing" of the James brothers' home in Missouri, because the agency wanted to publicly clarify its role. The agency understood that its history was what set the Pinkertons apart from newer firms, yet it was this same history that made the agency infamous. One solution was to plaster its advertising with images of Lincoln and Pinkerton together because, the company noted, the photo could "be used to great advantage" in attracting clients. Yet while the company stressed the founder's connections to Lincoln, it also downplayed Pinkerton's prewar abolitionism. This, after all, was an era of "Lost Cause" mythology, where both southern elites and northern businessmen convinced themselves that abolitionist "radicals" had ruined Reconstruction and triggered disorder. The company's literature seemed to feel that neither prospective clients nor the reading public would have any sympathy for a politically radical Allan Pinkerton. By connecting itself directly to the memory of Lincoln and the Civil War (but not radical abolitionism or Chartism), the Pinkerton agency tried to redeem its post-Homestead reputation and reconnected itself to the very state that now seemed to condemn it.[3]

But the tide of public sentiments and sympathies had turned against the agency; it was now largely the villain in the stories people told. While the agency tried to play up its connections to Lincoln, others continued to focus on the agency's role at Homestead. "Nothing more dramatic in the History of Labor and Capital is recorded than" the events at Homestead, stated one magazine. "The Hessians were to be imported," it wrote; "the Master of the Mill said: Hire Pinkerton's men. A foreign force was to settle the question of one dollar in wages." As the Pinkerton barge arrived in the steel town, up went "the long sad wail of the steam whistle . . . it is the voice of Labor shrieking to the wage-worker to rise and make haste, for armed Capital is to take possession of the workshop." In the midst of the chaos of that early morning "horsemen dash through the streets of Homestead yelling: To the river! To the river! The Pinkertons are coming!"[4] What had once been the counternarrative of the Pinkerton agent, the hired assassins and muscle of American capital, had become the dominant narrative. The agency was now out of step with American sympathies. Moreover, the agency was trying to defend its reputation within an entirely new venue. In 1893, *McClure's*, *Munsey's*, and *Cosmopolitan* dropped their prices to ten cents, shifting their revenue from sales to advertising. This ushered in a new era of popular middle-class magazines with a different audience and editorial voice than the older elite magazines such as *Harper's*. Professional advertisers, "realist" writers, and department store merchants were now targeting the parlors of the new middle class. Once subjected to this kind of public scrutiny and public scorn, the agency could no longer maintain its Victorian reputation, which meant that it could no longer maintain its power; they had become in the eyes of many the "hired Hessians of plutocracy" and the symbols of the larger dangers of Pinkertonism.[5]

In the aftermath of Homestead, many Americans agreed that the Pinkertons' role as armed guards needed to be eliminated. However, there was vast disagreement over how exactly the Pinkerton system could be done away with. Some, echoing earlier concerns of anarchism and criminal conspiracy, saw in the crowds of Homestead criminal action on the scale of 1877 or Haymarket—a criminality that perhaps the Pinkertons were no longer capable of subduing. Others saw the paramilitary actions of the agency as an unfortunate outgrowth of the times— labor conflict and the violence of strikers made the use of private guards necessary. Eliminate labor strife, they argued, and eliminate the need for Pinkertons. Some critics empathized with, even if they did not agree with, industrialists who felt the need to hire private armies to protect their property. If not for the failure of state and local officials to fulfill their obligations, they argued, such private guards would not be needed. The other side of this debate turned the equation around. Labor conflict did not create the need for Pinkerton agents; rather, the use of agents exacerbated labor strife and caused the violence. The arrival of the Pinkerton barge triggered the conflict, not the other way around. Eliminate the use of Pinkerton guards, this side argued, and you eliminate the violence of the strike. Yet this side too blamed the state for its lack of oversight. Instead of local officials who failed to maintain order, the state was responsible for empowering the Pinkertons by its lack of regulation of Pinkerton arms, importation, and deputization. No matter what the approach, the agency's meaning and impact were open to public interpretation. When the popular press, labor organizations, and social reformers debated the meaning of Homestead, they were rethinking the ideologies of private property, free labor, associationalism, reform, and artisanal labor in juxtaposition to Pinkertonism and plutocracy. When middle-class Americans read popular magazine articles about the Pinkertons, they were deciding what kind of social order they wanted, and increasingly the Pinkertons were not a part.

Protecting property from "the tyranny of the Homestead mob"

For its part, the *Independent* called the violence the "tyranny of the Homestead mob." In a July 21 article entitled "The Suicide of Labor" the paper argued that the crowd was "mob law pure and simple" and that "mob law is rebellion against civil law and civil rulers. The workmen at Homestead levied war against the institutions of the state of Pennsylvania." It lambasted those who sympathized

with the strikers, suggesting that the "fact that much sympathy has been ex-
pressed in public prints and public bodies with the course as well as the cause of
the strikers of Homestead impresses us as a dangerous symptom." While peaceful advocacy of workers' rights was one thing, "those who propose to do so 'through
smoke and blood' if necessary are as much the enemies of law and order and
human kind as the kind of fiends who set up the role of ruin in the name of the
Commune of Paris," the paper concluded. The *Independent* then quoted from a
letter it received from a minister critical of the Pinkertons. "The private interstate
and national police force of Pinkerton is subversive of one of the fundamental
principles of our National Government," the letter read. "A police force ought
to be, and must be, amenable to either the civil head of a city, county, State, or
the Nation, or otherwise we must inevitably drift into anarchy," it concluded.
"The whole system of Pinkertons, as now administered, is radically fundamen-
tally and viciously subversive of governmental safety and citizen freedom."[6]

In response, the *Independent* did not try to defend either the actions or the
presence of the Pinkertons. "Suppose all he says about the Pinkertons is true," the
paper retorted; "if the employment of the Pinkertons was an offense it was an
offense against the state of Pennsylvania and not against striking workmen." If
mill owners could not hire watchmen, the paper quoted the Pinkerton agency,
"then all capital so invested is practically at the mercy of secret labor organizations
whose tyranny and despotism exceed anything ever known in the history of the
world." The Pinkerton system may be deeply flawed and perhaps even an offense
to state sovereignty, but it seemed to the *Independent* a necessary evil for the time.
Given these alternatives of anarchy and the tyranny of labor, "who can say, without
thereby excusing crimes and encouraging criminals, that the agency which detects
and prevents such outrages is not a valuable ally of good government?"[7]

To the magazine, the conclusions about the crowd were simple. "When the
strikers at Homestead resolved to beat the Carnegie Company in the contest between them by the demonstration of physical force they became rioters," it concluded; "as rioters they advanced a step in crime and became murderers." Sympathetic coverage of the strike and criticism of the Pinkertons and Carnegie created
the conditions from which arose radicals such as Alexander Berkman, who tried
to assassinate Henry Frick. "Out of the loose talk of the newspapers and agitators
on this aspect of the Homestead strike has come the miserable sneaking assassin,"
it claimed. "So far as public opinion is concerned, the rioters and the murderers
at Homestead and the would-be assassin are to be condemned not because they
are arrayed against capital but because they are law breakers and criminals."[8]

Here was one response to the crisis of Homestead. Workers and strikers, the logic went, constituted a criminal class that threatened stability, order, and property. Moreover, the riots meant the possibility of (paradoxically) the anarchy of the crowd and the tyranny of labor. These were the kinds of threats that Pinkerton detectives (if not protectives) had long contained. Perhaps the agency was no longer capable of patrolling the industrial frontier on its own. Within this argument the use of Pinkerton guards may or may not have been justified or wise, but it was certainly understandable. Only an active state could protect private property and ensure property rights. Even as this seemingly countered the emerging ideology of laissez-faire economics, this argument complimented the recent legal decisions that gave corporations political standing under the Fourteenth Amendment. If corporations were people under the Constitution, then they had to be protected by the state, not by an overwhelmed private force.

Protecting free labor from "this gang of Hessians"

Breaking from the rest of the editorial tone of the magazine, Bishop Atticus Haygood was highly critical of both Andrew Carnegie and the Pinkertons in the pages of the *Independent*. How could Carnegie, he asked, leave "the settlement of these great and perplexing questions to underlings and the hireling Pinkertons?" "How long will the American people endure this gang of Hessians—a private army waiting to be hired?" Haygood asked. "Someday there will be a governor of some state who will deal with them as with foreign invaders, and put such as are not shot in fight, or hung by law, where they ought to be—among their sort, the convicts in the penitentiary," he concluded; "all the Pinkertons and all the money in the world cannot give permanence to any adjustment that in itself is contrary to righteousness."[9] It was not the tyranny or violence of the mob that threatened the stability and sovereignty of the state but the presence of an armed militia under Carnegie's employ that was the deep outrage of Homestead.

In the *Open Court*, General M. M. Trumbull declared that while Europe had traditions of soldiers with "a sword for hire," similar men existed in the United States, "but they go by the name of 'Pinkertons' and their military quality is the same as that of the bravo and the buccaneer." "They are soldiers without a flag, and without a cause beyond the hire of the day," concluded Trumbull. "They are armed with rifles and revolvers, and they shoot with promiscuous impartiality; at the Pinkerton rates for killing, which, I understand, are two dollars a day." The presence of the Pinkertons complicated all of the issues at Homestead. "The smoke of the battle of Homestead hides the dispute between Carnegie and his workmen so that we cannot say which of them was right or which of them was wrong," wrote Trumbull; "the merits of the controversy are smothered in the overwhelming folly of invading Pennsylvania with Pinkerton troops from Chicago."[10] While Americans condemned the mercenary tradition that had led the "Grand Duke of Hesse Something" to sell troops to King George, "right here in the United States, the Grand Duke of Hesse Pinkerton sells regiments of his American soldiers to anybody who desires to use them to suppress rebellious working men."[11]

Even apologists for Carnegie were reluctant to embrace the Pinkertons. "I do not approve of the Pinkerton system," one concluded, "but I do not feel justified in blaming Carnegie and his company for having had recourse to it."[12] Trumbull had "poured out the vials of wrath upon the Pinkertons; and I would say justly so," declared another. Yet had local officials fulfilled their obligations, "there would never have been any Pinkertons to denounce and to swear at." Given the failures of local officials, "can railroads or other industrial corporations be utterly condemned for appealing to the Pinkerton Bureau?" he declared. "Can they not at least plead mitigating circumstances?"[13]

"It is true that that I have a right to defend my property, but in so doing I have no right to incite or commit breaches of the public peace," responded General Benjamin Butler. "Assuming that the Pinkerton men were acting for the Carnegie Company," he continued, "that company prepared for a bloody riot." This was not a case of protecting private property, but rather one of organizing an armed band to intentionally disrupt the peace. "Now who are the Pinkerton detectives?" Butler asked. "They are, and have for several years been an organization of armed irresponsible men, ready to commence warfare whenever ordered by their officers—a conspiracy of men more harmful to the public peace than any other ever in this country and more dangerous to the liberty and welfare of our citizens than can otherwise be conceived." For Butler the conclusions were obvious: "no armed expedition for the purpose of violence in a state can be permitted to go from one state to another without the assent of the public authorities." Thus, Butler argued "that those having charge of the Carnegie Company and organizing this riotous invasion could be indicted and punished with great severity" because corporations "have no moral or legal right to proceed in a manner that would naturally create bitterness and tend to provoke hostility, riot, and bloodshed on the part of the men who have contributed so largely to their own fortunes." It was unfortunate, he concluded, that "in this evening tide of the nineteenth century" such "medieval methods of warfare" still existed.[14]

"The late quarrel at Homestead has revived a question of the utmost importance to the American people," wrote the *Zion's Herald* in August of 1892. "The
question is whether individuals or private corporations may arm men in their
own defence." Even "in the modern industrial world," it concluded, "individuals
and corporations, with their great wealth are coming to imitate the nobles of the
Middle Ages in securing defense by means of private arming." "The Pinkertons
are a body or organized, trained, and armed mercenaries who sell their services,
as the Swiss used to do and as the Hessians were sold to England in order to
subjugate America," the paper reported. "Mr. Frick exhibited his extreme unwis-
dom in employing these American Hessians to guard the company's property."
Such "millionaire's mercenaries" threatened the sovereignty of the state. "For
their own interest millionaires will do well to leave defense and the administration of justice to the State," the paper admonished. "They may be sure the American people will endure no such ursurption of the police power of the State. No
armed organization can be allowed in the private hands. All law-abiding citizens
must join in the demand for the suppression of the Pinkertons." Where the *Zion's
Herald* disagreed with the *Independent* and some of the writers from the *Open
Court*, however, was that it saw no justified reason that Carnegie and Frick
should have hired the agency in the first place. "'The way to abolish the Pinkertons is to abolish the need of them,' is the curt though inconsiderate putting of
the case by the Evening Post," reported the paper. "The reverse would convey a
more important truth. The use of the Pinkertons creates further use. If the capitalists may arm, the laborer will claim the same right." A powerful and respon-
sive state would be "far preferable to arming mercenaries by individuals or corporations" and would be "safest and best for all concerned."[15]

Others argued that the problem lay not in the state's inability to discharge its
duties, but rather that current laws were "never intended to cover the importation into a community of a private military force, armed and drilled to act as
soldiers rather than as watchmen." "For consider what the employment of these
Pinkerton detectives really means," the *Baptist Quarterly Review* continued: "the
end of democratic institutions and the rise of centralized power in the hands of
an industrial elite." "It is found, with reason," the paper concluded, "that either the
Pinkertons or the State must go," for clearly both could not coexist. The Pinkertons represented an "irresponsible force of hired mercenaries above the majesty
of the law"; thus, "there should be in every State . . . a statute forbidding private
individuals or corporations to arm and equip that which virtually amounts to
standing armies but subject wholly to private interests."[16] The *Social Economist*

noted that English critics had predicted that "when the day of our Manchesters and Birminghams should arrive, our democratic institutions would prove inadequate to the task of securing order and maintaining freedom, and we should be compelled to either sacrifice our civilization to save our freedom or to surrender our freedom to preserve our civilization." The paper went on to solemnly report that indeed "the day of our Manchesters and Birminghams, with their industrial conflicts, has arrived."[17]

The *Arena* was even more damning. "It is an incontrovertible fact," one columnist argued, "that the greatest menace which threatens the Republic to-day lies in the rapidly growing influence and the unscrupulous exercise of power on the part of plutocracy." A "significant illustration of the decadence of republican influence and the rise of plutocracy is seen in the toleration of the Pinkerton army of detectives," he continued, "a thoroughly irresponsible body, said to-day to be larger than the regular army of the Republic." The army at least was ordered, regulated, and answerable to the public; it attracted the best kind of men. "Standing in antithesis are the Pinkerton hirelings, who are, to say the least, of coarse fibre," he concluded, "for no man of refined sensibilities would enter the ranks as a hired Hessian of plutocracy, expecting to shoot down his brothers at the command of capital." Had a US soldier fired into crowds the way that Pinkertons had in Albany during the 1890 New York Central Strike, "he would have met with prompt and terrible punishment; had an officer in the United States Army, with no more provocation, ordered his men to shoot promiscuously into a body of American citizens, he would have been disciplined and dishonored." Although Pinkertons "were guilty of such anarchical and lawless proceedings," he declared, they were answerable to no one.[18] By using the imagery of the Hessians, these essays placed the resistance of the Homestead workers within a revolutionary tradition that traced back to the American Revolution instead of the Paris Commune or the workers' revolts of 1848. Moreover, for an age so sure that they were progressing into a better future, the accusation that society was regressing into the feudal systems of the past must have been cutting. The true villains of this argument were the hired mercenaries who threatened the sovereignty of the state and the dignity and independence of free labor. Only a state willing to curtail the impulses of plutocracy and protect free labor could ensure the future.

Protecting society from the "disgrace of Pinkertonism"

In an effort to see the larger issues at stake in the Homestead conflict, the *Forum* felt that "the question raised by the bloody encounter between the organized workingmen and the embodied Pinkertons on the Monongahela is one which cannot be put aside until there shall be found a satisfactory answer to it." Such acts were part of a longer struggle "whose persistent barbarity is the darkest reproach of the otherwise peaceful age in which we live." In these conflicts, "which have shamed this country in many instances, the state stands practically aloof, permitting each separate difference to degenerate, it may be, into a cruel and unequal combat between the capitalist and the workingman." While monopolies "actually constitute a menace to the free institutions of the country . . . the State has stood over their vast accumulations and their huge operations with all its police power affording them every possible security." This protection and security, in the shape of both militia and tariff, allowed Carnegie and Frick to build their empire. But when faced with resistance from strikers, these same companies "turned to a power beyond the territory and unknown to the laws of the state." "The Pinkertons have been compared to the Hessians, but the comparison is unfair to the latter," it concluded. "They resemble more the free companies of the middle ages, recruited by freebooters for freebooting and their services sold to the highest bidder." The agency "is a natural outgrowth of existing conditions. It, more than anything else, illustrates the barbarity of our methods, or rather our lack of methods in such contingencies."[19]

When the public peace was threatened with riot, corporations could "turn to the power of the State to crush the weaker" in the form of state militias and the US Army, "but in intermediate stages of the contest [between capital and labor] the employer must rely upon his own or hired force." Such a "private army duly disciplined and weaponed and open for engagement in any quarrel" allowed an industrialist to "make private war on his own account and in his own way." Companies would "naturally prefer to pursue unmolested the course which has so marvelously enriched them at the common expense of consumers and workingmen," the paper concluded. "They have cultivated the feudal spirit until it had become the master passion. They will be naturally reluctant, like the barons— which in many respects they are—to yield the privileges of private warfare." This fact made the increased power and oversight of the state even more important. Companies will, "beyond question, prefer the Pinkertons and the soldiers to the milder and fairer methods of the preferred law," but the public interest should deny this desire.[20]

Such an understanding that juxtaposed the public interest with the plutocratic desires of capitalists and Pinkertons was part of an emerging worldview in the last decade of the nineteenth century which used political pragmatism and

social science to understand the origins of industrial conflicts. Much like hous-
ing reformers who targeted the building of tenements or regulatory advocates
who campaigned against railroad rates and interstate trusts, these new labor
reformers believed that bad conditions caused conflicts; if one could create better conditions, then industrial conflicts (and the specter of Pinkertonism) would
cease to exist. The public interest had to deny bad desires, and the way to for-
mulate a "public interest" was through association. Civic-minded reformers, empowered by increasing the democratic sphere, could enact pragmatic reforms by
holding a middle ground between capital and labor. But this public interest had
to take the shape of an engaged but neutral state.

In response to this sense of crisis, the *American Journal of Politics* argued that
"when a difference arises between the corporation and its employees, it becomes
a matter of public interest for municipal recognition, and for action by the state."
A national tribunal was necessary, it argued, to arbitrate conflicts because "it is
the duty of the state, it having created the corporation, to provide the tribunal
and to require the causes of difference to be laid before it." In so doing, "lockouts
and strikes would go out of fashion and Pinkertons and the militia would not be
needed."[21] So too did the *Advocate of Peace* suggest the creation of a national police
force to maintain order in a more impartial and peaceful manner. "In view of the
national character which some of the late riots assumed," it concluded, "it would
be perfectly legitimate to establish a national constabulary, police of gendar-
merie [which would] render the obnoxious employment of Pinkertons and special deputies unnecessary."[22] Terence Powderly of the Knights of Labor publicly
called for federal arbitration of labor disputes. "The principle involved in the
Homestead trouble is the same as that by which the founders of this republic were
governed in rebelling against the British government," he argued. "In no case
should the introduction of an armed force, such as the Pinkerton detective agency
armed and equiped, be tolerated." Not only did Carnegie disregard the "laws of
Pennsylvania" when he introduced an "armed body of men at the onset" of the
conflict at Homestead, but "by the light of the blazing guns at Homestead it was
written that arbitration must take the place of 'Pinkertonism.' "[23]

"There has been much said and written in the last four weeks about the disgrace of Pinkertonism," stated *Scientific American*, and much of this "reference
has been made in this verdict to the character of the Pinkerton system and of the
Pinkerton guards." However, for *Scientific American* the issue was not the character of the Pinkertons but the social conditions that made their employment

necessary. "But there is another disgrace that ought to be emphasized in this connection," it continued: "the disgrace of a condition of things that requires the
importation of daredevil men to secure the rights which local authorities do not
guarantee." "It would be well for those who join in the general cry against Pinkertonism," the magazine warned, "to have a serious thought or two about the disgraces that are the occasion of Pinkertonism."[24] While "it has never been defi-
nitely known until now just what relations the Pinkerton men have sustained to
the corporations in the labor disturbances of the country," pointed out the *Chautauquan*, "it is not too much to expect the government to fulfill its functions and
when this becomes true to the letter, Pinkertonism will be abolished."[25] "It is
generally agreed that the Homestead riots and other similar events have shown
a weakness in our system of government," summarized *Current Literature*; "Pinkertonism, or the hiring of armed watchmen, is a natural outgrowth of the situation.
There is no room for debate between State and local authorities while a mob is
holding dynamite over an American citizen's property." Thus, the paper stated that
"it is generally agreed that the Pinkertons must go, but not before adequate protection can be had in their place."[26] To fail to do so might encourage even more
dangerous ideologies than Pinkertonism, concluded another, including the "various heresies that go under the general name of socialism or communism."[27] Perhaps overly optimistically, one editorial suggested that with the "enactment of
laws protecting the capital of labor just as the capital of corporations is protected
. . . all violence, disorder, and intimidation [would be] eliminated." As such, the
"era of Pinkertonism will have passed without having been reduced by the law of
extermination, and the way will open for the better and more peaceful settlement
of industrial disputes."[28] *Harper's Weekly* offered a similar conclusion. The fault for
Homestead, and indeed for the very existence of the Pinkertons, did not lay solely
with the leaders of corporations who felt the need to hire private muscle, nor with
members of the laboring classes who clashed with armed Pinkertons. "The main
point, however, for the consideration of the American people," *Harper's Weekly*
concluded, "is that we cannot admit the necessity of having and employing such
an armed force as the Pinkerton men without confessing to a condition of things
amongst us which we must be ashamed of." Modern industrial society may have
created the conditions of violence, but it was the American people who allowed
such outrages to occur. "A truly civilized community will not have to look to a
Pinkerton force," stated the paper, "to do under private pay that which is obviously
the business of the regularly constituted authorities."[29]

Conclusion: Lessons on corporate management from the mercenaries of the oligarchy

In a November 17, 1892, discussion, the Sunset Club of Chicago, an association of industrialists, tried to learn "the lessons of the Homestead troubles." This analysis ranged from outrage at the audacity of striker demands to a desire for social uplift to prevent such violence from occurring in the future. "Industrial unrest is a social malady," Holbrook continued, "and has its origins in a genuine desire of the lower classes to better their conditions." But lest the club's plans for social uplift look like a classless utopia, Holbrook made clear that workers should be taught the cold, hard rules of capital. "By education," he declared, "we mean that the laboring classes shall learn by heart these few eternal truths: . . . capital and labor are partners but capitalists and laborers are not." Yet despite these hard rules of capital, there was still plenty of blame ascribed to Carnegie. "When the Carnegie company prepared instead of a workshop, a factory in a free country for the employment of free men . . . they constructed a fort, an old-time castle to which were attached all modern agencies of destruction," concluded George Schilling in the same club discussion. "If they did that then I say they drew the sword, they issued the proclamation of war, and if they got the worst of it you ought to be satisfied." If Carnegie had called in the "modern agencies of destruction," then the blame for violence lay at his feet.[30] "What is nowadays called welfare work is not a benevolence or a charity," concluded another lesson on corporate management; "it is simple economy, common sense, and common humanity."[31] Industrial unrest and chaos created instability, and instability was bad business. A good industrialist, one conclusion ran, "took care of his workers, provided stable environments, and promoted tranquility thus eliminating labor strife and eliminating the need to hire private armies." This became the notion of scientific management and benevolent industrialism which would come to define industry between 1892 and 1929, symbolized by Carnegie's replacement of the notorious Frick with the young corporate manager Charles Schwab.[32]

Alongside corporate managers, social reformers also came to reject the morality and immorality of Victorian order or the implicit cruelty of social Darwinism, instead embracing scientific methods and pragmatic reforms to help explain and solve social issues such as poverty, pollution, and unrest. Urban and political reform became not a by-product of moral suasion but rather a scientific endeavor implemented by professional planners and social engineers. Chicago, emblematic of the new social and economic relations at the turn of the century, also became a center for this new form of pragmatic reform. Home to the Pinkerton agency, Chicago was also the social laboratory of reforms such as Jane Addams's Hull House, John Dewey's Laboratory School, the University of Chicago's experiments in urban sociology, and Daniel Burnham's vision for grand-scale urban planning, first in the 1893 World's Columbian Exposition and later in the 1906 Chicago Plan. Planning, sanitation, and the "Americanization" of settlement homes had come to replace the Pinkerton guard as the protector of social order.

Perhaps the most acclaimed attempt at this new kind of industrialism was the model city of Pullman, Illinois. Located just south of Chicago, Pullman promised to eliminate labor conflict through careful urban planning, benevolent paternalism, and targeted uplift. Pullman was to be a model city with a modern layout of educational facilities, "proper" sanitation, green spaces, and good entertainment—all to be controlled by George Pullman, and providing for the moral uplift of the workforce. These paternalistic controls, a series of wage cuts, and the continued high rents in company houses led to a major strike in 1894. By claiming that the strike was preventing the delivery of the mail, President Grover Cleveland secured a court order to end the conflict. He also sent in federal troops to uphold this order. The result was violence in Pullman between strikers and soldiers, resulting in twelve deaths. The violence in Pullman triggered yet another round of congressional investigations and focused blame. Although the agency was not directly involved with the Pullman strike, the specter of the Pinkerton agents still haunted the conflict. Chicago police superintendent Michael Brennan, for instance, testified that one instance of violence came not from a railroad man but from a local saloon keeper who "commenced to hoot, calling us Pinkertons, and inciting the mob to attack us." After its investigation, the Senate commission determined that the Railroad Managers' Association had acted out of arrogance and recklessness and that it had usurped power not granted in the city charter.[33] Other critics argued that it was court rulings that had empowered the Railroad Managers' Association, an organization that should "be classed with the other cutthroat organizations of hirelings and Hessians, who for money will start out to kill any citizens at the order of the corporations—the Pinkertons."[34]

Yet the Pullman strike was unlike the New York Central or Homestead strikes in important ways, because the result of the Pullman strike showed stark new truths. In the minds of social reformers such as Jane Addams and industrialists alike, the end of Pullman as a social experiment had demonstrated the "futility of social betterment schemes."[35] When US Steel looked to expand its midwestern steel production a couple of years later, it would build in Gary, Indiana, not a model town but an industrial fortress that would withstand labor conflicts. Furthermore, ideas about the role of the US Army were shifting as well. In 1883, General William Sherman had explained to Congress that the primary duty of the US Army was suppression of Indian rebellion and protection of western railroads. Yet in 1894 General John Schofield said just the opposite. "More than once in the last summer an infuriated mob in a single city was twice as formidable and capable of doing vastly greater injury to life and property," he told Congress, "than the most formidable of Indian warriors that ever confronted the Army in this country."[36] In the wake of Pullman, the army not only shifted its focus toward active intervention into factory town disputes but also dramatically changed its composition so that enlisted soldiers were US citizens and not unnaturalized immigrants. For social reformers, the failure of Pullman's experiment demonstrated that even benevolent industrialism could not prevent labor unrest or eliminate industrialists' need for armed guards. The solution, it seemed, was a regimented federal army, consisting of only citizens, which could provide order and protect property in mill towns filled with foreign labor. There was no need for Pinkertons if the army arrived before violence occurred. Disillusioned radicals, such as Jack London, saw in the legitimized actions of the Pinkertons a foreshadowing of a dystopian near future. "I have met men," London declared, "who invoked the name of the Prince of Peace in their diatribes against war, and who put rifles in the hands of Pinkertons with which to shoot down strikers in their own factories." In his 1907 novel *The Iron Heel*, London has his hero Ernest Everhard say the same thing. *The Iron Heel* purports to be the firsthand account of socialist Everhard as he fought the rise of a brutal oligarchy between 1912 and 1932. Under the rule of the oligarchy, whose power was solidified by the violence of the "Mercenaries," Everhard's story was lost. However, in London's telling, socialists in the far future would finally establish a "Brotherhood of Man" and rediscover the "Everhard manuscript." Editors from this socialist future would explain the Pinkertons in an annotation by saying that "originally they were private detectives; but they quickly became the hired fighting men of the capitalists, and ultimately developed into the Mercenaries of the Oligarchy."[37]

By 1894 the state took a direct and early role in the battle between capital and labor. Cynics looked at the pattern of labor intervention with the Pullman strike and saw a state that actively supported the consolidation of power in monopolies and trusts. The only step left, W. J. Ghent wrote satirically in the *Independent*, was a "benevolent feudalism" of concentrated wealth and medieval methods.

"Armed force will, of course, be employed to overawe the discontented and to quiet unnecessary turbulence," he wrote of the coming neo-feudalism. "Unlike the armed forces of old feudalism, the nominal control will be that of the State; the soldiery will be regular and not irregular," he declared. "Not again will the barons risk the general indignation arising from the employment of Pinkertons and other private armies." What company needs to hire Pinkertons, he concluded, when "the worker had unmistakably shown his preference, when he is to be subdued, for the militia and the Federal army"? Eugene Debs, who had led the American Railway Union strike in Pullman, would lament this new shift. "The private armies the corporations used some years ago such as Pinkerton mercenaries, coal and iron police, deputy marshals, etc.," he would later write, "have been relegated to second place as out of date." Instead, capitalists had found that court injunctions were "far more deadly to trades-unions and that they operate noiselessly and with unerring precision." While court injunctions had been threatened as early as 1888, it was not until the Homestead strike, "during which Pinkertonism reached its culmination and this brutal form of warfare upon labor by Carnegie and Frick excited the most intense indignation," that companies began turning to the court injunction and using the direct power of the state. With an active court system and army, "no longer was there any need for a private Pinkerton army." After all, "that was a clumsy contrivance compared to the noiseless, automatic, self-acting injunction. The Pinkertons were expensive, cumbersome, aroused hatred and sometimes missed fire." No such problems or outrage existed with the injunction; "one shock from the judicial battery and labor was paralyzed and counted out."[38]

{CHAPTER SEVEN}

In which the frontier closes
and Pinkerton practices are exposed

I N 1892, settlers and ranchers clashed violently in Johnson County, Wyoming. Because of the increasing demand for beef and the expanding network of rail transportation, cattle barons between 1865 and 1890 had been steadily moving northward from the ranges of Texas and New Mexico into Wyoming. At the same time, settlers and small ranchers who had received land through the Homestead Act were also arriving. Meanwhile, cowboys who had worked the big ranches were establishing their own holdings and, their former employers feared, rustling stock. Conflicts over water, land, fences, and most importantly ownership of unbranded maverick calves on the range quickly became violent. Leading cattle ranchers pooled together in 1879 to form the Wyoming Stock Growers Association to combat what they considered the rustling of calves. Their influence over the territorial government led to severe laws and periodic raids against small ranch owners by "stock detectives" hired by the association. In 1884, similar concerns in neighboring Montana led to the lynching of 100 suspected rustlers. In 1889, two Johnson county ranchers, James Avrell and Ellen Watson, who were accused of rustling by the association, were dragged from their home by stock detectives and lynched. The state legislature, heavily influenced by the powerful Stock Growers Association, formed the Wyoming Livestock Association in 1891 to seize the livestock of suspected rustlers.

In response, small ranchers and farmers formed their own association and announced their own roundup of unbranded calves. Shortly thereafter, two small ranchers were shot and killed, purportedly by stock detective Frank Canton. As tensions increased, the Stock Growers Association began to recruit more stock detectives, and in April of 1892, fifty "regulators" arrived in Wyoming, mostly from Texas, with a list of seventy suspected rustlers to kill. "It is said," went one rumor, "that they took oaths as Pinkerton detectives." The armed band first struck the ranch of Nick Ray and Nate Champion, killing both. In response, local residents formed a posse and pinned down the regulators at a nearby ranch. Governor Amos Barber, a political ally of the Stock Growers Association, sent an urgent telegraph to President Benjamin Harrison, who promptly dispatched one hundred federal troops to rescue the besieged regulators.[1]

In his angry exposé of the "Johnson County war," Asa Mercer categorized the "invasion of the state of Wyoming by a band of cutthroats and hired assassins in April 1892" as the "crowning infamy of the age."[2] In the complicated political and social world of the west, authority and power had long been seized far more than given. Yet at the root of the conflict in Wyoming was the expanding inequality in political and economic power between small and large ranchers. This was an industrial conflict with an armed plutocracy; the powerful Stock Growers Association could afford to hire its own guards and assassinate its political adversaries. Hence, when *Harper's* wrote of Wyoming's impending statehood, it mentioned that, although it had a fraction of the population of Pennsylvania, it faced many of the same issues, including the "Pinkerton problem."[3]

One remnant of the "Pinkerton problem" was the role of stock detectives such as Tom Horn. For much of his life, Horn had represented the blurry lines between lawman, outlaw, official of the state, and bad man. In the 1880s Horn had served as a scout and interpreter for the US Army in its wars against the Apache, and he had been part of a US military expedition that had crossed over into Mexico and clashed with the Mexican army. Following the Indian wars, he served as a deputy sheriff, before joining the Denver office of the Pinkerton agency in 1890. In his autobiography, Horn claimed that he left the Pinkertons in 1894 because he found their procedures and paperwork not to his liking ("too tame," he claimed), yet many others, including his friend and fellow agent Charlie Siringo, suspected that Horn still worked for the agency and that its political influence protected Horn.[4] In 1892, Horn was part of the posse of hired guns which came to Wyoming to take part in the Johnson County range war. After that debacle, Horn stayed in Wyoming and served as a stock detective and assassin for cattlemen associations. His job was to harass, punish, and terrify cattle rustlers and small ranchers; killing was, he would claim, "my stock-in-trade."

In 1903, Horn was arrested and tried for the shooting death of fourteen-year-old William Nickell; the young boy was found with Horn's calling card, a bloody rock beneath his head. US Marshal Joe LeFors (another lawman with suspected ties to the Pinkertons) testified that a drunken Horn admitted that Nickell's was "the best shot ever I made, and the worst trick I ever did." Horn declared that no such confession had taken place and that larger powers were conspiring to frame him for the killing. Speculation ran that Horn's actions were part of a Pinkerton investigation into the Wilcox train robbery and the agency's pursuit of Butch Cassidy, the Sundance Kid, and the Wild Bunch. Yet, by the turn of the century, the Pinkerton's political muscle was not what it once was, and some speculated that the agency seemed no longer willing to implicate itself with a man such as Horn. Based on the testimony of LeFors, Horn was convicted and executed for the shooting. Pinkerton's long arm, it seemed, could no longer protect Horn. Even in the cultural ethos of the west, long the incubator of flexible myths of Pinkerton men, outlaws, and bandits, the frontier was closing.[5]

The death of Tom Horn may have symbolized the end of a particular kind of cultural imagery of the lawless and vigilante west, but Horn's role as the hired muscle of powerful stock growers associations meant that a new kind of political violence was coming to define the west. In 1890, the superintendent of the US Census declared that, because of migration and settlement, the western frontier had closed, a remark that would catch the attention of young historian Frederick Jackson Turner, who in turn would argue that the existence of the frontier had formed the American spirit and was an important space in crafting American traits of self-reliance, rugged individualism, and independence. Thus, the closing of the American frontier also seemed to foretell the closing of an important American epoch.

It was certainly an important transition in Pinkerton history and folklore, because the notion of a lawless frontier was central to Pinkerton mythology. By 1908, the last of the great western bandits, Butch Cassidy and the Sundance Kid, had fled from the American west to resettle in the lawless frontiers of South America. Much of the rest of the Hole in the Wall Gang had been harassed, pursued, killed, or arrested by Pinkerton agents. However, the Johnson County war in Wyoming, combined with the brutal labor strikes and martial law in Colorado and Idaho and the rise of western labor radicalism in the form of the Western Federation of Miners (WFM) and the Industrial Workers of the World (IWW), showed that violence in the west had not come to an end. Instead, the closing of the frontier and the rise of industrial order had dramatically changed the context and meaning of the violence. Instead of the romantic individualism of the old west, the new violence looked like the consolidation of plutocratic control by a ranching and mining elite. For the agency the cowboy detective had been replaced by the labor spy.

As the politics of the "wild west" gave way to the struggles over industrial order, so too would critique, exposé, and embarrassment of "Pinkertonism" work their way into western cultural representations of the Pinkerton agent. As a Mercer's exposé publically denounced the abuses of the Stock Growers Association and their hired guns; in response, copies of Mercer's book went missing from libraries across the country, including the Library of Congress. From his jail cell, Horn lambasted "yellow journalists," cattle rustlers, and his own cattlemen association employers who had abandoned him. In an age of muckraking journalism, Pinkerton practices and the entirety of the Pinkerton system were laid bare for public eyes. As the frontier closed and Pinkerton guards and labor spies worked their way into the labor struggles in western mining districts, the carte blanche once possessed by the Pinkerton man in the west ceased to exist.

A cowboy detective and a labor spy

If there was a single figure who came to represent the agency's western transformation from trackers of bandits to breakers of mining unions, it was Charles Siringo. In 1886, Charlie Siringo came to Chicago with hopes of publishing his first of many memoirs. Siringo had written *A Texas Cowboy; or, Fifteen Years on the Hurricane Deck of a Spanish Pony*, which detailed his life as a cowpuncher in the American west. By sheer coincidence Siringo was in Chicago the night of the Haymarket bombing, and according to later autobiographies, the chaos and lawlessness of that night drove him to apply to Pinkerton's National Detective Agency. As a Pinkerton, Siringo spent the next few months living as a tramp in various industrial cities in an effort to infiltrate secret societies and criminal conspiracies. But Siringo found the east "too tame" and asked William Pinkerton to send him west. Pinkerton agreed, noting that the agency was about to open a new branch office in Denver and that "they would need a cowboy detective there, as they figured on getting a lot of cattle work."[6]

But the nature of politics, power, and the state in the frontier west was far more complicated than the "cattle work" that Pinkerton had promised. The Pinkertons of the Denver office were involved in the murky political struggles over land, race, and political power. On one such case in Colorado, Siringo infiltrated vigilante political organizations at the request of his politically powerful clients. Yet, in his summary of the case, Siringo remained sympathetic to the causes of both sides, including the society that he had infiltrated. They "had good cause for revolting, as politics in that county were rotten," he would later write; "most of them were honorable citizens, though a little rough and wild." "Of course," he added in his only complaint, "I felt 'sore' at them for wanting to hang me up by the neck." In 1891, after riders fired into the territorial legislature building in Santa Fe, New Mexico, territorial governor L. Bradford Prince hired

Siringo to investigate. When Siringo arrived, the committee responsible for his employment told him that a secret society of Mexican American ranchers called the Gorras Blancos, or "White Caps," was probably responsible. "I was told to work on the 'White Caps' and if possible join their order," Siringo would later write, "as there was no doubt about members of that lawless gang being the guilty ones, and that possibly the whole organization was in on the plot."[7]

Having gained the trust of several leaders of the White Caps, Siringo was taken to a private meeting where secret initiations were taking place, consisting of "weird chanting and gestures and sworn pledges to give up life if necessary for the good of the order or a brother in need." Like James McParlan (who in 1891 happened to be the superintendent in charge of the Denver office) had done before with the Molly Maguires, Pinkerton agent Charlie Siringo had pierced the veil of a secret organization bound by ethnicity, class, politics, and region— he had become a member of the White Caps. However, to the chagrin of the territory's Republicans (to whom the White Caps were also political adversaries), Siringo found no evidence of their participation in the shooting or of any other illegal activity. Instead, Siringo traced the crime to "the Borreago gang of 'bad' men." To the Republican committee overseeing this investigation, however, this not only failed to implicate the White Caps but also held political ramifications since the Borreagos had connections to many leading New Mexico Republicans. Given this new information, Siringo noted in wry understatement, "it was decided best to drop the matter and discontinue the operation."[8]

While cowboy detectives such as Charlie Siringo maintained steady employment in the struggle for power and land which defined the west, the agency was eager to reestablish its national reputation and further distance itself from the debacle of Homestead. The agency's chance for redemption came in June of 1899, when bandits stopped a Union Pacific train near Wilcox, Wyoming, and freed the contents of its safe with a liberal application of dynamite. Frustrated by the loss of money and railcars, railroad president E. H. Harriman unleashed the Pinkertons on the bandits. For the first time since their failure to capture Jesse James, the agency was given the chance to catch a high-profile train robber. For while they had continued to chase obscure bandits across the west, the Wilcox robbery had been attributed to the Wild Bunch of Butch Cassidy, a man whom the *Washington Post* had already declared the "boss bad man of the west."[9]

Born Robert Leroy Parker in 1866, Butch Cassidy had established himself as a unique kind of western outlaw. Dating back to the James gang, western outlaws seemed to originate as either vengeful killers or hunted lions; either way, they were driven into lives of crime. Only in fictional dime novels did charming young men choose a life of banditry. Yet Cassidy seemed intelligent, methodical, and precise in his planning; he avoided violence when he could, and he seemed to enjoy his chosen life as an outlaw. Raised in a very large and very poor farming family, young Parker had gravitated toward the freewheeling lifestyle of local rustler Mike Cassidy; when it came time to take an alias, Parker would name himself after this early influence. Graduating up from rustling, Butch Cassidy robbed the San Miguel Valley Bank in Telluride, Colorado, in 1889. Between 1894 and 1896 he would spend time in a Wyoming penitentiary for horse theft. Upon his release, he found his way into the canyons of the Outlaw Trail, where he would form his Wild Bunch. This gang would include young Henry Longabaugh, a kid raised in the mill towns of eastern Pennsylvania, where he fantasized about the lawless west he read about in dime novels; in the west Longabaugh would earn the nickname "the Sundance Kid." Once this gang (also sometimes referred to as the "Hole in the Wall Gang") escalated to train robbery, the Union Pacific decided to spare no expense in their capture.

And here is where the story of Butch Cassidy slips into not just mythology but multiple mythologies. Western outlaws were often constructed out of hagiography and half-truths, but the James brothers, for example, had sympathetic John Newman Edwards to create a central tale. The Wild Bunch has several different conflicting and overlapping stories depending on the teller of the tale. One version, the one popularized by the agency, said that after the Wilcox robbery the Pinkertons unleashed all of its resources, expertise, and manpower in a massive nationwide manhunt. Unlike the sporadic and unplanned posses that tried to follow tracks, the Pinkertons utilized all of the new modern technologies and techniques they had perfected. The company built detailed files on every member, which included their habits, tendencies, and networks of friends; long, detailed physical descriptions, often containing prison photos, were sent to every office. They traced the serial numbers of the stolen cash so that no money could be spent without the noose tightening around the bandits. When the gang brazenly had their picture taken in a Fort Worth studio, an agent noticed the photo and plastered the west with their updated images. The bandits were left with nowhere to hide. One by one the members of the gang were captured or killed, until Butch and Sundance fled the country for Argentina. Yet the long arm of the agency reached them there as well. Forced to flee into Bolivia by agent

Frank Dimaio, the duo died in a bloody shootout with Bolivian officials. The last of the gang, Ben Kilpatrick, was killed in an attempted train robbery in 1912. The Pinkertons, through modern scientific police methods, had hunted down the outlaws.

Variations on this narrative hinted that the Pinkerton pursuit of the gang was less scientific and systematic and more ruthless and relentless. Most western lawmen (such as Joe LeFors) and western bad men (such as Tom Horn) were assumed to be working the case in some form or another. In his description of the case, Charlie Siringo ridiculed the official tactics of the agency. While Siringo felt that he and his fellow cowboy detectives were skilled trackers, agency bureaucracy and convoluted orders kept them from making any real progress. Twice Siringo claimed to have almost infiltrated the gang, once posing as a murderer on the run and once by romancing the lover of gang member Lonnie Logan. Yet nothing came of these investigations. Instead, local officials and other incompetent agents stumbled across gang members out of sheer luck or coincidence, sometimes at the cost of their own lives. In sum, what Siringo described was four years of crisscrossing the west (25,000 miles on horseback, he claimed) in a fruitless search.[10]

A third version of the Wild Bunch myth does not attribute the breaking up of the gang to the methods of the Pinkertons. Rather, in this telling, the west closed around the gang; even as they were pulling their most impressive heists, they were becoming increasingly outdated and antiquated (not dissimilar to Tom Horn). Butch and Sundance did not so much flee the Pinkertons; rather, they were chasing a shifting (and dying) notion of the frontier. The fact that the gang, while supposedly avoiding the relentless pursuit of the Pinkertons, chose to have their picture taken in proper Victorian attire in Fort Worth, Texas, seemed to be both a recognition of their cultural status and a taunt to the agency; after all, the picture was left on display in the shop window. Before leaving the United States for South America, Butch and Sundance, along with the mysterious Etta Place, first traveled to New York City before departing for Argentina. Again, proper Victorian portraits were taken of the western outlaws. There is romantic irony in the image of Pinkerton agents, such as Siringo, hunting the caverns of the west while the duo cavorted in the shadow of the agency's Broadway office. It is this romantic imagery that also led to the persistent rumors that one (or both perhaps) of the bandits survived their Latin American adventure and moved back to the United States to live their lives in peace.[11] Given the variations of the tale, the Pinkertons had the victory they wanted but still did not control how the tale was told.

Surrounded with lice, Pinkerton detectives, and other vermin

While Butch Cassidy's west was closing, a new industrial west of labor conflict was opening. Before his four-year pursuit of the Wild Bunch, Siringo was asked to undertake a different assignment for the agency. With the growing possibility of labor troubles in the Idaho mining regions, mine operators had asked the Denver office to send labor spies to infiltrate their workers' unions. "Now Charlie you have to go to the Coeur d'Alenes," McParlan told him. "You're the only man I've got who can go there and get into the Miner's union. They are on guard against detectives and they became suspicious of the operative I sent up there, and ran him out of the county." Sensing that Siringo was reluctant to infiltrate a seemingly lawful community of miners, McParlan continued to press his case. "We know the leaders to be a desperate lot of criminals of the Molly Maguire type, and you will find it so," he noted. So Siringo ventured north into Coeur d'Alene to work among the miners.[12] When union miners uncovered Siringo, he fled into the surrounding hills. When strikers discovered that the company had imported strikebreakers, they stormed the mines and clashed with armed guards. At one site, miners rolled a car of powder into the mine and lit the explosives. The governor of Idaho declared martial law and called upon the president to send in the US Army. The army (assisted by Siringo, who had returned to town) began to detain strikers and placed them in military-style "bullpens," where they were held without charge. Military rule remained in Coeur d'Alene for the next four months.[13]

Deeply troubled by the outcome of the Coeur d'Alene strike, labor leaders met the following year to launch a new labor organization, the WFM. Intentionally more radical than the skilled trade organizations of the American Federation of Labor, the WFM tried to organize miners of all skills and ethnicities into a single and powerful labor union. Its first real test came in 1894 during a strike in Cripple Creek, Colorado. As the strike began, company officials in Cripple Creek formed the highly secretive Citizens' Alliance and built a private army of armed guards numbering upward of 1,200 men. One magazine summarized that in response "the miners, in their statement of the case . . . make no attempt to deny their armed resistance of the Sheriff, whose six-hundred deputies, recruited by the mine-owners from the large cities, they denounce as 'Pinkertons.'"[14] Populist governor Davis Waite intervened on behalf of the strikers and

served as their representative in negotiations with mine officials. The state militia, called out by Waite, also faced down the forces of local sheriff's deputies
and the Citizens' Alliance. The WFM had their first great victory.

Strikes in Leadville in 1896 and Telluride in 1901 established a different
pattern. At the first hint of labor conflict, companies would hire both labor spies
to infiltrate the union and armed guards to protect company property. Once
guards were established, the company would begin to import strikebreakers, violence would ensue, and the state militia or federal army would arrive to enforce
order, often with strikers rounded up and locked in bullpens. In 1899 a second
strike in Coeur d'Alene was similarly crushed when Governor Frank Steunenberg declared martial law and asked President McKinley to send in the US Army.
"We have taken the monster by the throat and we are going to choke the life out
of it," Steunenberg reported. "No halfway measures will be adopted. It is a plain
case of the state or the union winning, and we do not propose that the state shall
be defeated." As a result, several scores of labor leaders were arrested and held
in bullpens for months without charges.

In Cripple Creek in 1903, the United States Reduction & Refining Company
used information gathered by Pinkerton agent A. H. Crane to fire twenty-three
members of a new union, thus triggering a strike. Staunchly antiunion governor
James Peabody declared the region in chaos (even though no violence had yet
occurred) and sent in the state militia to restore order. After a massive explosion
in a mine killed several nonunion workers and mine officials, the state militia
again arrested strike leaders in mass. "The average citizen of the State has no idea
of the critical conditions in the two camps," explained General Sherman Bell.
"People of both camps are beginning to awaken to the danger they have been
placed in by the conspirators, and but for the military there would surely have
been a lynching bee or two before this."[15]

Although a coroner's jury could not determine the cause of the explosion and
a jury found the accused miners not guilty, Governor Peabody declared martial
law in Cripple Creek and suspended the writ of habeas corpus. The final act of
the Cripple Creek strike came in June, when an explosion rocked the Independence depot, killing several. Despite condemnations from the WFM leadership,
suspicion immediately fell on striking miners, and many within the community
formed themselves into vigilance committees and threatened lynchings. Angry
crowds, which included Pinkerton agent J. N. Londoner, armed themselves and
battled with strikers at Union Hall. Members of the Citizens' Alliance and the
Mine Owners' Association forced local officials to resign and quickly took their

places. Once in power, these new officials began arresting and deporting strikers and strike sympathizers from the state of Colorado. The mining districts of Colorado and Idaho were seemingly in open warfare against the WFM.

In Idaho one of the key figures of this conflict was Governor Frank Steunenberg, who declared martial law and established bullpens for arrested strikers. In 1905 the then former governor, returning home from a walk, tripped a bomb wired to his front gate and was killed by the explosion. Local officials and private detectives from the Boise Secret Service and Merchants Patrol quickly arrested vagrant Harry Orchard and charged him with the crime. Most of Boise, where the governor was still beloved, suspected that the assassination was retaliation for the governor's tactics in the Coeur d'Alene strike. James McParlan, who had overseen the agency's business in the Colorado and Idaho labor conflicts of the previous twenty years, soon took charge of the case and personally interrogated Orchard. After meeting with McParlan, Orchard confessed to not only the assassination of Steunenberg but also many of the acts of violence during the Cripple Creek strike. In addition, he claimed that the leadership of the WFM, especially Charles Moyer, George Pettibone, and "Big" Bill Haywood, had asked him to carry out these acts. Unwilling to wait for extradition hearings, Pinkerton agents seized Moyer, Pettibone, and Haywood in Wyoming, secreted them onto a train, and carried them into the state of Idaho, where they were arrested and charged with Steunenberg's murder. Much of the cost of the 1907 trial was paid for by the Mine Owners' Association. Arguing the case for the prosecution was Idaho senator William Borah. Although not a witness in the trial, James McParlan was a very visible presence in the courtroom and the town, accompanied by his Pinkerton bodyguard, Charlie Siringo. The trial became one of the first great legal spectacles of the new century.[16]

On its surface the trial of Bill Haywood, which was the first of the trials, looked a great deal like the Molly Maguire trials thirty years before, not only because of the presence of James McParlan but also because of the prominent role of mine operators in the trials of suspected labor agitators.[17] The *New York Times* made this connection directly by printing a full-page story on McParlan and the WFM entitled " 'Molly Maguires' of Pennsylvania Find a Parallel in the West."[18] Yet organized labor, the general public, and the reputation of the Pinkerton agency were far different in 1907 than they had been in 1876. Outraged by the kidnapping of the labor leaders, unions across the country raised defense funds and hired famed Chicago lawyer Clarence Darrow.

In his defense of Bill Haywood, Darrow intertwined three different perspectives on the case. First, Darrow explained the justified hostility of the miners and the necessary toughness of Haywood. There was a very real struggle taking place between labor and mine owners. All testimony, especially the motives of Pinkerton agents and mine owners, had to be understood within this context. "I don't claim that this man is an angel," Darrow would say of Haywood in his summation. "The Western Federation of Miners could not afford to put an angel at their head. Do you want to hire an angel to fight the Mine Owners' Association and the Pinkerton detectives, and the power of wealth?" Of course, the WFM would protest about the bullpens, Darrow argued, "in behalf of a thousand men placed there without charge, held without trial, denied the common necessities of life, covered with filth and dirt and mire, surrounded with lice, Pinkerton detectives and other vermin and left to rot." Yet, despite the constant attention of the "Pinkertons, with their million eyes focused upon him [Haywood], with their million ears trained to catch every sound that could come from his voice," the prosecution had little evidence of any crimes. "In all of their unions everywhere were the Pinkerton detectives, ready to report every act, every word, every letter," concluded Darrow. However, "this Pinkerton and all his cohorts—with the money of all the mines and all the mills behind them, and have produced nothing except the paltry story which you have heard upon this witness stand."[19]

It was clear, Darrow declared, that the mine owners desperately wanted to rid themselves of Haywood, Moyer, Pettibone, and the WFM. To what length, Darrow wanted the jury to ask, would the companies go to accomplish this goal? "But let us cut out the Western Federation men for a moment," Darrow said. Instead, he drew the jury's attention to the second part of his summation: Harry Orchard's shadowy past and biographical inconsistencies. Not only was Orchard's past filled with crimes, corruptions, vagrancy, and various aliases, but to believe Orchard, Darrow pointed out, was to dismiss the testimony of other witnesses with higher moral standards and less reason to lie. In addition, to believe the prosecution's case was to believe a vast and far-ranging criminal conspiracy in the face of far simpler and more believable answers. "I don't believe that this man was ever really in the employ of anybody," Darrow stated. "I don't believe he ever had any allegiance to the Mine Owners' association, to the Pinkertons, to the Western Federation of Miners, to his family, to his kindred, to his God, or to anything human or divine." The far easier conclusion was that Orchard had acted alone, and that his confession implicating the WFM was drafted by Orchard's personal confessor, whom Darrow mocked repeatedly as "Father McParlan."[20]

By questioning the motives of McParlan and both the methods and general reputation of the Pinkertons, Darrow brought in the third part of his defense. In seeking an explanation for Orchard's confession, Darrow notes that "Mr. Hawley tells us that McParlan had converted him." "He is a wonderful detective isn't he?" continued Darrow. "But here is a piece of work, gentlemen of the jury that will last as long as the ages last—McParlan's conversion of Orchard!" Sliding into playful mockery, Darrow questioned not only the morality of McParlan but, more importantly, the morality of private detectives in general. "Don't you think this detective is wasting his time down in the Pinkerton office in the city of Denver?" asked Darrow. "From the beginning of the world was ever any miracle like this performed before?" he mocked. Harry Orchard, "who has lived his life up to this time, and he had gotten over what religion he ever had," meets McParlan and finds God, even though McParlan was not a preacher but a detective, "who never did anything in his life but lie and cheat and scheme, for the life of a detective is a living lie, that is his business; he lives one from the time he gets up in the morning until he goes to bed; he is deceiving people and trapping people and lying to people and imposing on people: that is his trade." If Orchard's testimony was true, Darrow surmised, McParlan was wasting his time and skills with the Pinkertons. "What is the matter with McParlan changing the sign on his office, and going into the business of saving souls instead of snaring bodies?" he asked. "If he could convert a man like Orchard in the twinkling of an eye, I submit he is too valuable a man to waste his time in a Pinkerton detective office trying to catch men. He had better go out in the vineyard and go to work and bring in souls." The only purpose McParlan had with Orchard was using him to break the WFM. "Do you suppose he [McParlan] is interested in anything except weaving a web around these men so that he may be able to hang them by the neck until dead?" asked Darrow. "And to do it, like the devil, he quotes Scripture. To do it, there isn't a scheme or a plan or a device of his wily, crooked brain that he won't bring into action, whether it is the Bible or detective yarns—there is none too good for McParlan."[21]

As to the faith the jury should place in McParlan, concluded Darrow, "now, gentlemen so much for that. There are other witnesses in this case." After all, he continued, "McParlan is not under indictment. Mac is too slick." Although McParlan was the key to the prosecution's case, the jury did not hear directly from the detective. "He isn't indicted," Darrow concluded, "although he ought to be," because to Darrow's mind the prosecution's case "is a lie out of whole cloth, manufactured by the chief perjury manufacturer in this case, Mr. James McParlan, and manufactured in his perjury office down in Denver."[22]

Darrow's indictments of the Pinkerton methods were not limited to McParlan but extended to the competency of the entire agency. In dissecting a prosecution photograph, Darrow wondered where the prosecution had attained the evidence. "I will tell you where he got it," Darrow said of the prosecuting attorney. "He got it from these myriad eyes of the Pinkerton detectives." "Of course, anybody but a Pinkerton detective would have taken pains to find out when that photograph was made," Darrow continued, but the Pinkertons were too interested in framing Haywood to deal with details. "So these detectives helped fix up that choice hit of perjured testimony to hang Bill Haywood, and it is plain, plain as anything in this world can be." Likewise, when the prosecution pointed to a bomb in Colorado that Orchard claimed to have buried on orders from the union, Darrow again questioned the origin of the evidence. "That bomb was dug up by a party of men who went from the Pinkerton office," he pointed out; "The information was obtained from the Pinkertons. It was discovered by the Pinkertons. It was dug up and it was taken by the Pinkertons to the Pinkerton office. The exhibits were put together by the Pinkertons; everything was signed and sealed by the Pinkertons in the Pinkerton office." Darrow concluded, "It is suspicious to say the least, mighty suspicious."[23]

After hearing the summation from Darrow, the jury returned a verdict of not guilty. Pettibone and Moyer were likewise exonerated. Far from the Molly Maguire cases or the Haymarket trials, where Pinkerton agents' testimony seemed beyond reproach, in Idaho the very nature of detectives' subterfuge and motives made their actions and testimony questionable at best and reprehensible at worst. The legal understanding of Pinkerton labor spies and Pinkertonism had changed drastically from 1876 to 1907. Even the once impeccable reputation and legend of James McParlan could not withstand the sea change of public opinion toward the Pinkerton agency. Ironically, within a year of each other, the Pinkertons would celebrate one of their finest victories (the deaths of Butch Cassidy and the Sundance Kid in Bolivia and the taming of the west) and endure a humbling rebuke in Boise.

Pinking the Pinkertons

In Darrow's indictment of the Pinkerton agency and their tactics, one of his key witnesses was Morris Friedman, who had served as a private stenographer for James McParlan in the Denver office for several years. During this time, he had the opportunity to make copies of the documents created by Pinkerton labor spies during the Colorado labor wars. The introduction of Friedman's testimony and copies of his confidential internal correspondence created a buzz. The Pinkerton agency had long been famed for their secrecy and the devoted loyalty of their employees. This intense secrecy was a key part of the Pinkerton mythology, yet Friedman had infiltrated the heart of the Denver office, taken documents from the famed James McParlan, and exposed Pinkerton practices for a general audience. Friedman, the *New York Times* would point out, had been "pinking the Pinkertons." Senator Borah and the prosecution did little to oppose the introduction of the documents into the court record, for they felt that the documents actually weakened Darrow's case. Part of the defense was built on the assumption that Pinkerton operatives acted as agents provocateur; nowhere in the internal documents was there evidence of this. During cross-examination, the prosecution forced Friedman to admit that, to his knowledge, Pinkerton agents were not involved in any strikes or unions in Idaho before the personal intervention of James McParlan with Harry Orchard (even though Charlie Siringo had indeed infiltrated the union). For the jury and the court of public opinion, however, the testimony of Morris Friedman and the Pinkerton documents he presented were damning evidence against the agency.[24]

After the trial, Friedman collected these internal memorandums and published a scathing exposé of the agency entitled *The Pinkerton Labor Spy*. In this book, Friedman exposed the inner workings of the agency, including the methods of recruiting both agents and clients. But first Friedman took aim at the carefully constructed detective mythology that Allan Pinkerton had built. "The detective is a very interesting personality, both because of the secret nature of his calling and the mystery surrounding his movements," wrote Friedman. "However, stripped of all the glamour which fiction has so skillfully woven around his profession, he becomes another character."[25] To Friedman, detectives were men who lived lives of deceit and treachery. Allan Pinkerton, Friedman wrote, understood very early the depths of modern deceit and the fear that this deceit would create. "His superior intelligence and intimate knowledge of human nature enabled him to discover an inexhaustible gold mine in man's jealousy and suspicion of his fellow man," wrote Friedman. The fame and notoriety that followed the Molly Maguire case "paved a truly royal road to wealth and power for the Pinkerton family, a power which now extends across the entire length and breadth of the land." However, the mythology of the modern detective who pursued law and order with the highest morality was a creation of Pinkerton which hid the reality of the agency. "Underneath the impenetrable cover of a reputation gained by a skillful and systematic misrepresentation of facts," continued Friedman, "the

Agency meanwhile established and up to the time of the writing of this work has perfected a system of espionage, calumny and persecution of labor of all crafts and classes which is, if possible, even more intolerable and pernicious than the universally detested and infamous Secret Police of Russia."

Even the famous innovations of the agency which marked every popular description of the Pinkertons hid the true intentions of its operatives. Much credit had been given to the agency, Friedman noted, for developing the "Rogue's Gallery," an index of local criminals and the criminal underclass which existed in every branch office. "Even though criminal work is but an insignificant percentage of its business, it is but just and fair that a detective agency should at least have the semblance of a thief-catching institution," concluded Friedman, "and what will lend a truer color to this fiction than a Rogue's Gallery." The numbers, Friedman argued, made this reputation as the capturers of thieves and criminals a sham. Too much was paid out in salary and expenses, he pointed out, for the work of thief catching to cover. Instead, the Pinkertons were an organization of labor spies, the profits of which were often kept off the books.[26]

For Friedman, the pursuit of labor agitation and the practices of the labor spy not only represented the bulk of Pinkerton work but also demonstrated the depths to which the agency was willing to sink. It was bad enough that the agency was able to find a "secret operative [who] sells his honor and the interests of his brothers for eighteen dollars a week, net." But the corruption of the agency was systemic. In order to make profits, he argued, superintendents were responsible for rounding up their own business. This often meant overselling the threat of violent labor agitation and thus the need for Pinkerton spies. To make this case to clients, McParlan would have the clerical staff, including Friedman, rework the daily reports of agents so that they would reflect more of a threat from "dangerous union agitators." This reworking of the reports also helped justify the ten dollars per report that companies were charged. For the Pinkertons, bad labor relations, potential violence, and deep distrust between capital and labor were all good for business. "The justice or injustice of Labor's demands does not appeal to them; the immense losses of their clients do not worry them; and the suffering of the public does not interest them," wrote Friedman; only their profits seemed to matter. The WFM "aroused the fear and apprehension of mine owners; and these fears have been studiously fanned into flames of blind and furious hatred" by the agency to their satisfaction and "immense profit."

It was James McParlan himself who "has directed a war of extermination against the Western Federation of Miners." In Colorado McParlan found mine owners who were happy with the stability and profits and had peaceful relations with their employees. McParlan broke this peace by the "placing of the Murder's mark of Cain upon the forehead of every member of the Western Federation of Miners." McParlan was able to convince mine owners that every case of theft, accident, arson, murder, or death was attributable to an inner circle within the WFM. By inventing such a criminal conspiracy, the Pinkertons justified their presence in the Colorado mining fields and their tactics of infiltration. "As a matter of fact, if the files of the Pinkerton Agency were examined to-day not a report would be found showing a single item of actual incriminating evidence against the miners," concluded Friedman, "unless it is a crime of itself for work-ingmen to come together and transact lodge business." Friedman detailed the actions of several different Pinkerton agents who infiltrated unions in Colorado during the wave of strikes in 1903 and 1904. He also commented on the role Pinkerton agents played in the Citizens' Alliance, especially agent J. C. Frasier, who was a member and had his fees paid by the agency. It was this same Citizens' Alliance that seized power in the wake of the Independence depot explosion and began the series of deportations that would break the strike. Of this action Fried-man asked, "Is it not like a well planned coup d-etat?"[27] Pinkerton agents, who by necessity "conspire against the public welfare and peace," concluded Fried-man, "are a public menace while masquerading as a public necessity."[28]

For Pinkerton's National Detective Agency, never before had company se-crets been exposed from inside the agency. As a result, the agency became all the more obsessed with its public image and protective of the secrets held by its employees. The publication of Friedman's book on the Pinkertons and the agency's crackdown on leaked information could not have come at a worse time for Charlie Siringo. After finishing his service as James McParlan's bodyguard during the Boise trial of Bill Haywood, Siringo left the Pinkerton agency to write his memoirs of his time as a cowboy detective. When word of its impend-ing publication reached the Pinkerton offices, the agency balked at the idea of another exposé and fought hard to prevent the book from being printed. Even-tually, after many acrimonious discussions, Siringo, his publishers, and the Pinker-tons struck a deal. The content of the book would remain largely intact. Siringo still told of his time in Colorado, his dealing with the White Caps in New Mex-ico, and his undercover work in Coeur d'Alene in 1892. What had to be stricken, however, was any reference to the Pinkerton agency or any other Pinkerton agents. Hence, the name of the Pinkertons was removed from the subtitle, which

instead became "A True Story of Twenty-Two Years with a World-Famous Detective Agency." Other references in the book became the "Dickenson" agency
instead of the Pinkertons. James McParlan became James McCartney, and Siringo's fellow Pinkerton agent Tom Horn became Tim Corn. Despite these edits,
references to other Pinkerton officials, such as George Bangs, remained, as did
a few missed references to McParlan and Horn. However, the Pinkertons and
their lawyers felt that this compromise kept the agency's reputation safe.[29]

Charlie Siringo, however, did not take kindly to the editorial advice. Embit-
tered by the experience of trying to publish *A Cowboy Detective*, Siringo sent a
new manuscript to the Pinkerton office in 1914 to ask what objections they may
have to the new version of his Pinkerton experience. When the Pinkertons objected to the book in its entirety and attempted to stop its publication, Siringo
looked to publish his new book by himself. The result was Siringo's scathing
critique entitled *Two Evil Isms: Pinkertonism and Anarchism*. In total the book read
much like *A Cowboy Detective*; Siringo covers many of the same experiences, including his encounter with anarchism in Chicago, his time as a cowboy detective
in the west, and his introduction into the labor disputes of Idaho and Colorado.
Yet the tone and purpose of this volume were very different. Like Friedman
before him, Siringo set out to write an exposé of the unscrupulous business practices and unlawful procedures of the agency. On its cover, Siringo's book showed
Uncle Sam battling with a snake emboldened with the words "Anarchism" and
"Pinkertonism." The subtitle read "by Chas. A. Siringo, a Cowboy Detective,
who knows as he spent twenty-two years in the inner circle of Pinkerton's National Detective Agency." As in *A Cowboy Detective*, Siringo tells of his presence
in Chicago during the Haymarket bombing and how it drove him to join the
Pinkertons to take on the evils of anarchism. "Seeing some of those wounded
officers hauled to the hospital early next morning, chilled my blood, and I wanted
to help stamp out this great Anarchist curse," Siringo wrote. "I concluded the
best way to help in the righteous cause, was to join in that (to my ignorant mind)
model institution, Pinkerton's National Detective Agency, but little did I dream
that I was entering a school for the making of anarchists, and a disgrace to an
enlightened age."[30]

In taking on the Pinkertons, Siringo declared that "the object of this volume is only to show up evils which have crept into our beloved, free and easy
America." To do so, Siringo challenged the mythologies of Pinkerton detectives.
While Robert and William Pinkerton, like their father before them, claimed
that the agency only hired men of high moral standard and only "American

citizens," Siringo told lurid tales of detective quarters, which "contained dozens of men of all ages, colors and nationalities." In such a room "there were many good, conscientious men and others devoid of moral principle or character." Siringo also talked of the corruption that went into billing and the exaggerations that filled the daily reports, including fabricated details of agents' conversations with suspected Haymarket bomber Albert Parsons in a Chicago park. "The false reports written about anarchists as told to me by the writers themselves," he wrote, "would make a decent man's blood boil." Such exaggerations served a purpose for the agency. "The excuse was that these flashy reports suited the agency and pleased the clients who were having the work done," reported Siringo, "and also gave the detectives an excuse for rendering big expense bills for drinks and like." Much of the testimony provided by Pinkerton agents during the Haymarket cases came from such reports.[31]

Yet the word of Pinkerton agents was readily believed largely because of the mythology created by its owners. "How can a judge doubt the purity of this monster," Siringo said of the agency, "when shown an enlarged photograph of Allan Pinkerton and our dear beloved president, Abraham Lincoln, standing side by side near the bloody field of battle? These photographs are hung in conspicuous places in all the agency offices as emblems of purity." "Up to the time of the Homestead riot, and since the moral wave has been sweeping over the land," Siringo reminded his readers, "the Pinkerton National Detective Agency was above the law. A word from WA Pinkerton or one of his officers would send any 'scrub' citizen to the scrap heap or even to the penitentiary." He hoped that "the day is fast approaching when the American people will take a tumble and put this corrupt institution out of commission." While the agency may have positioned themselves as the defenders of Chicago and the larger industrial society against anarchists, "no doubt they feathered their dirty nest with a good share of the money, said to be one million dollars, put up by the Citizen's League of Chicago, to stamp out anarchy."[32]

His time in the west only further confirmed for Siringo that his agency was as much a creator of chaos and anarchy as an agency of order. "In truth," Siringo concluded, "it was anarchy against anarchy, with the school of anarchy, my agency, as the third party." Part of what made the Pinkertons in the west a "school of anarchy" was the quality of agent. "From time to time other operatives were sent from Chicago, one of whom was a murderer, as told to me by himself, smuggled from the laws clutches, to be kept in hiding as an operative," stated Siringo in reference to Tom Horn. "As the above killing had been committed in the interest of the agency, while drawing pay from the agency, it was no more than justice to protect the man." Horn shared the Denver office with Siringo and was one of Siringo's friends, yet, as Siringo points out, Horn was a hired killer who was once "sent into Wyoming by the Pinkerton National Detective Agency along with a gang of gunmen from the Indian Territory and helped to start the Great Johnson County War." The only worse men in the west, according to Siringo, were the leadership of the WFM. While Siringo stated that he was reluctant to take on the work in Coeur d'Alene because "my sympathy was with laboring men and against capitalists," his experience in Idaho changed his mind. Once in the union, Siringo had "to take a Molly Maguire oath to bleed and die for my noble order" and came into contact with a "true blue anarchist, George Pettibone." Once a part of the miners union, "I had nothing to do but drink booze and study anarchy at close range. My sympathies for labor unions had taken a genuine flop and I concluded to stay and see the war out." Indeed, here lay one of the great ironies of Siringo's time with the Pinkertons: the decision against the Haymarket anarchists was, to Siringo's mind, a miscarriage of justice because they were convicted. The trials of Haywood and Pettibone in Boise were miscarriages because the two went free.[33]

Overall, Siringo claimed that had the agency been what they claimed to be, "an organization for the ferreting out and running down of crime and for the upbuilding of society," he would not have become so disillusioned. He suggested that even "with all of the agency's faults, I must confess that they do a lot of good work in running down crime for money." But "if they didn't they could not keep their heads above the dirty water in which they constantly flounder." The Pinkertons, he summarized, "claim that they never do work which will retard justice, or put a stain on our social fabric, but that is not true." It need not be this way, he argued: "detectives are a necessary evil for the protection of society, and by rights should be an honorable calling, but ought to be kept out of the hands of unscrupulous men, and money-mad organizations." Siringo acknowledged,

> The question might be asked why I did not show my manhood by resigning and exposing this crooked agency in the beginning. Exposing it to whom, pray? Not to the officers of the law, I hope. In my cowboy simplicity I might have been persuaded to do so at that time. But I am glad I did not, for, with my twenty-two years behind the curtains, I can now see the outcome. It would have resulted in many "sleeps" in the city bull-pen, and a few doses of the "third degree" to try and wring a confession for blackmailing this notorious institution.

Before the turn of the twentieth century, the reputation and power of the Pinkertons were unmatched and unchallengeable. "A man without wealth and influence trying to expose the dastardly work of the Pinkerton National Detective Agency," concluded Siringo, "would be like a two-year-old boy blowing his breath against a cyclone to stop it." But by the early days of the twentieth century, the specter of Pinkertonism as a threat had changed this dynamic. Now, much like Friedman had before him, Siringo felt much more secure in exposing the inner workings and nefarious practices of the Pinkerton agency.[34]

Conclusion: Anarchists and detectives, reconsidered

By the end of the nineteenth century, the Pinkerton agency found itself on the defensive. Not only had Friedman, Darrow, and Siringo challenged the public perception of the agency, but anti-Pinkerton laws at the federal and state level had begun to limit the scope and legality of Pinkerton employment as both armed guards and labor spies. The city of Cleveland even added to its police reform an addendum that former Pinkerton agents could not be hired onto the force.[35] There were still plenty of international employment opportunities for Pinkerton detectives, however. As American business interests looked to consolidate their international holdings and interests, the Pinkertons and agencies like them provided both information and muscle. At the same time, foreign states also found Pinkerton spies to be useful allies. In the 1890s, Honduran president Luis Bogran consolidated his power by hiring Pinkerton agents; an ex-Pinkerton agent even became his director of the secret police. When Russian liberal Vladimir Korolenko toured the United States and visited the Chicago World's Fair in 1893, the Russian secret police, the *Okhrana*, paid the Pinkertons to follow him.[36]

During the Cuban insurrection beginning in 1895, the Spanish colonial government hired Pinkertons to keep track of Cuban rebels within the United States. At the same time, the US government used the agency to make sure that international neutrality laws were not violated by American filibustering expeditions leaving Florida for Cuba. During one high-profile trial of a crew contracted to move supplies and guns into Cuba, it was revealed that undercover Pinkerton agents had been on board. Because of the agency's connections to the Spanish government in Cuba, Pinkerton agents were also accused of providing the Spanish government with information about American defense plans, an accusation that William Pinkerton loudly denounced as "grossly malicious and tending to create an unjustifiable prejudice."[37] Once the United States declared war with Spain, the federal government contracted with the Pinkerton agency to provide intelligence for the United States against the Spanish.[38] Yet such actions did not bring the agency accolades and fame as much as suspicion and mistrust. Such public mistrust also began to cost the firm business; when the Diaz government of Mexico sought information on and the arrest of the anarchist Flores Magón brothers, the Mexicans contracted with the smaller and less notorious Saint Louis agency of Thomas Furlong.[39]

It was within this new context of mistrust that Robert Pinkerton tried to both craft a new role for his detectives and reconnect their practices to the interests of the nation-state. In an article for the *North American Review* in 1901 entitled "Detective Surveillance of Anarchists," Pinkerton argued that there was a grave and imminent threat to American society from violent anarchists and that such a threat could only be countered by constant surveillance by well-organized and efficient agents. "The police control of anarchists, while by no means a simple matter, may yet be accomplished," he wrote. However, "the matter must be undertaken in a clean-cut businesslike manner and the system kept absolutely free from the taint of political influence." His agents, he argued, were trained to watch the hands of suspicious characters and would never had allowed someone like Leon Czolgosz to get close to President William McKinley. In addition, his agency also had experience in infiltrating such organizations and uncovering their innermost workings. "The anarchists are something like the old 'Mollie Maguires' of Pennsylvania," he suggested. "If the Government is to take an active hand in the suppression of anarchism," Pinkerton argued, "I would advocate the forming of a special department for this purpose, whose attention could, at all times, be given to this very serious question." Such a department, modeled on the Pinkertons, could not be squeamish in its duties, however. "Kindly or halfway measures are thrown away entirely upon the 'Reds,'" Pinkerton concluded.

> They understand only one argument, and that is the argument of brute force. It is all very well to safe guard the rights of free speech and of free press; but sentimentalism in this direction should not be permitted to carry so far as to allow the open, or secret, advocacy of the overthrow of all government. Only a systematic campaign against this sort of thing can avert a serious condition, for these anarchists are becoming more and more numerous and those of the violent school are growing steadily bolder.

To curtail the political activities of dangerous anarchists, Pinkerton offered several suggestions. "At the very beginning," he suggested, "there ought to be a law passed to permit the deportation of every man and woman who preaches the overthrow of government and the principles of anarch." Second, there was a need for a "perfect system of police control . . . that would never lose touch with the anarchists already established here, and would pick up any foreigners that might come as soon as they reached any of our ports." In order to rid the country of dangerous anarchists, Pinkerton advocated the establishment of an anarchist colony, perhaps the Philippines, where anarchists can be both contained and controlled. Finally, a strong and potentially violent police presence was necessary to break up anarchists' meetings and rallies. While such an action "was reprehensible from the standpoint of the stickler for social and political rights . . . there are certain conditions that cannot be dealt with from the ordinary point of view, and anarchy is one of them." "Where that comes into question," he concluded, "we may well permit the authorities to stretch a point for its repression."[40]

However, by the turn of the century, those "sticklers for social and political rights" who loudly condemned the practices and policies of the Pinkerton agency dominated the public discourse on capital and labor. Despite Robert Pinkerton's efforts to connect early twentieth-century anarchism with "Molly Maguirism," public understandings of both the Pinkertons and the Molly Maguires had dramatically changed. In a 1903 muckraking article on Carnegie and US Steel, *Cosmopolitan* summarized this new public opinion on labor radicalism. When it described Homestead, it reminded readers that "we must bear in mind that this is 1892 of which we are speaking. Conceptions of business right and wrong were still crude. The general public had not been educated up to labor questions. The subject had received no full discussion. The press gave a great deal of the side of the employers and very little of that of labor. The public mind had a confused notion of Molly Maguirism when it talked of labor strikes." The Pinkertons were an essential part of the "confused notion of Molly Maguirism" which had governed the public's understanding of labor issues. The undermining of the Pinkerton's mythology had radically changed the public's perception of the firm and its history.[41]

CHAPTER EIGHT

In which the modern state takes on the duties of the Pinkerton agency

I N AN essay written in March of 1892, before the conflicts in Wyoming or the clash in Homestead, General James Weaver of the newly formed Populist Party warned that industrial oligarchs had "grown to be stronger than the government; and the army of Pinkertons, which is ever at their bidding, is greater by several thousand than the standing army of the United States," which meant that "instead of the government controlling the corporations, the latter dominate every department of State." A new political party was necessary because Congress seemed "bent on farming out its sovereign power to individuals and corporations," In their 1892 political platform for Weaver's presidential campaign, the Populists declared that "we regard the maintenance of a large standing army of mercenaries, known as the Pinkerton system, as a menace to our liberties, and we demand its abolition; and we condemn the recent invasion of the Territory of Wyoming by the hired assassins of plutocracy."[1] Only a direct intervention by a state that represented the interests of the people could limit such plutocratic powers.

By the end of the 1890s, as various reform movements coalesced into the loosely connected progressive movement, the very presence of the Pinkerton agency seemed symbolic of larger instabilities within industrial society. "In the middle ages the state supported no armies or navies. Private parties—dukes and earls and barons, the Pinkertons of the dark ages—furnished soldiers on contract," wrote John Commons, one of the major architects of progressive thought toward labor; "essential inequality was the result."[2] In an article entitled "A New Plea for a Square Deal" Edward Ross warned that if "laws guarding the interests of one class are enforced" while the underclasses are unprotected, or if "a law is enforced downward but not upward," then the state will inevitably perish "in the flame of class hate." The law had to be applied evenly, and "this is why it may be more imperative to cut out alike Pinkertons and sluggers," he concluded.[3] The progressive state needed to hold that middle ground between Pinkerton transgression and mob violence.

Some progressive reformers advocated outlawing the use of Pinkerton guards through anti-Pinkerton legislation, while others demanded that the state itself provide order and stability by usurping the power and practices of the Pinkertons. Some reforms suggested that good government demanded that the federal army take on some of the power and responsibilities of the Pinkerton agency in order to crush anarchism. What they could agree on was the central problem: it was not the tactics or actions of the Pinkertons as private guards, but the public reputation and perception of the agency. Progressive reformers were offended not by the Pinkertons but by accusations of Pinkertonism. The courts and the army, bolstered by new anti-anarchist legislation, could repress political radicalism. Other agencies such as the Thiel agency, the Baldwin–Felts, or the Bergoff Brothers could continue to do the same kind of strikebreaking work, so long as they did not carry the toxic "Pinkerton" name. The history of strikebreaking and industrial violence in the 1910s and 1920s demonstrates that the crisis of Homestead and the 1890s was the implicit threat that the Pinkertons posed to state authority; so long as smaller firms did not threaten the legitimacy of the state, industrial violence was still officially overlooked.

Not until the New Deal of the 1930s was there an attempt to construct a public trust by fully integrating the regulation of private economic power, the broad inclusion of political ideologies across the spectrum, and the reinvention of a shared industrial folklore. Such a public trust differed greatly from the idealism of John Dewey and earlier Progressives who understood the state to be a self-expression of an engaged public. Rather, the New Deal state tried to actively harness populist politics, consumerism, and folklore into a "symbolic theater" that controlled the discourse about industrialism and the state. Popular culture thus became an integral part of the New Deal state and created much of the voter loyalty and imagery that constituted the New Deal's influence. But to make this work, the New Deal state had to not just battle against the political specter of "Pinkertonism," but rather actively ensure the civil liberties of workers against private armed guards and labor spies, all while also providing a national police capable of chasing bandits and keeping the peace. In the mid-nineteenth century, the Pinkerton agency filled many of the new roles created by market expansion and industrialization; by the 1870s, the blurred lines between the Pinkertons and the state provided the firm with its authority and reputation. This very connection to the state became by the 1890s the most dangerous aspect of the agency. By 1937, however, these roles either had been banned by the state or were performed by the state itself. Moreover, the Pinkertons had long existed in a nexus that interconnected the needs of industrialists, the concerns of the public and the state, and the fantasies and folklore of popular culture. The New Deal state, with its active interventions, inclusive politics, and crafting of a national folklore, took on all of these new responsibilities.

Birdy Edwards and the last myth of the Pinkertons

Beginning in the first years of the new century, the agency tried once again to reinvent itself. The Colorado and Idaho labor wars, along with the Haywood trial, had complicated the agency's efforts to distance itself from Homestead and its labor-breaking past. Granted official access to confidential company files, journalist Charles Bourke avoided discussion of labor work and controversies over Pinkertonism. Instead, he recited the standard origin stories of Allan Pinkerton's war work and the agency's overall professionalism. In particular, Bourke focused on urban bank robberies and fraud cases and stressed the agency's use of the modern Bertillon method of scientific identification. One article did trace the case of the Reno brothers, but not James (although a photo of Jesse James did appear in the article, with the description "the notorious outlaw in criminal annals was in appearance slender, attractive, and somewhat dandified").[4] Instead, Bourke's articles rehashed Allan Pinkerton's books and mythologies for a new magazine-reading public.

A chance encounter on a trans-Atlantic steamer between William Pinkerton and Arthur Conan Doyle also led to the inclusion of Pinkerton lore in the canon of Sherlock Holmes. From his first appearance in 1887 until his "death" in 1893, Holmes had come to personify the Victorian gentleman detective. Reader outrage, however, had prompted Doyle to resurrect his beloved character in 1901. In the 1911 short story "The Adventure of the Red Circle," Holmes encounters Mr. Leverton of Pinkerton's American Agency, who is in London in pursuit of members of an Italian anarchist conspiracy. Doyle would return to the Pinkertons and the lore of the Molly Maguires in the 1914 novel *Valley of Fear*. While investigating the mysterious death of John Douglas, Holmes discovers that Douglas had actually killed his assailant and faked his own death. Once exposed, Douglas emerged from hiding and handed over his notes to Holmes and Watson to explain why he was a hunted man.[5]

Douglas's notes shift the tale of the *Valley of Fear* from the pastoral lands of the English countryside in 1902 to the coal regions of Pennsylvania of 1875. Jack McMurdo, a counterfeiter on the run, has recently arrived in the region and quickly integrated himself into both the local chapter of the "Eminent Order of Freemen" and the more sinister criminal organization of the "Scowrers," whose crimes are all overseen by local lodge "Boss" Jack McGinty. However, this world of crime is shaken by news from a fellow member who confides in McMurdo the details of a secret telegraph note. "There is a detective on our trail," laments the fellow member, and not just a local detective but a Pinkerton agent. "Well you can take it from me you've got no show when they are on your trail," he warns. This was no "take-it-or-miss-it Government concern," the miner points out; "it's a dead earnest business proposition that's out for results." The miner's conclusion was, "if a Pinkerton man is deep in this business, we are all destroyed." When he learns the same news, Boss McGinty is less impressed: "There is going to be a vacancy at Pinkerton's," he declares, "or I'm mistaken."[6]

The real surprise, however, is awaiting the Scowrers when they find themselves surrounded by the armed men of the Coal and Iron Police. It is then that Jack McMurdo reveals himself. "I guess we may not meet again until you see me on the stand in the courthouse," declares McMurdo. "I am Birdy Edwards of Pinkerton's. I was chosen to break up your gang. I had a hard and dangerous game to play. . . . But it's over to-night thank God, and I am the winner!" With these final words, Edwards left the coal region triumphant. He would go on to earn a fortune under the assumed name of John Douglas. Yet Scrower assassins continued to hunt him even to his English estate. Seemingly only Douglas's death would stop the Scrowers, which was why Douglas tried to fake his own death.[7]

For Holmes's adventure, Doyle reached back into the detective folklore of the Victorian age. Part of the mystery was an unexplained murder in a country estate; the other part was the lawlessness of the American interior. Such spaces called for the interventions of different detectives. Holmes, the scientific rational mind, analyzed the clues left at the scene of the crime. Birdy Edwards, the Pinkerton agent, went deep undercover to infiltrate a secret society dedicated to undermining civil society. However, by its publication, *Valley of Fear* was already out of date. Readers of the "modern age" cared less for the cool rationality and systemic order of the Victorian detective novel. When Allan Pinkerton wrote his account of the Molly Maguire case in 1876, readers were willing to take at face value the inherent goodness and moral standing of a Pinkerton agent. In the forty years since, Pinkerton agents, Pinkertonism, James McParlan, and private detectives in general were held in less regard.

The modern state and the detectives

By the turn of the century, a mushrooming of other detective agencies had cut severely into Pinkerton's business of armed guards and strikebreaking. At the same time, new patterns of intervention from the state changed the dynamics of union busting. Beginning with the Pullman strike in 1894 and accelerating through the first decades of the twentieth century, the state was far quicker to deploy police, the state militia, and the federal army early in strikes even before the onset of violence. In Pennsylvania, the Coal and Iron Police remained an important tool in strikebreaking; clashes during a 1902 anthracite strike resulted in the police killing at least fourteen people. Because the Coal and Iron Police still answered to private interests, the state legislature formed the Pennsylvania State Constabulary in 1905. Modeled on the British Constabulary of Ireland, the new force would keep "the turbulent foreign element under control" because "one state policeman should be able to handle 100 foreigners." Although formed as an alternative to the Coal and Iron Police, the State Constabulary served much the same purpose; miners declared them to be "Pennsylvania Cossacks." Not until 1931 would the governor of Pennsylvania abolish the use of the Coal and Iron Police.

Yet it would be incorrect to assume that the rise of the progressive state ended the private business of strikebreaking. Historians have previously argued that while direct action of the state in the Gilded Age served as a last resort after the failures of private interests, during the Progressive Era the state took a proactive role in crushing radical labor. While the more frequent intervention of state and federal officials did change the nature of strikebreaking, it did not end the business of private firms. Instead, new agencies that did not provide guards for strikebreakers but provided the strikebreakers themselves flourished. Between 1895 and 1907, this new business was dominated by James Farley, whose agency broke streetcar strikes by developing vast networks of strikebreakers (including southern African Americans and upper-class college students) who would have no sympathy with the strikers. Content with the fortune he had acquired, Farley retired in 1907. Between 1907 and 1914, strikebreaking contracts were dominated by two firms, Wadell & Mahon and the Bergoff Brothers. In 1914 these firms merged into Bergoff Brothers and Wadell. At its peak, the firm was rumored to have 40,000 men available and stockpiles of rifles, the same sort of rumors that had once been linked to the Pinkertons.[8]

Even more contentious was the brief and bloody history of the Baldwin–Felts Detective Agency. Formed in 1892 as a partnership between William Baldwin and Thomas Felts, the Roanoke, Virginia, based agency provided security for southern railroads. However, in 1899 Felts opened a new office in West Virginia dedicated to providing armed guards for coal companies. Between 1902 and 1912,

Baldwin–Felts guards earned a reputation for ruthless violence. Impressed by the agency's actions in West Virginia, coal operators hired the agency to patrol company towns in Colorado, including Ludlow, where Baldwin–Felts agents fired indiscriminately into workers' tents in what would come to be called the "Ludlow Massacre." In 1920, guards would again clash with strikers, as well as local sheriff Sid Hatfield, in Matewan, West Virginia. In a shootout that would leave ten dead, Hatfield shot and killed both Albert and Lee Felts (brothers of Thomas Felts). A year later, Baldwin–Felts gunmen ambushed and killed Hatfield on the steps of the McDowell County courthouse. The conflict that had begun in Matewan soon escalated into the "Battle of Blair Mountain," where for several days marching coal miners and an army of Baldwin–Felts agents battled each other; the armed Baldwin–Felts agents and the local sheriff even used machine gun nests and aerial bombardment.[9]

Yet none of the violence of the West Virginia coal wars or the organized strike-breaking of streetcar strikes evoked the same kind of outrage and soul searching that followed Homestead. Nor did the labor struggles of the age create public calls for investigations or accusations of "Pinkertonism." Rather, the Baldwin–Felts agency would slide into the historical record largely unnoticed after it disbanded in 1937. The fact that the Pinkerton agency was not involved probably helped to hide these conflicts; the agency had so long served as a metonym for corporate power that their absence from the conflict tempered the outrage. Public outrage, especially outrage driven by public exposé, had also been exhausted by the 1920s. Blair Mountain came not at the beginning of the Progressive age (with its calls for an increasingly interventionist state) but at the age's ragged end. Unlike Homestead, the labor conflicts of the 1920s did not seem to observers to be a crisis of state sovereignty, the rise of plutocracy, or the dangers of radical foreigners. Instead, in an age of post-Progressive cynicism, the conflicts seemed localized and unlikely to spread, even as the Baldwin–Felts assassinated a local sheriff. Moreover, the conflict in the mountains of West Virginia was understood by many outside of the coal region to be part of the long-standing blood feuds of the region, an idea popularized by T. C. Crawford's sensationalist 1889 "history" of the Hatfields and McCoys. The prominent role of Sid Hatfield in the Matewan shootout and his death on the courthouse steps made the story about the blood feud instead of the Baldwin–Felts. No one accused officials in West Virginia of Pinkertonism; no one spoke of Baldwin–Feltsism.[10]

Outside of the coal regions of West Virginia, other corporations had increasingly turned to scientific management, welfare capitalism, and company unions in order to alleviate the tensions between capital and labor. Such an emphasis on Taylorism and the "one best way" also reshaped cultural narratives and expectations. In 1901, for example, J. P. Morgan bought out Carnegie Steel and created the United States Steel Corporation; its new chairman was the corporate manager Judge Elbert Gary. When the corporation looked to expand, it built its own city in northwest Indiana, where physical structures such as the lakefront and the Grand Calumet River would protect the mill. Pinkerton guards would not be necessary. Likewise, Henry Ford created his own "Sociological department" to provide information about workers and a "goon squad" to crack down on agitation. Corporate brands such as the "General Motors family" were carefully crafted by advertising men such as Bruce Barton. Image-conscious companies could little afford to be seen hiring Pinkerton guards (although General Motors would indeed continue to hire Pinkerton spies). Even in times of industrial strife, other options emerged. During the 1919 steel strike, for instance, the governor of Indiana declared martial law and the US Army patrolled the streets of US Steel's fiefdom of Gary, Indiana. Both the need for and the justification for Pinkertons seemed limited.[11]

For better or worse, by the mid-1920s, the Pinkerton agency had lost not only its place as the primary firm involved in capital labor disputes but also its role as investigators and infiltrators of radical political groups. When dynamite ripped through the offices of the *Los Angeles Times* in 1910, city officials and Harry Chandler of the *Times* turned not to the Pinkertons but to the William J. Burns International Detective Agency (a one-upmanship of Pinkerton's National Detective Agency). It was also Burns's agents who would assist the new Bureau of Investigation after the 1920 Wall Street explosion. This connection with the Bureau of Investigation (the forerunner to the Federal Bureau of Investigation [FBI]) led to Burns's appointment as director of the bureau from 1921 to 1924, during which time he continued to run his private firm. Deeply implicated in the various scandals of the Harding administration, including the Teapot Dome scandal, Burns resigned his post in 1924. After his retirement, Burns turned, much like Pinkerton before him, to writing detective stories and slowly rebuilt his reputation. Just as Pinkerton had once been declared "America's Vidocq," Burns soon became known as "America's Sherlock Holmes."[12]

In response to this shifting political terrain, William and Robert Pinkerton refocused on providing private security. William specialized in investigating bank robberies, and Robert partnered with the Jockey Club to provide security for racetracks and investigate gambling corruption in New York. The brothers also took part in the formation of the "Protective Committee" of the American Bankers' Association; member banks could call upon Pinkerton agents to investigate crimes, holdups, and thefts from their banks. The agency also strengthened its ties with the Jeweler's Security Alliance and its service in investigating thefts and burglaries in member stores.[13] At the same time, both William and Robert positioned themselves as reformers by becoming vocal members of the Police Commissioners Association and advocates of prison reform. The Pinkerton agency, it seemed, had finally become a responsible member of Progressive society.

Stool pigeons, company gunmen, and the New Deal

Even as the company moved toward stressing its legitimate security work and police reform, others were less willing to forget the strikebreaking past (and present) of the agency. When the new Congress of Industrial Organizations (CIO) launched its effort to unionize steel in 1936, it drew direct analogies to the struggles of the 1890s. The CIO rallied in Homestead, Pennsylvania, alongside wreaths proclaiming "In Memoriam: The Spirit of 1892 Lives On." In his speech, which *Time* magazine reported as "paraphrasing the words of Thomas Jefferson at Philadelphia in 1776 and those of Franklin Roosevelt at Philadelphia in 1936," steelworker Charles Scharbo railed against the concentrated power of the steel industrialists. "The lords of Steel try to rule us as did the royalists against whom our forefathers rebelled," he stated. "They have interfered in every way with our right to organize.... They have sent among us stool pigeons.... They have kept among us armies of company gunmen." United Mine Workers district president Patrick J. Fagan made the connection to the past of Homestead even clearer. "Let the blood of the labor pioneers who were massacred here by Pinkertons in 1892," he said, "be the seed of this new organization in 1936."[14]

This all occurred as Franklin Delano Roosevelt was shifting the focus of the New Deal away from the collaborative and voluntary efforts of the so-called First New Deal and toward the broader reforms of the Second New Deal. Calling the New Deal "our covenant with ourselves" in his second inaugural speech, Roosevelt declared that a public trust had to "find practical controls over blind economic forces and blindly selfish men." This made the nation more democratic, Roosevelt argued, "for we have begun to bring private autocratic powers into their proper subordination to the public's government. The legend that they were invincible—above and beyond the processes of a democracy—has been shattered." As part of the process of breaking private autocratic powers, Roosevelt promised that "evil things formerly accepted will not be so easily condoned."[15] Such an era left little room for Pinkerton agents.

Moreover, by the mid-1930s the rhetoric of "Pinkertonism" had shifted toward the even more dangerous label of "fascism." In an analysis of New Deal rhetoric and practice, the *North American Review* argued that while the New Deal borrowed heavily from the rhetoric of Italian "corporatism," it was actually "die-hard big business—the conservative bankers, and industrialists, and mineowners" that represented "the spirit of Fascism in America." "The power of American big business to hire private armies—Pinkerton detectives, factory police, vigilantes, battling strike-breakers, etc.—has been shown through the whole course of our industrial history," it argued. "And it was with private 'black' and 'brown' armies, financed by big business, that Mussolini and Hitler and their industrial sponsors came into supreme power." To avoid the dangers of fascism, the new thinking went, the New Deal state had to limit the power of big business in the name of a broad new inclusive industrial democracy.[16]

It was within this spirit of industrial democracy that Senator Robert La Follette launched his investigation into the use of private detectives and labor spies within American industry. As part of this investigation, La Follette called before his committee current and former Pinkerton agents, as well as the agency's new president, to explain its labor espionage. After founder Allan Pinkerton died in 1884, the company passed to his two sons. Robert Pinkerton died in 1907; William passed in 1923, after which sole direction of the family business passed to Robert's son Allan.[17] After Allan's death in 1930, his son Robert, who had been working as a stockbroker, assumed control of the company, and it would be this Robert Pinkerton who would come to Congress in 1936 to answer for his company's practices in providing labor spies. Unlike the Homestead hearings that Robert's grandfather attended, which addressed the legality of Pinkerton guards, La Follette's committee was looking into labor espionage because it considered labor spies a violation of worker's civil liberties.

In their first round of testimony, Pinkerton officials admitted that various industries had paid the agency $1,750,000 for labor spy and strikebreaking services since 1933. Their largest customer, General Motors, had contracted with the agency for $419,850 worth of espionage, including, a former Pinkerton agent admitted, surveillance on "a man named McGrady, a Government mediator" (who turned out to be assistant secretary of labor Edward F. McGrady) during the 1935 Chevrolet strike in Toledo. In an article entitled "Pinkertons Pinked,"

Time magazine documented the growing evidence that Pinkerton agents had intentionally circumvented both state laws governing the registration of private detectives and the federal anti-Pinkerton law that forbade the federal government from doing business with the agency. "Last week it was the embarrassing task of the Pinkerton National Detective Agency's fourth-generation head to discuss that law in Washington before the Senate committee investigating labor spying and coercion," wrote the magazine; "From the agency's instruction book, Committee Chairman La Follette read an item ordering operatives to submit their bills to Government officials on 'plain paper.' 'That,' snapped the inquisitor, 'clearly was intended to indicate a method of evading the law, wasn't it, Mr. Pinkerton?' 'Yes,' said unhappy Robert Allan Pinkerton." Instead, the committee seemed to support John L. Lewis's contention that if General Motors would recognize workers' rights to organize, "it will no longer be necessary for the Corporation to spend hundreds of thousands each year on labor spies."[18]

In total the La Follette commission found that labor espionage was a "common, almost universal practice in American industry . . . large corporations rely on spies. No firm is too small to employ them." Some corporations, such as General Motors, had several layers of labor espionage where plant managers hired their own spies, personnel managers hired their own spies, and general management also contracted with still other spies. The La Follette commission also investigated Corporations Auxiliary Co., which used former Pinkerton agents to infiltrate United Auto Workers unions for Chrysler. The committee found that at least 304 Pinkerton agents were active union members, including one vice president of a national union, fourteen presidents of locals, and several other union officials. "There is no gathering of union members large enough to be called a meeting that is small enough to exclude a spy," reported one labor leader. "Not only is the worker's freedom of association nullified by employer's spies but his freedom of action, of speech and assembly is completely destroyed," concluded the report. "Fear harries his every footstep, caution muffles his words. He is in no sense any longer a free American. In a constitutional sense his very position reflects the mockery and contempt which those who demand constitutional rights for themselves deny to others."[19] In response to the embarrassing details of the La Follette committee reports and in light of the shifting political realities of the New Deal state, Robert Pinkerton and the board of directors vowed, in 1937, to eliminate labor investigations. That same year, Thomas Felts dissolved the Baldwin–Felts agency. The era of the labor spy, it seemed, had come to an end.

The 1930s represented an important transformation for the Pinkerton agency. Henry Ford's goons, led by Harry Bennett and infamous for beating strikers in Detroit, would become the new face of antilabor thuggery. Likewise, between 1933 and 1936, the federal government launched its own "war on crime," in particular the crimes of bank robbery and kidnapping. Instead of subcontracting with private agencies, the war on crime was to be fought with the highly professionalized FBI. However, one of the ironies of the New Deal state is that while it created its own authority by reining in the powers of the private police, it maintained order by creating institutions that borrowed the same techniques as the Pinkertons. Under the leadership of J. Edgar Hoover, the FBI would rise to national and cultural prominence. Like Allan Pinkerton before him, Hoover understood the need to combine ruthless tactics with cultural propaganda to help popularize the agency and control its reputation. Among Hoover's key innovations at the FBI was the standardization and professionalization of department agents. This meant not only distancing the agency from the red-baiting, corruption, and patronage of Burns and Attorney General A. Mitchell Palmer but also controlling the imagery and reputation of the agency. Hoover recruited white, middle-class, college-educated men who shared his politics. He demanded uniformity in dress and style, in particular the black suit and hat. The agents were "government men" (or "G-Men") and as such had to represent the professionalism and incorruptibility of the state. Juxtaposed to these agents were lawless and dangerous bandits. Although embraced by folk cultures as social bandits and celebrities, outlaws such as John Dillinger, Clyde Barrow, and Bonnie Parker were classified by Hoover as "public enemies."

The "war on crime" then was as much a battle for the hearts of the American people as it was enforcement of the law. Hoover formed a public relations staff, called the "Crime Records Division," to create good press. Hoover's own byline went onto hundreds of magazine articles describing agency cases. Beginning in 1935, the Crime Records Division helped create a pulp detective magazine called "Public Enemy: The Thrilling Exploits of the G-Men" and gave journalist Courtney Riley Cooper access to its files. Cooper's books also contained a picture of and an introduction by Hoover. Soon Hollywood came to embrace the image of the federal agent. James Cagney and Edward G. Robinson, who earlier in the decade had played iconic gangsters in *Public Enemy* and *Little Caesar*, respectively, starred as lawmen in *G-Men* and *Bullets or Ballots*. Yet, as scandals in the 1970s would unearth, beneath this façade of order and respectability Hoover's FBI was willing to adopt many of the same tactics that once made the

Pinkertons notorious, including infiltration, misinformation, factionalization, agents provocateur, entrapment, and paramilitary violence.[20]

Conclusion: Dashiell Hammett, Pinkerton

The G-Men of the FBI were not the only agents and lawmen of 1930s political culture, however. At the same time that Hollywood films glorified the federal agents responsible for chasing America's public enemies, a new form of crime fiction created a series of private detectives who worked not in the public's interest but for their own. The hard-boiled detective reveled in the seedy underbelly of crime and corruption. Unlike the aristocratic detective or the western lawman, the hard-boiled detective was not an outsider imposing order and law; rather, he was a product of the criminal milieu and experienced daily corruption, violence, and betrayal. Filled with sex, violence, double-crossings, and naked self-interest, the new private detective novels depicted a gritty world in which the hard-boiled detective moved easily from order to violence and from legality to illegality. One of the chief architects of this new genre was Dashiell Hammett, who fittingly had actually been a Pinkerton agent. Hammett would later describe his Pinkerton work as less exciting and dangerous than comical and surreal. For instance, Hammett told of spending the day shadowing a suspect as he wandered in the countryside. By the end of the day, the man had gotten so lost that Hammett had to give him directions back to the city. "I was a pretty good sleuth," Hammett would later remember, "but possibly a bit overrated because of the plausibility with which I could explain away my failures."[21] Hammett told two very different stories about why he left the agency in 1921. His public story was boredom with the work and comedic disillusionment about finding stolen money on an ocean liner right before it was scheduled to depart, thus cheating himself out of a free trip. But Hammett's longtime companion Lillian Hellman told a different version. To her, Hammett relayed a story of his time in Montana working for the Anaconda Copper Company. He was offered five thousand dollars by an officer of the company to kill labor leader Frank Little. Though Hammett refused, Little was later lynched by unidentified masked men.[22]

In his time as a Pinkerton operative lay the context for Hammett's literary detectives who move through a sordid world of corruption, power, wealth, and violence. Unlike Birdy Edwards or the literary creations of Allan Pinkerton, Hammett's detectives are not middle-class agents bringing order to disordered frontiers. Rather, they are willing to bend rules and break the law because they understand that both rules and law are creations of corruption and power. These detectives, such as the nameless "Continental Op" (an operative for the Continental Detective Agency), walked the blurry line between law and crime, work and revenge, and operating within the system versus going "blood simple." Consolidated from earlier short stories, the novel *Red Harvest* introduced the Continental Op. The story is set in the western mining town of Personville, a recognizable space for a Pinkertonesque agent, but the Op is not there to break the IWW (although its members, the Wobblies, are present). Rather, the corruption comes from his recently killed client's father, the mine owner Elihu Willson. "For forty years," the Op is told, "old Elihu Willson had owned Personville, heart, soul, skin and guts." In addition to owning the mining company, the bank, and the town newspapers, Willson also "owned a United States senator, a couple of representatives, the governor, the mayor, and most of the state legislature. Elihu Willson was Personville, and he was almost the whole state." The root of this power was the Personville Mining Corporation, yet this power had been challenged by the rise of organized labor. "Back in the war days the I.W.W.—in full bloom then throughout the West—had lined up the Personville Mining Corporation's help," the Op learned. "Old Elihu gave them what he had to give them and bided his time. In 1921 it came." Willson chose to close down the mines and break the IWW. When the conflict came, "both sides bled plenty," the Op notes; "The wobblies had to do their own bleeding. Old Elihu hired gunmen, strike-breakers, national guardsmen, and even parts of the regular army to do his. When the last skull had been cracked, the last rib kicked in, organized labor in Personville was a used firecracker." Here lay the origins of Personville's lawlessness. The bad men and hired guns that Willson had brought into town had chosen to stay. It is into this dark underbelly of crime and corruption that the Continental Op wades, not to bring justice or order but to settle scores.[23]

Within *Red Harvest*, Hammett both utilized and undermined several different tropes of American popular fiction, especially those narratives most connected to Pinkerton detective lore and mythology. The story is part western, part detective tale, and part gangster drama.[24] All of these genres are presented by Hammett and then subverted. Instead, the Continental Op was among the first of what would become the genre of "hard-boiled detectives," men whose cynicism helped them survive a morally ambiguous and corrupt world. Hammett's *The Maltese Falcon* (1930) introduced the similarly inclined private detective Sam Spade, and *The Thin Man* (1934) starred his third detective, Nick Charles, formerly of the Transcontinental Detective Agency.

All of these literary detectives rejected the all-knowing presence of the Gilded

Age sleuth. Instead, the private detective was hired to do a job; they had to find someone to blame. Truth and/or justice mattered less. When Nora Charles challenges her husband's conclusions by calling them "just a theory," the jaded detective retorts, "Call it any name you like. It's good enough for me." When Nora returns with ideas about innocence and reasonable doubt, Nick replies, "That's for juries not detectives. You find the guy you think did the murder and you slam him in the can and let everybody know you think he's guilty." Despite its flaws, "it's neat enough to send him to the chair," Nick finally summarizes, "and that's what counts." Here was a private detective for the modern age.[25]

Pinkerton's Inc.

AFTER 1937, the institutions of the liberal state largely came to fulfill any perceived needs for order, investigation, and infiltration. No longer, it seemed, would agencies such as the Pinkertons serve in quasi-official government roles. American industry, especially industries such as automotive and steel, which were central to the New Deal compact, no longer felt the need to hire their own mercenary armies. Yet in the last half of the twentieth century, the "Pinkerton agent" remained a part of American cultural and political mythology. In their 1952 sci-fi satire *The Space Merchants*, for example, Frederick Pohl and C. M. Kornbluth imagined a future where senators represented individual corporations, workers toiled in debt peonage, and the entire system was controlled by grand advertising agencies that contracted with private security firms such as Brinks, Burns, and Pinkertons. Thus, when the advertising executive who narrates the story visits the launchpad of the US government's Venus rocket, he is pleased to see the armed guard. "I could see from his insignia and shoulder flashes that he was a Contract Specialist, Intelligence, on his third five-year option from the Pinkerton Detective Agency," he says. "He was a regular; he wore the class ring of the Pinkerton Graduate School of Detection and Military Intelligence, Inc. It's pine with an open eye carved on it; no flashy inlay work. But it's like a brand name. It tells you that you're dealing with quality."[1] So too would Ian Fleming's spy hero James Bond continue to receive the help of his friend Felix Leiter in the 1956 novel *Diamonds Are Forever*, even after Leiter had left the CIA and become a Pinkerton agent; his intelligence bona fides were still the same. The Pinkerton agency was still part of the intelligence community. Although the Pinkerton agency last had any real political resonance in 1937, the reputation and imagery of the Pinkerton detective remained relevant to mid-century cultural debates.[2]

By the 1960s, as the New Deal political consensus crumbled under the pressures of civil rights and Vietnam and American popular culture shifted toward romantic visions of outlaws and countercultural bandits, so too would the image of the Pinkerton agent change. Just as they had in the late nineteenth-century genre of the dime novel, the villainous Pinkerton agent would return to the American western as a force of retribution and an agent of unrelenting order. In the 1969 western *Butch Cassidy and the Sundance Kid*, the heroes of the film are chased by a faceless band of railroad detectives, which leads the duo to repeatedly ask the question, "Who are those guys?" This was a question that had long been asked about Pinkerton agents within the symbolic theater of American popular culture, and it was a question that remained resonant within American politics.

Between 1861 and 1937, the Pinkerton agency sat at the nexus of capital's desire for order, the state's fluctuating methods of authority, the power implicit in defining dangers (such as criminality, conspiracy, or anarchism), and the use of folklore to both explain and critique these categories. Despite long-standing historiographical assumptions that the Gilded Age state played little role in the rise of industrial power, state authority and resources were actively involved in promoting market growth and providing order (either overtly or quietly) through their use of the agency. Ideologies such as the promotion of free labor, the protection of private property, or the crackdown on dissent served as a way for the state to legitimize and hide its involvement. Laissez-faire was a constructed mythology promoted by capitalists in the Gilded Age and perpetuated in American memory. Little about the rules of capital, labor, property, or law in the Gilded Age was naturally occurring; the Pinkerton agency created and enforced these new rules in collaboration with both capitalists and the state. Even as first the Progressives and then the New Deal state came to usurp much of the power and authority once reserved for the Pinkertons, the core questions about the concentrated power of the state (what would come to be called the "garrison state" by the 1940s) and its connection to private industry remained relevant. Accusations of "Pinkertonism" have outlasted the relevance of the actual agency.

At the same time, modern folklore and political culture left enough interpretative room for dissent, disagreement, and renegotiation of not only market "rules" but also the very nature of the modern state. Even as the state took on a more active role, the questions of who constituted or threatened free labor, whose property the state protected, whose rights it ensured, and what dissent it cracked down on remained open to interpretation. Through the constructed narratives of criminals, thugs, bandits, Hessians, plutocrats, and detectives, the new communities of the dislodged crafted a folklore of industrial society. The Pinkertons, who were both heroes and villains within these stories, gave American readers a way to read the new market and negotiate power. Dime novels, detective stories, Lincoln biographies, weekly newsmagazines, sensationalist police gazettes, and other forms of pulp fiction were not peripheral to the agency's purpose and reputation; rather, they combined with the agency's actions on behalf of the state and capital to create a metonym for the age.

After 1945, Cold War rhetoric of anticommunism abroad (handled by the CIA) and antiradicalism at home (handled by the FBI) gave an ideological cover to any covert operations in support of American business interests. Not until after the end of the Cold War would exposés and concerns about the collaboration between private "economic hitmen" and American commercial interests challenge the connection between American industry and foreign policy.[3] Since the retreat of the liberal state after 1980, the issues of plutocracy and state authority (and concerns over private funded mercenaries) have re-arisen. No firm has more epitomized the both lucrative and unpopular rise of corporate mercenaries in the twenty-first century than Blackwater USA. Founded by former Navy SEAL Erik Prince, Blackwater originated as a training ground and shooting course for law enforcement officials. Soon, however, the employment of former military special operatives and the arrival of lucrative governmental contracts meant the expansion of business into providing private security. In particular, Blackwater provided security for US officials within the "Green Zone" of Baghdad and other Iraqi cities in the years that followed the 2002 American occupation; such work also resulted in first the high-profile death of four Blackwater operatives in Fallujah in March 2004 and then, in September 2007, Blackwater guards firing into a crowd while escorting diplomats through Nasour Square in Baghdad, killing fourteen and wounding twenty-four.[4] Investigations into Blackwater soon exposed the degree to which the federal government contracted not only with Blackwater but also with other private security companies, such as DynCorp, Intercon, Triple Canopy, American Security Group, Blackhawk, Wackenhut, Instructive Shooting International, and Bodyguard and Tactical Security, as well as major international corporations such as Aegis.[5]

Since 2001, private security has been a booming business for former special service members and retired soldiers.[6] Much like the Pinkertons and their relationship to the Burns agency, the Baldwin–Felts, and the Thiel agency, Blackwater is but the most visible company of a new industry that provides armed services for private individuals, corporations, and governments. Much like the Pinkertons a century before, critics would expose the inner workings of the company ("the world's most powerful mercenary army," said one), and the founder, Erik Prince, would counter the accusations (they were "civilian warriors," he said). Prince's defense even cites the use of the Pinkertons as Lincoln's private guards as evidence of a long tradition of private arms. All of this led one critic to say of Blackwater, "Black is the new pink."[7] Interestingly, while the Pinkerton family struggled for decades to defend their name, brand, and reputation, in the wake of congressional investigations into the company contracts, Erik Prince dropped the name Blackwater and rechristened the company Xe Services. New owners changed the name again to Academi. Yet the company still provides protection services to the government and still remains a key employer of former CIA agents and military personnel—just like Felix Leiter, only more sinister.

Rebranding the Pinkertons

So what became of the Pinkerton agency in both American politics and American memory in the twentieth century? In 1914, the same year that Sir Arthur Conan Doyle published *Valley of Fear*, mystery writer Mary Roberts Rinehart introduced her new sleuth, Hilda Adams, who combined home nursing and snooping to earn the affectionate nickname "Miss Pinkerton." Likewise, the exploits of Nat Pinkerton, the protagonist of a series of short novels and adventure tales mass-produced by writers in postwar Germany, evoked the reputation of, while not having any real connection to, the famous agency. Immigrants in the first two decades of the twentieth century often associated the name Pinkerton with these novels. One immigrant would later remember, "When I was a boy every week I bought books by American detective, Nat Pinkerton. There were three, Nat Pinkerton, Nick Carter and somebody else in Russian translation. I bought every week and we heard these stories." So influential was the series that the Bolsheviks worried that their popularity would corrupt Russian youth and undermine the revolution. Rather than ban the series, however, the Soviets used the basic formulas of the pulp series to create heroes of the revolution and showcase the corruption of western industrialism in a series of books and films known as "Red Pinkertonism."[8]

Meanwhile, Hollywood films in the 1910s and 1920s tried to craft an American western mythology. Former lawmen such as Wyatt Earp and Charlie Siringo came to California to sell their stories and their authenticity. Although he joined the agency after witnessing the Haymarket bombing in hopes of battling political anarchism, Siringo soon became one of the "cowboy detectives" of the agency's Denver office (under the supervision of McParlan). As such, he was involved in many of the agency's murky western cases of political disputes, land grabs, cattle thefts, and labor wars. He was also McParlan's bodyguard in Boise during the Steunenberg trials. Yet "Charlie Siringo" was also a kind of fictional character crafted by Siringo through a constant rewriting of his autobiography. Siringo was in Chicago in 1886 to sell his first autobiography, *A Texas Cowboy; or, Fifteen Years on the Hurricane Deck of a Spanish Pony*, which described his time as a cowboy and his acquaintance with Billy the Kid. Over the next decades, Siringo would continue to reshape and resell his life story, including *A Cowboy Detective: A True Story of Twenty-Two Years with a World-Famous Detective Agency* and its vitriolic sequel, *Two Evil Isms: Pinkertonism and Anarchism by a Cowboy Detective Who Knows as He Spent Twenty-Two Years in the Inner Circle of Pinkerton's National Detective Agency*. To recover from the personal economic disaster that was *Two Evil Isms* (blocked by the Pinkerton agency, Siringo had decided to pay for publication himself), Siringo moved to Los Angeles to rework his history of Billy the Kid. While there, Siringo befriended "cowboy" actors William James and William Hart, along with storyteller Will Rogers; all three were drawn to Siringo's western "authenticity." Siringo even lent an air of authority to Hart's 1925 film *Tumbleweeds* by serving as a consultant. In the meantime, Siringo had managed to republish his earlier autobiographies (with the blocked Pinkerton material replaced by Siringo's "history" of western bad men) as *Riata and Spurs, the Story of a Lifetime Spent in the Saddle as Cowboy and Ranger*. When Hollywood reinvented the mythology of the American cowboy, Siringo was there.

The political and cultural transformations of the 1930s changed these reputations, however. Following the public embarrassment of the La Follette hearings, the Pinkerton agency again opened its files to a sympathetic writer who might redeem their public standing. Beginning in 1940, true crime writer Alan Hynd wrote a series of short tales taken from the Pinkerton files. These stories skipped the more controversial aspects of the Pinkerton past; there were none about the James gang, the Reno brothers, or Homestead. Instead, Hynd focused on murder, bank robberies, insurance fraud, and racetrack corruption. In Hynd's telling Pinkerton operatives were not official agents of the state, nor did they usurp the power of the state. "When the Pinkertons are called in on a major criminal case, they always work in close cooperation, never in opposition, with the public officials who are charged with solution of the crime," he stressed. "The entrance of the Agency into a public crime picture does not imply failure on the part of those officials in whose jurisdiction the crime has been committed"; instead, the Pinkertons, according to Hynd, brought unique abilities, manpower, and experience that only assisted the local authorities.[9]

Moreover, "Pinkerton detectives, or operatives, as they are called within the organization, all have one thing in common—personal integrity," Hynd declared.

"The rules for the conduct of an ethical detective agency, drawn up and laid down by the Scotch-American a century ago, are faithfully followed by every Pinkerton operative today." Such rules included not only the standard concerns of avoiding rewards, divorce cases, and issues of political corruption but also the new decree that the Pinkerton agency "will not investigate lawful activities of labor unions or supply strike guards." Any agency investigation, Hynd concluded, "whether it be on behalf of a private individual or in cooperation with official peace-enforcement authorities, must be carried out within a rigid framework of ethics laid down by the Agency's founder." This structure, however, did not hamper the success of the agency. "The Pinkertons, like the Northwest Mounted Police," he reiterated, "always get their man."[10]

Hynd's history tried to distance the agency from both its labor-breaking past and Hollywood's image of the western Pinkerton agent. In the film *Days of Jesse James* (1939), for instance, Roy Rogers protects the unfairly accused James against an unscrupulous railroad detective; yet, the following year in *Colorado*, Rogers played a moral Pinkerton agent bringing federal authority to the western territory. Part of this ambiguity stems from the fact that midcentury westerns borrowed heavily from the story lines of dime novels. Nowhere was this more prevalent than in the celluloid persona of Jesse James. The 1939 film *Jesse James*, starring Tyrone Power as Jesse and Henry Fonda as Frank, opens with a railroad agent forcing Missouri farmers to sell their land to the railroad. When the James brothers refuse and stand up to the agent, he returns with the infamous fire bomb and throws it into the home. It is this action, set early in the film, that triggers the life of crime, revenge, and banditry for the James brothers. And of course, within the Robin Hood tales of Jesse James, the Pinkertons never get their man.[11]

While trying to counter the romantic portrayals of bandits, Hynd's book also tried to stress the patriotism of the agency by reprinting in its entirety Robert Pinkerton's official response to Pearl Harbor. "Our country is at war," he wrote; "the undivided will of the whole people now is to contribute whatever is necessary to fight the war." Because of the importance of industrial factories to the war effort, their protection was a vital necessity. "The Agency will receive many calls for such protection," Pinkerton assumed; "whether employed alone or as a supplement to other protection services, the protection we will furnish can only be regarded as a necessary part of the national war effort." Considering that in the 1940 presidential campaign Wendell Willkie had to deny accusations that, while he was president of the power company Commonwealth & Southern, he and his subsidiaries had spent thousands on Pinkerton guards and spies, Robert Pinkerton's task of realigning the actions of his agency to the interests of the state was substantial.[12]

Robert, who would oversee this reinvention of the agency, had taken over the family business in 1930 at the age of 26. The company regained some of its public acceptance by providing security for industrial plants during the Second World War, and slowly the agency did away with its capacity for criminal detection in order to focus instead on security services. This transformation and reinvention was capped by the agency's name change in 1965 to Pinkerton's Inc. Two years later, Pinkerton resigned as president and became chairman of the board of the now public company. *Time* magazine noted that the company drew a high price per share owing to the "fact that the agency, presently known as Pinkerton's Inc., is profiting from the growing demand for unblinking private police services." Revenues were up at the agency, but that owed "less to derring-do involving rustlers and train robbers than to routine protection services for industrial plants and exhibitions." While this was a far cry from the high-profile protection of Lincoln or the pursuit of Jesse James, it was also a long way from Homestead, the "tarnished spot on the Pinks' badge of honor." "Still sensitive about those years," *Time* noted, "Pinkerton's Inc. today turns down labor-relations cases as quickly as it does divorces."[13] In 1967, Robert Pinkerton's death ended familial control of the agency.

Robert's death came right in the middle of yet another cultural reinvention of the agency. During the 1950s, Cold War paranoia and fear of social breakdown spurred the cultural return of the western lawman, including Pinkertons; for instance, Randolph Scott infiltrated the Reno gang in *Rage at Dawn* (1955). Yet bandits like the Reno brothers could still be the heroes of films, such as *Love Me Tender* (1956; with Elvis Presley as naïve Clint Reno).[14] However, as Cold War anxiety gave way in the 1960s to romantic countercultural banditry, Pinkerton agents became the relentless force of repression and law in, for example, *Butch Cassidy and the Sundance Kid*, *The Great Northfield Raid*, *The Train Robbers*, and *The Outlaw Josey Wales*. To counter such films, the Pinkerton agency again chose an author, this time New York journalist James Horan, to document their exploits. While "we have received over the years many requests from authors and editors to examine these records," wrote Robert Pinkerton in the preface to Horan's book, "we have refrained from allowing anyone outside of the agency to examine the complete files." "In the last few years, however, numerous motion pictures, television shows, books and magazine articles on the life of the Jameses and Youngers and other Western outlaws have appeared," Pinkerton continued; "Many of them glorified the bandits as misjudged Robin Hoods. To offset this erroneous conception, we decided to open our complete century-old files dealing with Western outlaws for the first time to Mr. Horan." "Although we have cooperated with him to the fullest extent," Pinkerton assured the reader, "Mr. Horan's conclusions are his own."[15]

Despite this disclaimer, Pinkerton had little to worry about regarding Horan's conclusions. The book explicitly set out to counter the myths and legends of the bandits and to show the gangs as ruthless and lawless killers. "Romance and legend aside, it is best now that our desperate men of the Middle Border be introduced," he wrote about the James brothers; "For sixteen years they will thunder across the West in America's greatest crime wave; they will rob trains, stagecoaches and banks; they will murder and plunder; they will be merciless and ruthless; they will halt a civilization, wreck businesses, and drive innocent men to ruin; they will defy their own government; they will kill and be killed; in their own lifetime they will become legends." Only an organization such as the Pinkertons could stop such ruthless men as Jesse James and Butch Cassidy. Yet for all of Horan's protests, Jesse and Frank James remained the folk heroes and social bandits of American popular culture.[16]

While American film embraced the outlaw, reactionary politics rethought the Pinkerton agent. By the 1970s, fear of crime and violent political protest led to increased employment opportunities for Pinkerton's Inc. "Some of the radical young complain about their revolution being co-opted by the Establishment," noted one news report. "But on the other hand, countering revolution head-on has stimulated equal amounts of Establishment enterprise," it continued. "Pinkerton's, the venerable private constabulary that hunted down Butch Cassidy and was McClellan's private OSS in the Civil War, is marketing the new Pinkerton Bomb Blanket to smother incendiary bombs."[17] Not only had the Pinkertons come to battle the radicals of the New Left, but they were once again an integral part of the law and order of the "Establishment." Indeed, a significant percentage of the business and funding for private security forces in the late 1960s and early 1970s came directly from state and federal governments. In 1967, for instance, the governor of Florida contracted with the Wackenhut Corporation, founded by former FBI agent George Wackenhut in 1954, to investigate, in Wackenhut's words, "everyone and anyone who needs investigating."[18]

Such use of Pinkertons and other private security agencies certainly seemed to violate the 1893 Anti-Pinkerton Act, which forbad the federal government from contracting with the Pinkertons or "similar agencies."[19] The most thorough reevaluation of the act came in 1963 during a congressional proposal to repeal the anti-Pinkerton law, which passed the Senate but failed in the House. In these debates, Congress concluded that the original Anti-Pinkerton Act concerned intrusive work in labor disputes and did not mean to prohibit the employment of Pinkerton guards for security purposes. In its discussion in 1963, Congress quoted the author of the original 1893 bill, who said that "nobody objects to the legitimate use of Pinkerton detectives as such. It is their use as armed guards that is objected to, and it is the sending of their armed guards from one state into another that is objected to."[20]

The courts borrowed this same logic in the first legal revision to the Anti-Pinkerton Act. In *Jacob Weinberger v. Equifax* (1977), the Fifth Court of Appeals determined that to make sense of the Anti-Pinkerton Act it must consider the Pinkerton agency as it was in 1892 and not how it existed in 1977.[21] Thus, the court felt compelled to return to the political context of the 1890s. "The Anti-Pinkerton Act is an expression of legislative frustration," the court concluded. Because "the nascent labor movement was increasingly involved in sometimes violent confrontations with factory owners over wages and working conditions," owner's efforts at legal remedies "proved fruitless," and local police were "ineffectual," capitalists had little choice but to engage "the Pinkerton Agency to supply large bodies of armed men to discourage strikers from interfering with the orderly operation of business." What Congress wanted to do, the court determined, was "ban the employment of Pinkertons as a private mercenary force," yet it "concluded that it lacked the power to enact such a ban and looked to the states to control Pinkerton conduct." Instead, Congress passed the Anti-Pinkerton Act, which began as an amendment preventing the government from "contracting with entities that employed 'Pinkerton detectives or any other association of men as armed guards' and . . . from employing the Pinkerton Detective Agency or any similar agency." Although the Senate in 1893 rejected the wording of "armed guards," the Fifth Court of Appeals in 1977 took this as evidence that "Congress clearly generally intended to prohibit employment" by the government of the Pinkerton Agency as then constituted, or any similar agency." The original amendment convinced the court that "the purpose of the Act and the legislative history reveal that an organization was 'similar' to the Pinkerton Detective Agency only if it offered for hire mercenary, quasi-military forces as strikebreakers and armed guards." Thus, the court concluded that "an organization is not 'similar' to the (quondam) Pinkerton Detective Agency unless it offers quasi-military armed forces for hire. Because Weinberger fails to allege that Equifax provides so much as an armed guard, much less an armed quasi-military unit, Equifax's employment is not illegal under the Anti-Pinkerton Act." After consideration of the ruling, the Government Accountability Office agreed that government contracts could indeed go to investigative firms (such as Equifax) so long as they did not constitute a "quasi-military armed force."[22]

In the twenty-first century, the close connections between Blackwater and the federal government led some to claim that government contracts with Blackwater violated the 1893 Anti-Pinkerton Act. In June of 2007, the courts briefly revisited the Anti-Pinkerton Act when a federal judge temporarily halted the awarding of a government contract for intelligence and security in Iraq to Blackwater. The suit argued that the contracts violated the Anti-Pinkerton Act because Blackwater was clearly a military force. However, the court dismissed the complaint because it found that the plaintiff had no standing as an interested party (they were not competing for the same contracts) and thus had no legal standing to sue. This also meant that the court did not have to actually decide the issue of whether the contracts did or did not violate the Anti-Pinkerton Act.[23]

Even as the courts distinguished between nineteenth-century Pinkertons and modern private firms, the underlying assumption was that the Pinkertons of the Gilded Age were indeed a quasi-military armed force employed by capital to crush labor. Given this new cultural ethos, not only was the Pinkerton mythology of the west open for reinterpretation, but so was its crowning achievement of uncovering the Molly Maguires. Literary descriptions of the Molly Maguires, outside of a few morally ambiguous dime novels, followed the same story line that Franklin Gowen had laid out and Arthur Conan Doyle had followed. The Mollies were, the narrative went, a vast and dangerous criminal conspiracy driven to acts of violence based on their Irish ethnicity and old-world hatreds. In such a tale the Pinkerton detective remained the hero. Despite academic reconsiderations of the Mollies in the 1930s which placed them in the context of Pennsylvania labor conflicts, this remained the popular thinking about the Mollies well through the mid-1960s, as in the 1964 popular book *Lament for the Molly Maguires*.[24] For his part Alan Hynd would refer to the "notorious Mollie Maguires" as "an organization that was, among other things, a sort of an early-day Murder, Incorporated."[25]

However, the countercultural ethos of the late 1960s challenged this interpretation. The 1970 film *The Molly Maguires* embraced far more of the nuances and contradictions of the Pennsylvania coalfields; neither Richard Harris's James

McParlan nor Sean Connery's Jack Kehoe is fully hero or villain.[26] In 1979, nine years after the film, supposed ringleader Kehoe received a posthumous pardon from the state of Pennsylvania. A plaque outside the Schuylkill County prison in Pottsville, erected in 1980, declared that the pardon reflected "the judgment of many historians that the trials and executions were part of a repression directed against the fledgling mineworker's union of that historic period." In 2006 a new plaque commissioned by the Pennsylvania Historical and Museum Commission updated the interpretation. "On June 21, 1877, four 'Molly Maguires,' an alleged secret society of Irish mineworkers, were hanged here," it reads. "Pinkerton detective James McParlan's testimony led to the convictions for violent crimes against the coal industry, yet the facts of the labor, class, and ethnic conflicts, even the existence of the organization, remain contested." Seemingly, the last pillar of Pinkerton mythology had collapsed.

In 1999, Swedish security conglomerate Securitas bought the Pinkerton company and merged it with its other security offerings; the following year, the firm also acquired Pinkerton's longtime rival the Burns International Detective Agency. Within its "government services" division, Securitas continues to use both the Pinkerton name and logo; it also proudly traces its history back to Allan Pinkerton. By the end of the century, the Pinkerton agency had ceased to have deep political implications. Yet public opinion was still unsure about both private security and the security state. When Ward Churchill declared the US Patriot Act of 2001 the apex of political policing, he traced the origins of this power not just to Hoover's FBI but back to Pinkerton's National Detective Agency.[27] The FBI became, he argued, "state-sponsored Pinkertons." Another exposé of immigration practices would complain of abuses by union-busting "Pinkertons" within the Department of Homeland Security.[28] Being called a "Pinkerton" remained an accusation. Moreover, within American popular culture, the Pinkerton remains a mercenary thug; in HBO's recent drama *Deadwood* even ruthless antihero Al Swearengen fears the diabolical violence of the Pinkertons. "I don't like the Pinkertons," he declares. "They're muscle for the bosses, as if the bosses ain't got enough edge."[29]

Rewriting the Pinkertons

All of this leads us back to the question posed in *Butch Cassidy and the Sundance Kid*: Who are these guys? Gilded Age authors wrote often of the agency, and in the twentieth century writers tended to repeat the same assumptions and story lines about the agency. Midcentury writers mined the company archives (with agency approval) to tell thrilling tales of bandits, lawmen, and true crime. Newer popular biographies of Pinkerton have repeated this same kind of either simple admiration for Pinkerton and his agents (and scorn for their adversaries) or dismissal. Some popular histories, such as Jay Bonansinga's *Pinkerton's War*, heap praise on Pinkerton's wartime service; others, such as Gavin Mortimer's *Double Death*, have nothing but scorn for the bumbling spymaster. The same contradictions exist for the postwar legacies of Pinkerton agents and guards. A 1996 biographer of Pinkerton declared that "the popular image which lingers to this day is that the Pinkertons were strike-breakers when, in fact, they were acting within the law in the protection of industrial premises against a violent mob ten times their number." Furthermore, he concluded that while "today the Molly Maguires are often held up as martyrs of the labor movement . . . the plain fact is that the Molly Maguires were gangsters and hoodlums without any redeeming features." Yet Mahanoy City, Pennsylvania, recently dedicated the Molly Maguire historical park, which includes a statue of a condemned and hooded miner unjustly convicted. Authors have been surprised to find the contrast between the valiant lawmen presented in Pinkerton's own self-told tales and, as another recent biographer put it, "the larger legacy of the Pinkerton organization (not to mention the sour taste that the name leaves in the mouths of many of my lefty friends)."[30]

These contradictions were and are essential to the meaning of the Pinkerton agency, and as often as they confuse biographers and hagiographers, they have fascinated the American public and its historians. They took on so many different forms and meanings and existed in so many different genres that a single version of the Pinkerton tale is impossible to discern. They were and remain the apotheosis of industrial violence precisely because their origin, impact, and benevolence or malevolence were uncertain. They lurked in Victorian parlors, city streets, western landscapes, mill towns, rail yards, and other diverse places because industrialization (and the violence connected to industrialization) impacted so many different places. The mills of Homestead, Pennsylvania, the rail yards of Albany, New York, coal mines in Pennsylvania and silver mines in Idaho, the railroads of postwar Missouri, the streets of postfire Chicago, the immigrant neighborhoods of industrial cities, the Canadian border, the cattle ranches of Wyoming, and the political terrain of Arizona were all spaces that Pinkerton agents patrolled. "The history of all places which had a rapid growth is full of incidents of crime," Allan Pinkerton wrote in 1876 to justify his agency's employment. Any locations "where the incoming population has been of such a mixed character, and opportunities for criminal deed so numerous as to sometimes create an epidemic of wrong-doing" were spaces of Pinkerton employ. A place with a history of rapid growth and with an incoming population of a mixed character is a pretty apt description of the United States in the Gilded Age, which made it an age of and for the Pinkertons.[31]

Notes

INTRODUCTION: Pinkerton's National Detective Agency, or heroes and villains of the Gilded Age

1. Testimony of Andrew C. Johnson (first appearance), July 24, 1886, in Illinois v. August Spies et al. trial transcript no. 1 (Chicago History Museum); Testimony of Andrew C. Johnson (first appearance resumed), July 26, 1886, in Illinois v. August Spies et al. Timothy Messer-Kruse offers a correction to the long-assumed nature of the trial as presented by Paul Avrich and others. The prosecution did provide evidence and followed the standard procedures for courtrooms of their time. Still, it was the testimony of undercover agents that tied it all together. Timothy Messer-Kruse, *The Trial of the Haymarket Anarchists: Terrorism and Justice in the Gilded Age* (Basingstoke: Palgrave Macmillan, 2011); Paul Avrich, *The Haymarket Tragedy* (Princeton, NJ: Princeton University Press, 1986).

2. Illinois governor Roger Oglesby commuted the death sentences of Samuel Fielden and Michael Schwab to life sentences. Louis Ligg committed suicide by triggering a blasting cap in his mouth. George Engel, Adolph Fischer, Albert Parsons, and August Spies were executed.

3. *Reasons for Pardoning Fielden, Neebe and Schwab by John P. Altgeld, Governor of Illinois* (Pamphlet, Chicago Historical Society, 1893).

4. The company's official name was "Pinkerton's National Detective Agency." Both advocates and critics would refer to both the company (singular) and its agents (plural) as "Pinkertons." Because I study the history of the firm, its public reputation, and the intersections of its actions and meanings, I have chosen to use the terms interchangeably.

5. According to Michel Foucault, surveillance "should be considered a faceless gaze . . . that transforms the entire social body into a field of vision . . . thousands of eyes placed everywhere, everywhere attentive and always alert, a long hierarchical network." As cited in John Merriman, *Police Stories: Building the French State, 1815–1851* (Oxford: Oxford University Press, 2005). The unblinking eye is also similar to the logo of the abolitionist "Wide Awakes" of the 1850s, a party with which self-proclaimed abolitionist Pinkerton should have been familiar.

6. The "Wide Awakes" were a loosely organized set of militias connected to the Republican Party during the 1860 election. Young men who joined the Wide Awakes bought matching capes, caps, and torches and marched under banners that prominently displayed an unblinking eye. Given his self-proclaimed abolitionism, Allan Pinkerton certainly must have been familiar with the iconography of the Wide Awakes.

7. US Congress, House, Judiciary Committee, "Investigation of the Employment of Pinkerton Detectives in Connection with the Labor Troubles at Homestead, Pa.," House Report 2447, 52nd Congress, 2nd Session, 1892, 222; *Illustrated American*, July 16, 1892.

8. The idea of a cultural logic of capitalism comes from Fredric Jameson. I apply the idea of a cultural logic of capitalism to the nineteenth century instead of the late capitalism of the twentieth century. Lawrence Levine suggests how we might look at the folklore of an industrial society. James Scott shows us how to read the "hidden transcripts" of power (the things left unsaid from both the powerful and the subaltern). Fredric Jameson, *Postmodernism; or, the Cultural Logic of Late Capitalism* (Durham, NC: Duke University Press, 1992); Lawrence Levine, "The Folklore of Industrial Society: Popular Culture and Its Audiences," *American Historical Review* 97, no. 5 (1992): 1369–99; James C. Scott, *Domination and the Arts of Resistance: Hidden Transcripts* (New Haven, CT: Yale University Press, 1990).

9. If one definition of "folklore" is a recurring tale with a recognizable structure that can still be adapted and changed, then the story of the Pinkertons is certainly folkloric. See Richard Dorson, ed., *Handbook of American Folklore* (Bloomington: Indiana University Press, 1986).

10. Hayden White, *Tropics of Discourse: Essays in Cultural Criticism* (Baltimore: Johns Hopkins University Press, 1986); Hayden White, *Metahistory: The Historical Imagination of Nineteenth-Century Europe* (Baltimore: Johns Hopkins University Press, 1973).

11. Eric Rauchway talks of Kipling's compliment and the meaning of Roosevelt in *Murdering McKinley: The Making of Theodore Roosevelt's America* (New York: Hill & Wang, 2003).

12. Included among these mysteries about Allan Pinkerton are his activities (and maybe exile) as a Chartist, the persistent and unfounded rumors that his brother helped build the agency (and Allan wrote him out of the fortune and fame), fabricated tales of his father's career as a Scottish policeman who was severely hurt while putting down a Chartist riot, the lurid possibilities of an illicit affair between Pinkerton and agent Kate Warne, etc. Part of this came from Pinkerton's own capacity for self-invention, and part came from the family's tendency to repeat the same names across generations. Allan had a father (William), brothers (William and Robert), sons (William and Robert), grandsons (William, Robert, and Allan), and great-grandsons who all shared names. Jesse James biographers in the 1870s, for instance, often misidentified William Pinkerton as Allan's brother instead of his son.

13. The Chartists were a British working-class movement most active between 1838 and 1848 which demanded electoral reform, including expanded suffrage, the secret ballot, the removal of property requirements for Parliament, and annual parliamentary elections. Allan Pinkerton left Scotland in 1842 as part of a large-scale emigration of Chartists, liberals, and free thinkers who fled Europe in the 1840s. Many of these emigrants chose the United States as their destination, infusing it with new radical politics that would combine with and transform many of the reform movements of antebellum America.

14. Originating from southern apologists almost immediately after the Civil War and gaining widespread acceptance by the turn of the century through the work of southern historians, the Lost Cause was an ideology that redefined the origins, meanings, and outcomes of the Civil War. In this telling, the benevolent institution of slavery was not a primary factor in the war; rather, southern states were defending states' rights against tyranny. Southern generals, especially Robert Lee, were models of cavalier gentlemen who, despite their tactical brilliance, were overwhelmed by the sheer numbers of their much more vulgar Union counterparts. Despite the loss of the war, the ideology declared, the south had been right to secede and southern soldiers had proven themselves valorous, chivalrous, and brave.

15. Alfred D. Chandler, *The Visible Hand: The Managerial Revolution in American Business* (Cambridge, MA: Harvard University Press, 1993).

16. Karl Polanyi, *The Great Transformation: The Political and Economic Origins of Our Time* (Boston: Beacon Press, 1971).

17. Jean-Christophe Agnew, "Anonymous History," in *Capitalism Takes Command: The Social Transformation of Nineteenth-Century America*, ed. Michael Zakim and Gary J. Kornblith (Chicago: University of Chicago Press, 2011).

18. The debate over the role of government in allowing monopoly capitalism to rise (or in being incapable of stopping its abuses) largely begins with Wallace Farnham, "The Weakened Spring of Government: A Study in Nineteenth-Century American History," *American Historical Review* 68, no. 3 (1963): 662–80.

19. Brian Balogh, *A Government Out of Sight: The Mystery of National Authority in Nineteenth-Century America* (Cambridge: Cambridge University Press, 2009); Max Weber, "Politics as a Vocation," in *From Max Weber: Essays in Sociology*, ed. H. H. Gerth and C. Wright Mills (Oxford: Oxford University Press, 1944).

20. Merriman, *Police Stories*.

21. One of the agents of the Special Irish Branch was William Melville, whose career has several parallels to Pinkerton's. He rose quickly to the top of the Special Branch, largely on the reputation of exposing the Walsall anarchist plot—a conspiracy that Melville and other agents probably constructed themselves. He mysteriously retired in 1903, only to reappear as one of the chief architects of the newly formed British national security agency MI5.

22. Benedict Anderson, *Imagined Communities: Reflections on the Origins and Spread of Nationalism* (New York: Verso Books, 1983).

23. "Companies Use Immigration Crackdown to Turn a Profit," *New York Times*, September 28, 2011.

24. Walter Johnson, *Soul by Soul: Life inside the Antebellum Slave Market* (Cambridge, MA: Harvard University Press, 1999).

25. While this quote began to circulate as early as the 1890s, its attribution to Gould was solidified by Philip Foner, *History of the Labor Movement in the United States*, vol. 2 (New York: International, 1975), 50.

26. Charles Francis Bourke, "The Story of the Pinkertons; the History of the Most Remarkable Detective Agency in the World, Taken from Original Sources and Now Told Comprehensively for the First Time," *Leslie's Monthly Magazine* 59, no. 6 (April 1905).

CHAPTER ONE: In which Allan Pinkerton creates his agency

1. Allan Pinkerton, *Spy of the Rebellion: Being a True History of the Spy System of the United States Army during the Late Rebellion* (New York: G. W. Carleton, 1883), 156.

2. "Detective Pinkerton's Last Case," *Harper's Weekly*, March 30, 1872.

3. Lorien Foote, *The Gentlemen and the Roughs: Violence, Honor, and Manhood in the Union Army* (New York: New York University Press, 2010).

4. On self-promotion and the "peddler," see Jackson Lears, *Fables of Abundance: A Cultural History of Advertising in America* (New York: Basic Books, 1994).

5. Paul Boyer, *Urban Masses and Moral Order in America, 1880–1920* (Cambridge, MA: Harvard University Press, 1978); Eric Monkkonen, *Police in Urban America, 1860–1920* (Cambridge: Cambridge University Press, 2004).

6. The concept of the flâneur stems from the poetry of Charles Baudelaire and Walter Benjamin's interpretations of this poetry. Walter Benjamin, *The Writer of Modern Life: Essays on Charles Baudelaire* (Cambridge, MA: Belknap Press, 2006).

7. Frank Morn, *The Eye That Never Sleeps: A History of the Pinkerton National Detective Agency* (Bloomington: Indiana University Press, 1982).

8. Allan Pinkerton, *Professional Thieves and the Detectives* (New York: G. W. Dillingham, 1880), 54.

9. "Astounding Post-Office Robbery," *New York Times*, July 7, 1855.

10. Morn, *Eye That Never Sleeps*.

11. *Chicago Daily Tribune*, June 24, 1857; "Railway Embezzling," *Railway Times*, February 6, 1864; Morn, *Eye That Never Sleeps*.

12. Allan Pinkerton, *The Expressman and the Detective* (Chicago: W. B. Keen, Cooke, 1874); "The Express Robber; Story of His Detection and Conviction," *New York Times*, July 4, 1860; "The Adams Express Robbery," *New York Times*, February 6, 1864.

13. Allan Pinkerton, *History and Evidence of the Passage of Abraham Lincoln from Harrisburg, Pa., to Washington, D.C., on the 22d and 23d of February, 1861* (Chicago: Republican Print, 1868); A. K. McClure, "The Night at Harrisburg; A Reminiscence of Lincoln's Journey to Washington in 1861," *McClure's Magazine* 5, no. 1 (June 1895): 91; Cleveland Moffett, "How

Allan Pinkerton Thwarted the First Plot to Assassinate Lincoln; Stories from the Archives of the Pinkerton Detective Agency," *McClure's Magazine* 3, no. 6 (November 1894): 519.

14. Pinkerton, *History and Evidence.*

15. *New York Times,* February 25, 1861.

16. *New York Times,* February 25 and 27, 1861.

17. George Brinton McClellan, *Report on the Organization and Campaigns of the Army of the Potomac* (New York: Sheldon, 1864), 119–20. He wrote, "I organized a secret service force under Mr. EJ Allen, a very experienced and efficient person," in use until "I was relieved of command."

18. Rose O'Neal Greenhow, *My Imprisonment and the First Year of Abolition Rule at Washington* (London: Spottiswoode, 1863), 204.

19. Most of Pinkerton's war work during this period was the much less glamorous job of watching ferry crossings of the Potomac.

20. There was some controversy over exactly how and from whom the Richmond authorities learned of Webster's double life. Pinkerton was convinced that Lewis had confessed his role and exposed both Webster and Lawton. For the remainder of his life Lewis insisted that he had done no such thing, but rather Pinkerton's hubris of sending Lewis, a recognizable agent, into Richmond to make contact with Webster had tipped off the authorities. On the life and writings of Pryce Lewis, see Gavin Mortimer, *Double Death: The True Story of Pryce Lewis, the Civil War's Most Daring Spy* (New York: Walker, 2010).

21. Edwin Fischel, *Secret War for the Union: The Untold Story of Military Intelligence in the Civil War* (Boston: Houghton Mifflin, 2006).

22. Pinkerton details much of his wartime work in the 1884 book *Spy of the Rebellion,* paying close attention to the work of Timothy Webster and other spies in and around Richmond, Washington, and Baltimore. In this work Pinkerton also tries to defend McClellan's Peninsula Campaign and his own troop estimates during that campaign. Mostly the book reads like romantic fiction, with Webster as the grand hero of multiple adventures infiltrating secret societies, wooing southern women, and defying rebels. Pinkerton himself admits in the book that since his files burned in the 1871 Chicago Fire, many of the anecdotes and details are from memory.

23. Parmenas Taylor Turnley, *Memoir of Parmenas Taylor Turnley, in Reminiscences of Parmenas Taylor Turnley, from the Cradle to Three-Score and Ten: By Himself, from Diaries Kept from Early Boyhood. With a Brief Glance Backward Three Hundred and Fifty Years at Progenitors and Ancestral Lineage* (Chicago: Donohue & Henneberry, 1892), 383.

24. The records of vouchers for Secret Service fund monies demonstrate that the vast majority of monies went to Allan Pinkerton and L. C. Baker and nearly all the Secret Service funds were spent by the Army of the Potomac in 1861–1863. Record Group 110 [Provost Marshal General Bureau Records], Entry 95 Accounts of Secret Service Agents, 1861–1870, National Archives Building, Washington, DC. My thanks to Stephen Towne, who shared this information from his own work on wartime espionage in the middle west. See also Stephen E. Towne, *Surveillance and Spies in the Civil War: Exposing Confederate Conspiracies in America's Heartland* (Athens: Ohio University Press, 2015).

25. Benson John Lossing, *Pictorial History of the Civil War in the United States of America,* vol. 1 (Philadelphia: G. W. Childs, 1866), 278–81.

26. Benson John Lossing, *Pictorial History of the Civil War in the United States of America,* vol. 2 (Hartford, CT: T. Belknap, 1868), 147–49; Benson John Lossing, *Pictorial History of the Civil War in the United States of America,* vol. 3 (Hartford, CT: T. Belknap, 1868), 565–67.

27. Issac A. Arnold, "The Baltimore Plot to Assassinate Abraham Lincoln," *Harper's New Monthly Magazine* 37, no. 217 (June 1868): 123–28.

28. Ward Hill Lamon, *The Life of Abraham Lincoln from His Birth to His Inauguration* (Boston: James R. Osgood, 1872), 512–27.

29. Lossing, *Pictorial History*, vol. 1; Pinkerton, *History and Evidence*; "Detective Pinkerton," *Harper's New Monthly Magazine* 47 (October 1873): 720–27.

30. "Detective Pinkerton," *Harper's New Monthly Magazine* 47 (October 1873): 720–27.

31. Ibid.

32. *General Principles and Rules of Pinkerton's National Police Agency* (Chicago: Geo. H. Fergus, 1867), 5; copy in Library of Congress.

33. Ibid.

34. Pinkerton, *Expressman and the Detective*, 5–19.

35. Ibid., 24–30, 49.

36. Ibid., 94–96, 103. The idea that femininity was a set of limitations which some exceptional women could rise above, becoming nearly masculine, has a long history, stretching from Joan of Arc to Rosie the Riveter.

37. Ibid., 90, 157.

38. Mark Twain, *The Stolen White Elephant* (Boston: James R. Osgood, 1882), 17–19, 30.

39. Allan Pinkerton, *The Somnambulist and the Detectives* (New York: G. W. Carleton, 1874); Allan Pinkerton, *Claude Melnotte as a Detective and Other Stories* (Chicago: W. B. Keen, Cooke, 1875); Allan Pinkerton, *The Model Town and the Detectives* (New York: G. W. Carleton, 1876); Allan Pinkerton, *The Molly Maguires and the Detectives* (New York: G. W. Carleton, 1877); Allan Pinkerton, *The Spiritualists and the Detectives* (New York: G. W. Carleton, 1877); Allan Pinkerton, *Criminal Reminiscences and Detective Stories* (New York: G. W. Carleton, 1878); Allan Pinkerton, *Strikers, Communists, Tramps, and Detectives* (New York: G. W. Carleton, 1878); Allan Pinkerton, *Gypsies and the Detectives* (New York: G. W. Carleton, 1879); Allan Pinkerton, *The Mississippi Outlaws and the Detectives* (New York: G. W. Carleton, 1879); Allan Pinkerton, *Bucholz and the Detectives* (New York: G. W. Carleton, 1880); Allan Pinkerton, *Professional Thieves and the Detectives* (New York: G. W. Carleton, 1880); Allan Pinkerton, *The Railroad Forger and the Detectives* (New York: G. W. Carleton, 1881); Allan Pinkerton, *Bank Robbers and the Detectives* (New York: G. W. Carleton, 1882); Allan Pinkerton, *The Burglar's Fate and the Detectives* (New York: G. W. Carleton, 1883); Allan Pinkerton, *Spy of the Rebellion* (New York: G. W. Carleton, 1883); Allan Pinkerton, *A Double Life and the Detective* (New York: G. W. Carleton, 1884); Allan Pinkerton, *Thirty Years a Detective* (New York: G. W. Carleton, 1884).

40. "Mr. Cummings," *National Police Gazette*, January 8, 1887. Other examples of the *National Police Gazette*'s coverage of Pinkerton cases include "Shocking Case Indeed," *National Police Gazette*, August 2, 1879; "Notorious Philly Crock in London," *National Police Gazette*, September 6, 1879; "Our Illustrations," *National Police Gazette*, April 2, 1881; "Swindler and Bigamist," *National Police Gazette*, September 3, 1881; "William A. Pinkerton," *National Police Gazette*, October 29, 1881; "Tot Dunkle's Capture," *National Police Gazette*, November 4, 1882; "Murder Will Out," *National Police Gazette*, February 2, 1884. On the origins of the magazine, see Guy Reel, *The National Police Gazette and the Making of the Modern American Man, 1879–1906* (Basingstoke: Palgrave Macmillan, 2006).

41. Pinkerton, *Criminal Reminiscences*.

42. Ward Hill Lamon, *Recollections of Abraham Lincoln, 1847–1865*, ed. Dorothy Lamon Teillard (Washington, DC: A. C. McClurg, 1895).

43. For examples of Lincoln biographies (which are legion), see Josiah Gilbert Holland, *Life of Abraham Lincoln* (Springfield, MA: Gurdon Bill, 1866); Frank Crosby, *Life of Abraham Lincoln* (Philadelphia: John E. Potter, 1865); William Cunningham Gray, *Life of Abraham Lincoln* (Cincinnati: Western Tract & Book Society, 1869); Joseph Hartnell Barrett, *Life*

of Abraham Lincoln (Cincinnati: Moore, Wilstach & Baldwin, 1864); Ida Tarbell, *Life of Abraham Lincoln* (New York: S. S. McClure, 1895); Henry Ketcham, *Life of Abraham Lincoln* (New York: A. L. Burt, 1901).

44. "Detective Pinkerton," *Harper's New Monthly Magazine* 47 (October 1873): 720–27; Pinkerton's National Detective Agency Files, Library of Congress, box 23, folder 4.

CHAPTER TWO: In which Pinkerton Men become the antiheroes of the middle west

1. Herman Melville, *The Confidence-Man* (London: Longman, Brown, Green, Longmans, & Roberts, 1857), 9–10.

2. Allan Pinkerton, "Hard Life of the Detective," in *The Model Town and the Detectives* (New York: G. W. Carleton, 1876).

3. Richard Slotkin, *Regeneration through Violence: The Mythology of the American Frontier, 1600–1860* (Norman: University of Oklahoma Press, 1973).

4. On pioneer myths of the early nineteenth century, see John Mack Faragher, *Daniel Boone: The Life and Legend of an American Pioneer* (New York: Henry Holt, 1992); Howard Means, *Johnny Appleseed: The Man, the Myth and the American Story* (New York: Simon & Schuster, 2011).

5. By the late 1840 and 1850s, as possibilities for adventure and self-determination dwindled in Kentucky and Tennessee, men sought their futures in new frontiers such as California, Mexico, or, if in a filibustering mood, Nicaragua. Amy S. Greenberg, *Manifest Manhood and the Antebellum American Empire* (Cambridge: Cambridge University Press, 2005).

6. Allan Pinkerton, *The Mississippi Outlaws and the Detectives* (New York: G. W. Carleton, 1879).

7. There was a fifth brother, Clint, who, because he was never involved with the gang, was known as "Honest" Reno, and a sister, Laura, who did have close connections to her outlaw brothers. Cleveland Moffett, "The Destruction of the Reno Gang: Stories from the Archives of the Pinkerton Detective Agency," *McClure's Magazine* 4, no. 6 (May 1895): 549.

8. Ibid.

9. The location just outside of Seymour is still referred to as Hangman Crossing.

10. "Robbery of an Express Car on the Ohio and Mississippi Railroad," *New York Times*, September 30, 1867; "Adams Express Robbers Arrested," *New York Times*, October 21, 1866; "Attempt to Capture a Safe of the Adams Express Company on the Ohio and Mississippi Railroad," *New York Times*, July 13, 1868.

11. Allan Pinkerton, "Extradition Cases of Reno and Anderson," letter to editor of *Toronto Telegraph*, *New York Times* reprint, October 5, 1868.

12. "Lynch Law in Indiana," *New York Times*, July 24, 1868; "Express Robbers," *New York Times*, August 26, 1868; "Seymour Thieves," *New York Times*, July 25, 1868; "Lynch Law," *New York Times*, July 22, 1868; "The Seymour Express Robbery," *New York Times*, January 9, 1869.

13. Senate Bill 705, Bills and Resolutions, Senate, 40th Congress, 3rd Session, December 17, 1868.

14. Allan Pinkerton to George Bangs (Pinkerton Collection, Library of Congress); Frank Morn, *The Eye That Never Sleeps: A History of the Pinkerton National Detective Agency* (Bloomington: Indiana University Press, 1982), 78–79.

15. *Saint Louis Globe*, March 20, 1874; T. J. Stiles, *Jesse James: Last Rebel of the Civil War* (New York: Alfred Knopf, 2002), 257–58.

16. Stiles, *Jesse James*.

17. John Newman Edwards, *Shelby and His Men: Or the War in the West* (Cincinnati: Miami Printing, 1867); John Newman Edwards, *Shelby's Expedition to Mexico: An Unwritten Leaf of the War* (Kansas City: Kansas City Times Steam Book & Job Printing House, 1872); "A Traduced Gentleman: Mr. Jesse James, the Accomplished Outlaw, Comes to His Own Defense in the Public Prints," *New York Times*, July 20, 1875; "An Outlaw's Plea," *New York Times*, July 22, 1875.

18. E. J. Allen to Samuel Hardwicke, December 28, 1874, Pinkerton Papers; Stiles, *Jesse James*, 279.

19. Local rumor, often repeated in James biographies, declared that a pistol marked "P.G.G." (for Pinkerton Governmental Guard) was found. No such division of Pinkerton's ever existed, but the accusation tied Pinkerton's agency back to its time as the Union's Secret Service and tied the agency to the federal state overseeing Reconstruction.

20. *Nashville Republican Banner*, July 11, July 28, and August 4, 1875.

21. As early as 1876, some writers were already crafting the Younger brothers as outlaw heroes of the west. See, e.g., Augustus C. Appler, *The Guerrillas of the West; or, The Life, Character and Daring Exploits of the Younger Brothers* (St. Louis: Eureka, 1876).

22. John N. Edwards, *Noted Guerrillas; or, The Warfare of the Border* (St. Louis: W. S. Bryan, 1877).

23. R. T. Bradley, *Outlaws of the Border; or, The Lives of Frank and Jesse James* (St. Louis: J. W. Marsh, 1882); Joseph Dacus, *Life and Adventure of Frank and Jesse James: The Noted Western Outlaws* (St. Louis: W. S. Bryan, 1880); James William Buel, *The Border Outlaws: An Authentic and Thrilling History of the Most Noted Bandits of Ancient or Modern Times* (Cincinnati: Forshee & McMakin, 1882).

24. Bradley, *Outlaws of the Border*; Dacus, *Life and Adventure of Frank and Jesse James*; Buel, *Border Outlaws*.

25. Michael Denning, *Mechanic Accents: Dime Novels and Working-Class Culture* (New York: Verso Books, 1987); Richard Slotkin, *Gunfighter Nation: The Myth of the Frontier in Twentieth-Century America* (New York: Atheneum, 1992).

26. W. B. Lawson, *Jesse James, the Outlaw: A Narrative of the James Boys*, in *The Jesse James Stories: Original Narratives of the James Boys*, no. 1 (New York: Street & Smith, 1901).

27. William A. Pinkerton, "Highwaymen of the Railroad," *North American Review*, November 1893, 530.

28. Cleveland Moffett, "The Rock Island Express Robbery: Stories from the Archives of the Pinkerton Detective Agency," *McClure's Magazine* 4, no. 3 (February 1895): 245.

29. So successful was Allan Frank Pinkerton that many contemporaries and numerous historians since have assumed that Frank was one of Allan Pinkerton's sons and that the novels were a continuation of Allan's writings.

CHAPTER THREE: In which Pinkerton agents infiltrate secret societies

1. Allan Pinkerton, *The Model Town and the Detectives* (New York: G. W. Carleton, 1876).

2. Ibid.

3. The life of James McParland, who would go on to head the Pinkerton office in Denver and would reemerge several times in company folklore, is traced in Beau Riffenburgh, *Pinkerton's Great Detective: The Amazing Life and Times of James McParland* (New York: Viking, 2013).

4. Allan Pinkerton, *Strikers, Communists, Tramps, and Detectives* (New York: G. W. Carleton, 1878).

5. Mark C. Carnes, *Secret Ritual and Manhood in Victorian America* (New Haven, CT: Yale University Press, 1989).

6. Allan Pinkerton, *The Molly Maguires and the Detectives* (New York: G. W. Carleton, 1877), 13–14.

7. Ibid., 14–17.

8. Ibid., 17–18.

9. Ibid., 19–24.

10. Franklin B. Gowen, *Argument of Franklin B Gowen, Esq: Of Counsel for the Common-wealth, in the Case of the Commonwealth vs. Thomas Munley* (Pottsville, PA: Chronicle Book & Job Rooms, 1876); *A Full Account: The Lives and Crimes of the Mollie Maguires* (Philadelphia: Barclay, 1877); Herman Marsdorf, *Thirty Days among the Mollie Maguires* (Philadelphia: Barclay, 1877).

11. Gowen, *Argument of Franklin B. Gowen*, 16.

12. Ibid., 19–26.

13. Ibid., 20, iii, 33–36; John T. Morse, "The 'Molly Maguire' Trials," *American Law Review*, January 1877, 233.

14. "Coal Miners Troubles," *New York Times*, September 4, 1875; "A Murderer's Confession," *New York Times*, February 5, 1876; "The Mollie Maguires," *New York Times*, February 15, 1876; "Mollie Maguire Murderers," *New York Times*, March 30, 1876; "Murderous Mollie Maguires," *New York Times*, May 9, 1876; "The Mollie Maguires," *New York Times*, May 14, 1876; "Trial of the Mollie Maguires," *New York Times*, February 8, 1877; "Molly Maguires Excommunicated," *New York Times*, February 12, 1877; "A Case of Mistaken Sympathy," *New York Times*, February 13, 1877; "The 'Molly Maguires' Convicted," *New York Times*, February 25, 1877; "Sentences of Organized Murderers," *New York Times*, April 3, 1877; "Murder in the First Degree," *New York Times*, April 14, 1877; "A Molly Maguire to Be Hanged," *New York Times*, April 17, 1877; "Ten Men to Be Hanged: Mollie Maguires Brought to Justice at Last," *New York Times*, June 18, 1877; "The Prisoners at Mauch Chunk," *New York Times*, June 21, 1877; "Hunting Down the Mollie Maguires," *New York Times*, June 27, 1878.

15. Kevin Kenny, *Making Sense of the Molly Maguires* (New York: Oxford University Press, 1998), 206.

16. Ibid.

17. Ernst Lucy, *The Molly Maguires of Pennsylvania; or, Ireland in America* (London: George Bell & Sons, 1877); Francis Dewees, *The Molly Maguires: The Origin, Growth and Character of the Organization* (New York: Burt Franklin, 1877).

18. Michael Denning, *Mechanic Accents: Dime Novels and Working-Class Culture* (New York: Verso Books, 1987); Kenny, *Making Sense of the Molly Maguires*.

19. Denning, *Mechanic Accents*; Kenny, *Making Sense of the Molly Maguires*; "Coal Region Thugs Denounced," *National Police Gazette*, March 15, 1879, 13.

20. Committee Reports, 1887, Citizens' Association, Chicago Public Library (CPL), Chicago, Illinois; Citizens' Association Papers, box 5, folder 1, Chicago History Museum, Chicago, Illinois; *Chicago Tribune*, July 24, 1877.

21. Pinkerton, *Strikers, Communists, Tramps, and Detectives*, 23–24.

22. Ibid., 87–88.

23. Ibid., 88, 95–96, 85.

24. Ibid., ix–x.

25. Ibid.

26. People's Exhibit 89, *Arbeiter-Zeitung* (newspaper) article, editorial, 1886 April 20 (Chicago History Museum); People's Exhibit 44, *The Alarm* (newspaper) article, "Bombs," 1885 May 2 (Chicago History Museum); Albert R. Parsons, *Anarchism: Its Philosophy and Scientific Basis as Defined by Some of Its Apostles* (Chicago: Mrs. A. R. Parsons, 1887), 46–47.

27. *New York Times,* July 22, 1886; "The Anarchists' Trial," *New York Times,* July 27, 1886; "Watching the Anarchists," *New York Times,* July 24, 1886; "The Prosecution Closes," *New York Times,* August 1, 1886.

28. Testimony of William A. Pinkerton, July 26, 1886, in Illinois v. August Spies et al. trial transcript no. 1 (Chicago History Museum); Testimony of Andrew C. Johnson (first appearance), July 24, 1886, in Illinois v. August Spies et al. trial transcript no. 1, Chicago History Museum; Testimony of Andrew C. Johnson (first appearance resumed), July 26, 1886, in Illinois v. August Spies et al. trial transcript no. 1 (Chicago History Museum).

29. People's Exhibit 83, *Arbeiter-Zeitung* (newspaper) article, untitled, December 31, 1885 (Chicago History Museum); People's Exhibit 75, *Arbeiter-Zeitung* (newspaper) article, "Editorial," October 8, 1885 (Chicago History Museum).

30. People's Exhibit 80, *Arbeiter-Zeitung* (newspaper) article, "Editorial," December 28, 1885 (Chicago History Museum).

CHAPTER FOUR: In which the Pinks serve as a private army for capital

1. *General Principles of Pinkerton's National Detective Agency* (Chicago: Fergus Printing Co., 1873), copy in Library of Congress; *The Rules and Regulations for the Government of the Preventive Force of Pinkerton's National Police Agency* (Chicago: George H. Fergus, 1867), copy in Library of Congress; *The Rules and Regulations for the Government of the Preventive Force of Pinkerton's National Detective Agency* (Chicago: JMW Jones Printer, 1873), copy in Library of Congress.

2. Prints and Photographs Department, Chicago Historical Society, Chicago, Illinois; Carl Smith, *Urban Disorder and the Shape of Belief: The Great Chicago Fire, the Haymarket Bomb, and the Model Town of Pullman* (Chicago: University of Chicago Press, 1995), 313.

3. "Allan Pinkerton, Detective," *Harper's Weekly,* July 12, 1884; "The Pinkerton Force," *Michigan Farmer,* November 1, 1890.

4. Sven Beckert, *The Monied Metropolis: New York City and the Consolidation of the American Bourgeoisie, 1850–1896* (Cambridge: Cambridge University Press, 2003); Jeffrey Haydu, *Citizen Employers: Business Communities and Labor in Cincinnati and San Francisco, 1870–1916* (Ithaca, NY: Cornell University Press, 2008).

5. H. W. Brands, *American Colossus: The Triumph of Capitalism, 1865–1900* (New York: Knopf Doubleday, 2011).

6. Frank Morn, *The Eye That Never Sleeps: A History of the Pinkerton National Detective Agency* (Bloomington: Indiana University Press, 1982).

7. Mary Harris Jones, *The Autobiography of Mother Jones* (Chicago: Charles H. Kerr, 1925), 242; "Pinkerton's Men Denounced," *New York Times,* January 22, 1887; "Pinkerton's Men," *Nation,* January 27, 1887; Henry George, "Labor in Pennsylvania," *North American Review* 143, no. 358 (September 1886): 268; Samuel Gompers, "Trade-Unions: Their Achievements, Methods and Aims," *Journal of Social Science* 28 (October 1891): 40.

8. The number of conflicts and strikes that Pinkerton guards took part in was massive between 1877 and 1900. The blurry lines between official actions of the agency, the use of Pennsylvania's Coal and Iron Police (which often included Pinkerton agents), and local vigilante committees (which also included Pinkertons) can lead us to oversummarize and overcategorize the violence of this era, even though each act of violence came from a particular context with a particular progression. For example, John Davies describes a specific confrontation between strikers and a combination of C&I police and Pinkerton detectives in Shenandoah, Pennsylvania, during an 1887–1888 strike. John Davies, "Authority, Community, and Conflict: Rioting and Aftermath in a Late-Nineteenth Century Pennsylvania Coal Town," *Pennsylvania History* 66, no. 3 (Summer 1998): 339–63.

9. Testimony of William A. Pinkerton, July 26, 1886, in Illinois v. August Spies et al. trial transcript no. 1 (Chicago History Museum); Testimony of Andrew C. Johnson (first appearance), July 24, 1886, in Illinois v. August Spies et al. trial transcript no. 1 (Chicago History Museum); Testimony of Andrew C. Johnson (first appearance resumed), July 26, 1886, in Illinois v. August Spies et al. trial transcript no. 1 (Chicago History Museum).

10. Albert R. Parsons, *Life of Albert R. Parsons: With Brief History of the Labor Movement in America: Also Sketches of the Lives of A. Spies, Geo. Engel, A. Fischer, and L. Lingg* (Chicago: Mrs. Lucy E. Parsons, 1889), 46–47.

11. August Vincent Theodore Spies, *The Accused, the Accusers: The Famous Speeches of the Eight Chicago Anarchists in Court When Asked If They Had Anything to Say Why Sentence Should Not Be Passed upon Them. On October 7th, 8th and 9th, 1886* (Chicago: Socialistic Publishing Society, 1886).

12. *An Appeal to the People of America, Albert Parsons, Defendant, Dated Sept. 21, 1887 in Prison Cell No. 29* (Chicago: s.n., 1887).

13. "A Long Strike," *Harper's Weekly*, December 27, 1884.

14. Ibid.; "Ohio Miners Becoming Desperate," *New York Times*, September 18, 1884.

15. C. H. Salmons, *The Burlington Strike: Its Motives and Methods, Including the Causes of the Strike, Remote and Direct, and the Relations to It, of the Organizations of Locomotive Engineers, Locomotive Firemen, Switchmen's M. A. A., and Action Taken by Order Brotherhood R. R. Brakemen, Order Railway Conductors, and Knights of Labor* (Aurora, IL: Press of Bunnell & Ward, 1889), 8, 212, 233.

16. "Bold Lake Shore Strikers," *New York Times*, September 12, 1886.

17. *New York Times*, October 27, 1886.

18. *Chicago Tribune*, October 20–22, 1886, November 5, 1886, November 21, 1886.

19. *New York Times*, January 22, 1887; "Thomas Hogan's Funeral," *New York Times*, January 23, 1887; "Hogan's Inquest," *New York Times*, January 28, 1887; "Don't Like Detectives," *New York Times*, July 17, 1887.

20. *New York Times*, January 22, 1887.

21. "A Labor Convention," *New York Times*, August 16, 1887.

22. *New York Times*, January 22, 1887.

23. *New York Times*, July 17, 1887

24. "Knights and Detectives," *New York Times*, July 21, 1887.

25. "Pinkerton's Men," *Nation*, January 27, 1887.

26. Ibid.

27. Mayor Orestes Cleveland of Jersey City, Governor David B. Hill of New York, Governor Robert S. Green of New Jersey, and Governor Richard Oglesby from Illinois; ibid.

28. "Compulsory Arbitration," *Atlantic Monthly* 67, no. 399 (December 1891); "A Sure Sign," *Puck* 24, no. 610 (November 14, 1888): 195; "Two Causes of Closed Mills," *Puck* 25, no. 629 (March 27, 1889): 75.

29. William Schuyler, "Shakespeare on the Labor Question," *Open Court* 4, no. 170 (November 27, 1890): 1; Thos. Stoughton Potwin, *New Englander and Yale Review* 17, no. 248 (November 1890): 411.

30. Terence Powderly, *Thirty Years of Labor* (Philadelphia: Ranking & O'Neal, 1890), 253, 147.

31. Theresa A. Case, *The Great Southwest Railroad Strike and Free Labor* (College Station: Texas A&M University Press, 2010).

32. Terence Powderly, *The Path I Trod* (New York: Columbia University Press, 1940), 151, 154.

33. *New York Times*, September 3, 1890.

34. *New York Times*, August 11, 1890.

35. "Circular That Makes a Stir," *New York Times*, May 9, 1889; "Stoned by the Strikers," *New York Times*, August 14, 1890; "Firearms Freely Used," *New York Times*, August 18, 1890; "Pinkerton Men Killed," *New York Times*, August 19, 1890; "A Quiet Day in Albany," *New York Times*, August 19, 1890; "Two Strikers Arrested," *New York Times*, September 8, 1890; "More Strikers Arrested," *New York Times*, September 9, 1890; *Atlanta Constitution*, August 18, 1890.

36. *Chicago Daily Tribune*, August 19, 1890.

37. US Congress, House, Judiciary Committee, "The Employment of Pinkerton Detectives," House Report 2447, 52nd Congress, 2nd Session, 1893, 228.

38. "Appeal to the People," *New York Times*, August 22, 1890.

39. US Congress, House, Judiciary Committee, "The Employment of Pinkerton Detectives," House Report 2447, 52nd Congress, 2nd Session, 1893, 222–23. The shared interests of capital and labor and their shared victimization by the Pinkertons were very much in line with Powderly's notion of producerism.

40. Ibid., 22.

41. "A Bit of Ancient History," *New York Times*, September 3, 1890.

42. "Watched by Pinkerton Men," *New York Times*, July 24, 1888.

43. *New York Times*, May 9, 1889.

44. *Reasons for Pardoning Fielden, Neebe and Schwab by John P. Altgeld, Governor of Illinois* (Pamphlet, Chicago Historical Society, 1893).

CHAPTER FIVE: In which Pinkerton myrmidons invade Homestead

1. Emma Goldman, *Living My Life*, vol. 1 (New York: Alfred A. Knopf, 1931), 86; Myron R. Stowell, *Fort Frick, or the Siege at Homestead* (Pittsburgh, PA: Pittsburgh Printing, 1893), 111; Terence Powderly, *The Path I Trod* (New York: Columbia University Press, 1940), 260–61.

2. *Social Economist* 4, no. 1 (January 1893): 55; "Treason," *American Journal of Politics 1* (November 1892): 558; Belva Lockwood, "A Woman's View," *American Journal of Politics 2* (January 1893): 36; B. O. Flower, "The Menace of Plutocracy," *Arena*, no. 34 (September 1892): 508.

3. Arthur G. Burgoyne, *The Homestead Strike of 1892* (Pittsburgh, PA: Rawsthorne Engraving & Printing, 1893), 42–45; Stowell, *Fort Frick*.

4. US Congress, House, Judiciary Committee, "Investigation of the Employment of Pinkerton Detectives in Connection with the Labor Troubles at Homestead, Pa.," House Report 2447, 52nd Congress, 2nd Session, 1892, 224, 237.

5. Burgoyne, *Homestead Strike*, 24–25, 33–34, 37.

6. *Pittsburgh Post*, July 8, 1892.

7. "Mob Law at Homestead," *New York Times*, July 7, 1892; "The Homestead Riots," *Harper's Weekly*, July 16, 1892.

8. Phillip S. Foner, *American Labor Songs* (Champaign: University of Illinois Press, 1975).

9. "As for Pinkerton," the letter continues, "he was a marplot during the war and was either disloyal or a very poor detective. During the Peninsular campaign of Gen. McClellan … he kept the otherwise able general fully impressed with the idea that 300,000 rebel troops were constantly in his front." *New York Times*, July 11, 1892; "An Anti-Pinkerton Bill," *New York Times*, July 15, 1892.

10. Burgoyne, *Homestead Strike*, 76.

11. *New York Times*, July 7, 1892.

12. "The Homestead Riots," *Harper's Weekly*, July 16, 1892.

13. *New York Times*, July 7, 1892; "Burgess McLuckie Surrenders," *New York Times*, July

19, 1892; "Labor Questions in the Senate," *New York Times*, July 23, 1892; "O'Donnell on Trial," *New York Times*, February 14, 1893; "Hugh O'Donnell Acquitted," *New York Times*, February 19, 1893.

14. "The Homestead Riots," *Harper's Weekly*, July 16, 1892.

15. "The Pinkerton Men," *Harper's Weekly*, July 23, 1892.

16. US Congress, House, Judiciary Committee, "Investigation of the Employment of Pinkerton Detectives in Connection with the Labor Troubles at Homestead, Pa.," House Report 2447, 52nd Congress, 2nd Session, 1892.

17. US Congress, Senate, Committee on Labor and Education, "Investigation in Relation to the Employment for Private Purposes of Armed Bodies of Men, or Detectives, in Connection with Differences between Workmen and Employers," Senate Report 1280, 52nd Congress, 2nd Session, 1892.

18. Ibid.

19. Ibid; William C. Oates, "The Homestead Strike: A Congressional View," *North American Review* 155, no. 430 (September 1892): 355; T. V. Powderly, "A Knight of Labor's View," *North American Review* 155, no. 430 (September 1892): 370.

20. US Congress, House, Judiciary Committee, "Investigation of the Employment of Pinkerton Detectives in Connection with Labor Troubles at Homestead, Pa.," House Report 2447, 52nd Congress, 2nd Session, 1892; US Congress, Senate, Committee on Labor and Education, "Investigation in Relation to the Employment for Private Purposes of Armed Bodies of Men, or Detectives, in Connection with Differences between Workmen and Employers," Senate Report 1280, 52nd Congress, 2nd Session, 1892.

21. *Age of Labor*, September 1, 1892, as quoted in J. Bernard Hogg, "Public Reaction to Pinkertonism and the Labor Question," *Pennsylvania History* 11, no. 3 (July 1944): 184.

22. "Provoked by Carnegie," *New York Times*, July 7, 1892.

23. "Mob Law at Homestead," *New York Times*, July 7, 1892.

24. David Dudley Field, "Solutions of the Labor Problem," *North American Review* 156, no. 434 (January 1893): 61.

25. H. L. Wayland, "Has the State Abdicated?," *Journal of Social Science* 30 (October 1892): 5.

26. Ibid.

27. Alan Kraut, *Silent Travelers: Germs, Genes, and the Immigrant Menace* (Baltimore: Johns Hopkins University Press, 1995).

CHAPTER SIX: In which the disgrace of Pinkertonism is subjected to public scrutiny

1. Cleveland Moffett, "How Allan Pinkerton Thwarted the First Plot to Assassinate Lincoln; Stories from the Archives of the Pinkerton Detective Agency," *McClure's Magazine* 3, no. 6 (November 1894): 519; Cleveland Moffett, "The Overthrow of the Molly Maguires; Stories from the Archives of the Pinkerton Detective Agency," *McClure's Magazine* 4, no. 1 (December 1894): 90; Cleveland Moffett, "The Rock Island Express Robbery; Stories from the Archives of the Pinkerton Detective Agency," *McClure's Magazine* 4, no. 3 (February 1895): 245; Cleveland Moffett, "The Pollock Diamond Robbery; Stories from the Archives of the Pinkerton Detective Agency," *McClure's Magazine* 4, no. 5 (April 1895): 437; Cleveland Moffett, "The Destruction of the Reno Gang; Stories from the Archives of the Pinkerton Detective Agency," *McClure's Magazine* 4, no. 6 (May 1895): 549; Cleveland Moffett, "The American Exchange Bank Robbery; Stories from the Archives of the Pinkerton Detective Agency," *McClure's Magazine* 5, no. 2 (July 1895): 179; Cleveland Moffett, "The Susquehanna Express Robbery; Stories from the Archives of the Pinkerton Detective

Agency," *McClure's Magazine* 5, no. 4 (September 1895): 366; A. K. McClure, "The Night at Harrisburg; A Reminiscence of Lincoln's Journey to Washington in 1861," *McClure's Magazine* 5, no. 1 (June 1895): 91.

2. Charles Francis Bourke, "The Story of the Pinkertons; the History of the Most Remarkable Detective Agency in the World, Taken from Original Sources and Now Told Comprehensively for the First Time," *Leslie's Monthly Magazine* 59, no. 6 (April 1905): 6.

3. Clippings from several other newspapers fill a file in the Pinkerton papers, along with notes on how the company should respond to protect its image. Box 20, folder 2, box 119, folder 32, box 23, folder 4, Pinkerton Collection, Library of Congress, Washington, DC.

4. *Illustrated American*, July 16, 1892.

5. Ellen Gruber Garvey, *The Adman in the Parlor: Magazines and the Gendering of Consumer Culture, 1880s to 1910s* (New York: Oxford University Press, 1996).

6. "The Homestead Mob," *Independent* 44, no. 2276 (July 14, 1892): 18; "The Suicide of Labor," *Independent* 44, no. 2277 (July 21, 1892): 10; "A Clerical Apologist," *Independent* 44, no. 2278 (July 28, 1892): 11.

7. "A Clerical Apologist," *Independent* 44, no. 2278 (July 28, 1892): 11; *Independent* 44, no. 2278 (July 28, 1892): 12.

8. "Guiteauism," *Independent* 44, no. 2278 (July 28, 1892): 10.

9. Atticus G. Haywood, "Without Justice Strikes without End," *Independent* 44, no. 2298 (December 15, 1892): 4.

10. M. M. Trumbull, "Current Topics," *Open Court* 6, no. 255 (July 14, 1892): 3315.

11. Ibid.

12. E. C. Hegeler, "The Homestead Affair," *Open Court* 6, no. 259 (August 11, 1892): 1.

13. G. K., "A Current Topic," *Open Court* 6, no. 259 (August 11, 1892): 1.

14. B. O. Flower, "The Menace of Plutocracy," *Arena*, no. 34 (September 1892): 508.

15. "The Millionaire's Mercenaries," *Zion's Herald* 70, no. 32 (August 10, 1892): 252; "Law and Legislation," *American Law* 26 (September/October 1892): 658; *Life* 20, no. 505 (September 1, 1892): 116; "On Picket Duty," *Liberty* 9, no. 51 (April 21, 1894): 1.

16. "Lessons of the Strikes," *Baptist Quarterly Review* 14, no. 54 (October 1892): 497; "The Recent Strikes," *California Illustrated Magazine* 2, no. 6 (November 1892): 851; F. E. Goodrich, "The Cost of a Labor Strike," *Current Literature* 11, no. 1 (September 1892): 42.

17. "Economics of Strikes and Boycotts," *Social Economist*, May 1893, 257.

18. B. O. Flower, "The Menace of Plutocracy," *Arena*, no. 34 (September 1892): 508; Atticus Haywood, "Organizations and Personal Freedom," *Zion's Herald* 71, no. 1 (January 4, 1893): 1; David J. Brewer, "The Liberty of Each Individual," *Independent* 45, no. 2328 (July 13, 1893): 2.

19. Chauncey F. Black, "The Lesson of Homestead," *Forum*, September 1892, 14.

20. Ibid.

21. C. H. Reeve, "The Ethics of Strikes and Lockouts," *American Journal of Politics* 2 (January 1893): 75.

22. Philip Garrett, "The Promotion of Peace," *Advocate of Peace* 56, no. 9 (September 1894): 199; "The Outlook," *Christian Union* 46, no. 23 (December 3, 1892): 1029.

23. T. V. Powderly, "A Knight of Labor's View," *North American Review* 155, no. 430 (September 1892): 370.

24. "Disgrace of Pinkertonism," *Scientific American* 67, no. 18 (September 24, 1892): 200.

25. *Chautauquan* 16, no. 4 (January 1893): 484.

26. "Protection against Strikes," *Current Literature* 11, no. 1 (September 1892): 4.

27. *Central Law Journal* 35, no. 20 (November 11, 1892): 375.

28. Edward Arden, "Organized Labor and the Law," *Chautauquan* 17, no. 2 (May 1893): 140.

29. "The Pinkerton Men," *Harper's Weekly*, July 23, 1892.

30. Z. S. Holbrook, "The Lessons of the Homestead Troubles," address to the Sunset Club of Chicago, November 17, 1892, Chicago History Museum, Chicago, Illinois.

31. Charles W. Eliot, "'The Ethics of Corporate Management' and Address before the Merchants Club of Chicago," March 10, 1906, 21, miscellaneous pamphlets, Merchants Club of Chicago, Chicago History Museum.

32. Miscellaneous pamphlets, 1897–1905, Merchants Club of Chicago, Chicago History Museum.

33. US Strike Commission Report, Senate Executive Document, no. 7, 53rd Congress, 3rd Session, "Report on the Chicago Strike of June–July 1894."

34. Eugene Debs, *Debs: His Life, Writings and Speeches* (Chicago: George Renneker, 1908), 56.

35. Jane Addams, "A Modern Lear," *Survey* 29 (November 2, 1912): 131–37. Addams wrote her piece in 1894 and first delivered it as an address. Graham Romeyn Taylor, "Satellite Cities: Pullman," *Survey* 29 (November 2, 1912): 117–31.

36. As cited in Eric Rauchway, *Blessed among Nations: How the World Made America* (New York: Hill & Wang, 2006), 136.

37. Jack London, "What Life Means to Me," *Cosmopolitan* 40, no. 5 (March 1906): 526; Jack London, *Iron Heel* (New York: Regent Press, 1907).

38. W. J. Ghent, "Next Step: A Benevolent Feudalism," *Independent* 54, no. 2783 (April 3, 1902): 781; Debs, *Debs: His Life, Writings, and Speeches*, 131, 317–18.

CHAPTER SEVEN: In which the frontier closes and Pinkerton practices are exposed

1. Marilynn S. Johnson, *Violence in the West: The Johnson County Range War and the Ludlow Massacre* (Boston: Bedford/St. Martin's, 2008).

2. A. S. Mercer, *The Banditti of the Plains; or, The Cattlemen's Invasion of Wyoming in 1892: The Crowning Infamy of the Ages* (1894; repr., Norman: University of Oklahoma Press, 1954), 28, 39.

3. Julian Ralph, "Wyoming—Another Pennsylvania," *Harper's New Monthly Magazine* 87, no. 517 (June 1893): 63–78.

4. Charles A. Siringo, *A Cowboy Detective: A True Story of Twenty-Two Years with a World-Famous Detective Agency* (Chicago: W. B. Conkey, 1912).

5. Tom Horn, *Life of Tom Horn* (Denver, CO: Louthan, 1904), 273, 297.

6. Howard R. Lamar, *Charlie Siringo's West: An Interpretive Biography* (Albuquerque: University of New Mexico Press, 2005), 135–36; Siringo, *Cowboy Detective*, 17.

7. Lamar, *Charlie Siringo's West*, 144; Siringo, *Cowboy Detective*, 34–35, 117.

8. Siringo, *Cowboy Detective*, 121, 132–33.

9. *Washington Post*, April 24, 1898.

10. Lamar, *Charlie Siringo's West*, 201–2.

11. Such a legend is not uncommon for bandits and outlaws. The story lines of bandits such as Billy the Kid, Jesse James, Butch Cassidy, and Mexican revolutionary Emiliano Zapata all include legends of their survival and long lives.

12. Siringo, *Cowboy Detective*, 136–40.

13. Lamar, *Charlie Siringo's West*, 176–77.

14. *Outlook* 49, no. 24 (June 16, 1894): 1085.

15. Morris Friedman, *The Pinkerton Labor Spy* (New York: Wilshire, 1907), 88–91.

16. J. Anthony Lukas, *Big Trouble: A Murder in a Small Western Town Sets Off a Struggle for the Soul of America* (New York: Simon & Schuster, 1997).

17. Oscar King Davis, "Ex-Pinkerton Man Talks for Haywood," *New York Times*, January 30, 1907; Oscar King Davis, "Pinkerton Reports Are Read at Boise," *New York Times*, July 2, 1907; "20,000 Parade for Accused Miners," *New York Times*, May 5, 1907; "Adams Told of Trade in Murder," *New York Times*, February 24, 1907; Oscar King Davis, "Orchard's Story Denied in Detail," *New York Times*, July 3, 1907; Oscar King Davis, "Orchard Was Angry over Banishment," *New York Times*, July 10, 1907.

18. "'Molly Maguires' of Pennsylvania Find a Parallel in West," *New York Times*, June 16, 1907.

19. "Darrow's Speech in the Haywood Case," *Wayland's Monthly*, no. 9 (October 1907): 36–38, 60.

20. Ibid., 15, 56.

21. Ibid., 28–33.

22. Ibid., 68.

23. Ibid., 78, 87, 93.

24. Oscar King Davis, "Ex-Pinkerton Man Talks for Haywood," *New York Times*, June 30, 1907.

25. Friedman, *Pinkerton Labor Spy*, 1.

26. Ibid., 2–5.

27. Ibid., 18–23, 49, 114.

28. *Pinkerton's National Detective Agency and Its Connection with Labor Troubles at Homestead, Penn., July 6th, 1892: With Extracts from Proofs before the Judiciary Committees of the U.S. Senate and House of Representatives* (New York, 1892); Friedman, *Pinkerton Labor Spy*, 69, 23–24.

29. Siringo, *Cowboy Detective*.

30. Charles A. Siringo, *Two Evil Isms: Pinkertonism and Anarchism* (Chicago: C. A. Siringo, 1915), 2–4, 13.

31. Ibid., 4–5, 13.

32. Ibid., 4–5, 18–19.

33. Ibid., 11, 36–42, 94–97.

34. Ibid., 4–5, 34–35, 107.

35. Arthur Reed Kimball, "Cleveland's Reformed Police Force," *Outlook* 48, no. 27 (December 30, 1893).

36. Alex Butterworth, *The World That Never Was: A True Story of Dreamers, Schemers, Anarchists, and Secret Agents* (New York: Vintage Books, 2010).

37. *New York Times*, March 22, 1898.

38. *New York Times*, March 8, 1895; "Captured in the Bay-Filibustering Expedition Ready to Sail," *New York Times*, February 26, 1896; "Filibuster Went to Sea," *New York Times*, October 18, 1897; "Hunt for Spanish Spies," *New York Times*, June 2, 1898; "A Spanish Detective in Jail," *New York Times*, October 28, 1896.

39. Thomas Furlong not only tried to compete with the Pinkerton agency but also tried to one-up Allan Pinkerton's *Thirty Years a Detective* by publishing his own memoir in 1912, entitled *Fifty Years a Detective* (St. Louis, MO: C. E. Barnett, 1912). The trials of the Flores Magón brothers are traced in Colin MacLachlan, *Anarchism and the Mexican Revolution: The Political Trials of Ricardo Flores Magón in the United States* (Berkeley: University of California Press, 1991).

40. Robert Pinkerton, "Detective Surveillance of Anarchists," *North American Review* 173, no. 540 (November 1901): 609.

41. John H. Bridge, "The Story of the World's Largest Corporation," *Cosmopolitan* 36, no. 1 (November 1903): 120.

CHAPTER EIGHT: In which the modern state takes on the duties of the Pinkerton agency

1. J. B. Weaver, "Threefold Contention of Industry," *Arena* 28 (March 1892): 427; "People's Party Platform," *Omaha Morning World-Herald*, July 5, 1892.

2. John R. Commons, "Progressive Individualism," *American Magazine of Civics* 6, no. 6 (June 1895): 16.

3. Edward Ross, "A New Plea for a Square Deal," *Current Literature*, no. 5 (November 1907): 528.

4. Charles Francis Bourke, "The Story of the Pinkertons; the History of the Most Remarkable Detective Agency in the World, Taken from Original Sources and Now Told Comprehensively for the First Time," *Leslie's Monthly Magazine* 59, no. 6 (April 1905): 6; Charles Francis Bourke, "The Pinkertons; The Story of the Enterprising Bidwell Brothers and of the Reno Family," *Leslie's Monthly Magazine* 60, no. 1 (May 1905): 36; Charles Francis Bourke, "The Pinkertons; Protecting Banks against Yeggmen; Adam Worth's Career," *Leslie's Monthly Magazine* 60, no. 2 (June 1905): 205.

5. Arthur Conan Doyle, "A Reminiscence of Sherlock Holmes: The Adventure of the Red Circle, Part I," *Strand Magazine*, no. 243 (March 1911): 259–66; Arthur Conan Doyle, "A Reminiscence of Sherlock Holmes: The Adventure of the Red Circle, Part II," *Strand Magazine*, no. 244 (April 1911): 428–34; Arthur Conan Doyle, *Valley of Fear* (New York: George H. Doran, 1914).

6. Conan Doyle, *Valley of Fear*, 282, 297.

7. Ibid., 310.

8. Stephen Norwood, *Strikebreaking and Intimidation: Mercenaries and Masculinity in Twentieth-Century America* (Chapel Hill: University of North Carolina Press, 2002).

9. Thomas G. Andrews, *Killing for Coal: America's Deadliest Labor War* (Cambridge, MA: Harvard University Press, 2008).

10. Altina Miller, *Feud: Hatfields, McCoys, and Social Change in Appalachia, 1860–1900* (Chapel Hill: University of North Carolina Press, 1988).

11. Roland Marchand, "The Corporation Nobody Knew: Bruce Barton, Alfred Sloan, and the Founding of the General Motors 'Family,'" *Business History Review*, Winter 1991, 825–75. On the building of Gary as a new form of industrial order, see S. Paul O'Hara, *Gary, the Most American of All American Cities* (Bloomington: Indiana University Press, 2011).

12. Beverly Gage, *The Day Wall Street Exploded: A Story of America in Its First Age of Terror* (Oxford: Oxford University Press, 2010).

13. "The Pinkertons and the American Bankers' Association," *Independent* 68, no. 3073 (October 24, 1907): 1020; "Safe Cracking Has Become Unpopular," *Bankers' Magazine* 80, no. 1 (January 1910): 107; George S. Dougherty, "The Public the Criminal's Partner," *Outlook* 104, no. 17 (August 23, 1913): 895.

14. *Time*, July 13, 1936.

15. Second Inaugural Address of Franklin D. Roosevelt, Wednesday, January 20, 1937, transcript, The Avalon Project, Lillian Goldman Law Library, Yale University.

16. Roger Shaw, "Fascism and the New Deal," *North American Review* 238, no. 6 (December 1934): 559–64.

17. "A Family of Sleuths," *Outlook*, December 26, 1923, 705.

18. "Pinkertons Pinked," *Time*, February 22, 1937.

19. "National Affairs: Espionage Exposed," *Time*, January 3, 1938.

20. Claire Bond Potter, *War on Crime: Bandits, G-Men, and the Politics of Mass Culture* (New Brunswick, NJ: Rutgers University Press, 1998), 125–38.

21. *Time*, April, 27, 1931.

22. Dashiell Hammett, *Selected Letters of Dashiell Hammett, 1921–1960* (Berkeley, CA: Counterpoint Press, 2001).

23. Ibid.

24. Sinda Gregory, *Private Investigations: The Novels of Dashiell Hammett* (Carbondale: Southern Illinois University Press, 1984).

25. Dashiell Hammett, *The Thin Man* (New York: Alfred A. Knopf, 1934).

CONCLUSION: Pinkerton's Inc.

1. Frederick Pohl and C. M. Kornbluth, *The Space Merchants* (New York: St. Martin's Press, 1958), 46.

2. Ian Fleming, *Diamonds Are Forever* (London: Jonathan Cape, 1956).

3. For example, see John Perkins, *Confessions of an Economic Hitman* (New York: Plume, 2004).

4. Jeremy Scahill, *Blackwater: The Rise of the World's Most Powerful Mercenary Army* (New York: Avalon, 2008); "Before Shooting in Iraq, a Warning on Blackwater," *New York Times*, June 29, 2014; Matt Apuzzo, "Blackwater Guards Found Guilty in 2007 Iraq Killings," *New York Times*, October 22, 2014.

5. Jeremy Scahill, "Blackwater Down," *Nation*, October 10, 2005.

6. Scahill, *Blackwater*; Alec Klein and Steve Fainaru, "Judge Halts Award of Iraq Contract," *Washington Post*, June 2, 2007; Scott v. United States, 78 Fed. Cl. 151, 156–57 (Fed Cl. 2007); Scahill, "Blackwater Down"; *Daily Kos*, October 4, 2007.

7. Erik Prince, *Civilian Warriors: The Inside Story of Blackwater and the Unsung Heroes of the War on Terror* (New York: Portfolio, 2013).

8. Alexander Alland, interview by Edward Applebome, June 3, 1986, in Ellis Island Oral History Project, Series AKRF, no. 185 (Alexandria, VA: Alexander Street Press, 2003), 31; Ronald A. Fullerton, "Toward a Commercial Popular Culture in Germany: The Development of Pamphlet Fiction, 1871–1914," *Journal of Social History* 12, no. 4 (Summer 1979): 489–511; Robert Russell, "Red Pinkertonism: An Aspect of Soviet Literature of the 1920s," *Slavonic and East European Review* 60, no. 3 (July 1982): 390–412.

9. Alan Hynd, *Pinkerton Casebook* (New York: Signet, 1940).

10. Ibid.

11. Richard Slotkin, *Gunfighter Nation: The Myth of the Frontier in Twentieth-Century America* (Norman: University of Oklahoma Press, 1998).

12. "Governor Attacks Willkie's Record," *New York Times*, October 31, 1940; "Flynn Challenges Willkie on Labor," *New York Times*, September 3, 1940; "Willkie Denounces Labor Spies Story," *New York Times*, September 4, 1940; "Willkie Shift Seen on Industry Draft," *New York Times*, September 7, 1940.

13. "US Business: Public Private Eye," *Time*, April 7, 1967.

14. In neither film is the Pinkerton agency actually mentioned. In *Rage at Dawn*, Scott's agent works for the thinly veiled "Peterson Detective Agency." In *Love Me Tender*, only the name "Reno" bears any resemblance to the actual case. Instead, the brothers are Confederate raiders from Texas who rob the Union payroll before they learn that the war has ended. The conflict and violence come from within the gang, not with the benevolent railroad detective named Siringo.

15. James Horan, *Desperate Men: Revelations from the Sealed Pinkerton Files* (New York: Doubleday, 1962), 8.

16. Ibid.

17. "Bomb Blanket," *Time*, December 14, 1970.

18. *New York Times,* January 8, 2005.

19. 5 United States Congress, Sec. 3108.

20. S. Rep. No. 447, 88th Congress, 1st Session (August 20, 1963).

21. Jacob Weinberger claimed that Equifax, because it employed investigating detectives, was a firm similar to the Pinkertons.

22. S. Rep. No. 447, 88th Congress, 1st Session (1963), a report on a bill to repeal the Anti-Pinkerton Act, S1543 (1963); Government Accounting Office, June 7, 1978, comp. gen. 524.

23. Government Accounting Office, August 18, 2006, B-298370; B-298490; Brian X. Scott v. US, US Court of Federal Claims, no. 07-216C, August 23, 2007; Government Accounting Office, March 2007, B-299524; Alec Klein and Steve Fainaru, "Judge Halts Award of Iraq Contract," *Washington Post,* June 2, 2007; Scott v. United States, 78 Fed. Cl. 151, 156–57 (Fed Cl. 2007).

24. Arthur Lewis, *Lament for the Molly Maguires* (New York: Harcourt, Brace & World, 1964).

25. Hynd, *Pinkerton Casebook,* 12.

26. Kevin Kenny, "The Molly Maguires in Popular Culture," *Journal of American Ethnic History* 14, no. 4 (Summer 1995): 27–46. *The Molly Maguires* was Hollywood's effort to make sense of not only late 1960s radicalism and violence but also the role of the informer, a significant point because both director Martin Ritt and writer Walter Bernstein were blacklisted for their refusal to name names in front of the House Un-American Activities Committee.

27. Ward Churchill, "From the Pinkertons to the Patriot Act: The Trajectory of Political Policing in the United States, 1870 to the Present," *CR: The New Centennial Review* 4, no. 1 (2004): 1–72.

28. T. A. Frank, "Pinkertons at DHS: Are Immigration Officials Undermining U.S. Labor Law?," *Washington Monthly,* May 1, 2008.

29. James Mackay, *Allan Pinkerton: The First Private Eye* (Edison, NJ: Castle Books, 1996); Jay Bonansinga, *Pinkerton's War: The Civil War's Greatest Spy and the Birth of the US Secret Service* (Guilford, CT: Lyons Press, 2012); Gavin Mortimer, *Double Death: The True Story of Pryce Lewis, the Civil War's Most Daring Spy* (New York: Walker, 2010); Daniel Stashower, *Hour of Peril: The Secret Plot to Murder Lincoln before the Civil War* (New York: Minotaur Books, 2013).

30. Bonansinga, *Pinkerton's War.*

31. Allan Pinkerton, *The Model Town and the Detectives* (New York: G. W. Carleton, 1876).

Index